# GAME PROGRAMMING FOR TEENS, THIRD EDITION

## MANEESH SETHI

**Course Technology PTR**

*A part of Cengage Learning*

COURSE TECHNOLOGY
CENGAGE Learning™

Australia • Brazil • Japan • Korea • Mexico • Singapore • Spain • United Kingdom • United States

## COURSE TECHNOLOGY
CENGAGE Learning

**Game Programming for Teens, Third Edition**
**Maneesh Sethi**

**Publisher and General Manager, Course Technology PTR:** Stacy L. Hiquet

**Associate Director of Marketing:** Sarah Panella

**Manager of Editorial Services:** Heather Talbot

**Marketing Manager:** Jordan Casey

**Acquisitions Editor:** Mitzi Koontz

**Project Editor:** Jenny Davidson

**Technical Reviewer:** Michael Duggan

**PTR Editorial Services Coordinator:** Erin Johnson

**Interior Layout Tech:** ICC Macmillan Inc.

**Cover Designer:** Mike Tanamachi

**CD-ROM Producer:** Brandon Penticuff

**Indexer:** Katherine Stimson

**Proofreader:** Sara Gullion

For product information and technology assistance, contact us at
**Cengage Learning Customer & Sales Support, 1-800-354-9706**

For permission to use material from this text or product, submit all requests online at **www.cengage.com/permissions**
Further permissions questions can be emailed to
**permissionrequest@cengage.com**

BlitzMax and BlitzPlus/Blitz3d are either trademarks or registered trademarks of Blitz Research. Corel and Paint Shop Pro are registered trademarks of Corel Corporation or Corel Corporation Limited. MilkShape 3D is a trademark of chUmbaLum sOft. CoolEdit Pro/Adobe Audition is a registered trademark of Adobe Systems Incorporated. All other trademarks are the property of their respective owners.

Library of Congress Control Number: 2008929222

ISBN-13: 978-1-59863-518-8

ISBN-10: 1-59863-518-2

**Course Technology**
25 Thomson Place
Boston, MA 02210
USA

Cengage Learning is a leading provider of customized learning solutions with office locations around the globe, including Singapore, the United Kingdom, Australia, Mexico, Brazil, and Japan. Locate your local office at: **international.cengage.com/region**

Cengage Learning products are represented in Canada by Nelson Education, Ltd.

For your lifelong learning solutions, visit **courseptr.com**

Visit our corporate website at **cengage.com**

Printed in the United States of America
3 4 5 6 7 16 15 14 13

*For Ramit Sethi—Never stop motivating me.*

# ACKNOWLEDGMENTS

Jeez, there are so many people to thank. This feels like I'm accepting an Oscar: I'm afraid the band will start playing and usher me off the stage. Anyway, first of all thank you André LaMothe for giving me a chance and taking me out to lunch. I will get you back for that one day. Thank you everyone at Course Technology PTR: my copy editor Jenny Davidson; my acquisitions editor, Emi Smith; and my CD editor, Brandon Penticuff.

Special thanks to everyone who helped me through this book—my parents, who keep telling their friends how proud they are of me (even though they both still tell me every day to come home!), my brother Ramit and sisters Nagina and Rachita, who always offered me support. Thanks, guys!

Finally, thanks to Edgar L. Ibarra (Feo) for his artwork and Thomas Stenbäck for his work on music. Also, to Ari Feldman, for allowing me to use his sprite library on the CD.

And to everyone whose name I forgot, you know who you are. Thanks!

# ABOUT THE AUTHOR

**Maneesh Sethi** is a student at Stanford University, an author, and a freelance programmer. Maneesh runs a freelance company, developing custom enterprise software. Maneesh has taught game programming on TechTV's "Call for Help" and at game programming conferences such as the XGDX. He is the author of *PHP for Teens, Web Design for Teens,* and a coauthor of *3D Game Programming for Teens.* Additionally, he authored *How to Succeed As A Lazy Student.* If you want to learn more about him or contact him about your needs for software development, visit www.maneeshsethi.com. Maneesh is currently living in Buenos Aires, Argentina, while continuing to write and code.

# Contents

# INTRODUCTION

Hey, reader. Thanks for reading and/or buying my book. I am really thankful for it.

What is programming? Programming, according to Dictionary.com, is "a set of coded instructions that enables a machine, especially a computer, to perform a desired sequence of operations." In other words, programming allows you to make your computer do whatever you want it to do. Programming is used in everything related to the computer, but there are many distinct flavors of programming. This book teaches Game Programming.

Game programming is very different from the other types of programming. When you turn on your computer, you often see static programs—programs that sit there and wait for you to do something. Not with games. Games are running constantly, and they don't need the player to do anything to keep it running.

Of course, does this mean that game programming is a bit tougher than other styles of programming? Yes and no. While it can be difficult at times, this book strives to turn the difficult into second nature. We use a language of programming called BASIC, which, as you can probably guess, is pretty darn basic.

## What's in the Book?

This book is meant to be a guide to teach any beginner how to design and develop games. Inside the book you will find a wealth of knowledge all written to help you reach the goal of making a game. Each chapter adds on the previous chapters and makes the book seem like a staircase—you move up step by step.

**Part I** discusses the BlitzMax language. During this time, the book does not discuss graphical programs, but instead uses text-based programs to get the language points across.

**Part II** teaches the reader all about graphics within games. There is such information as varying colors, loading and displaying images, making scrolling backgrounds, and things like that.

**Part III** examines other related parts to game programming. The reader can learn how to use keyboard input, sounds and music, and take into account artificial intelligence. This part also creates the final game that the book has been leading up to.

**Part IV** contains all the appendixes for the book. You will find all of the key codes (for handling input), a list of websites to further your knowledge in the field, and what is on the CD.

## Who Are You?

I suppose you can answer this question better than I, but let me tell you what I am looking for in a reader. First of all, I am guessing that you are either a teenager who is interested in game programming or a parent who is interested in having your child learn game programming. That is pretty much all that is required: interest. This book is not made to be difficult. It is made to help introduce the reader into the world of game programming.

There are literally very few requirements. All you really need is a basic knowledge of math, like addition, subtraction, multiplication, and division. If you know those techniques, you are pretty much set! I also suggest that the reader asks his or her parent for help whenever necessary. I use some rudimentary algebra, but those instances are few and far between, and should be easily comprehended within the book.

What do I require of the reader in order for him to read this book? Besides the mathematical knowledge I discussed earlier, simply interest. You don't need to have any knowledge of other programming languages. Not that it won't help, of course. If you do know any other languages, you can learn from this book as well. But, *Game Programming for Teens* teaches the language of game programming along with the ability to actually implement games.

If you are the parent of a child you want to learn programming, this book is the way to go. General programming is a long and boring subject, but game programming allows your child to create things that are **fun.** Help your child with programming while he reads this book, as well. Not only will you both learn programming and keep interest together, but who knows, it may serve as a bond between parent and child (this comes from my psychologist side).

## Who Am I?

Hey everybody, I am Maneesh Sethi. I am a student at Stanford, and the reason I am writing this book is because I believe that, because I was just a teenager myself (less than a year ago, *sigh* I'm so old now), I would be the best one to help other teens learn about it as well. I began programming in 1999 in C and C++. Five years ago I discovered BlitzMax and I have studied it ever since. BlitzMax seems to be the easiest way for any novice to begin writing games, and I want to help the reader progress as fast as possible. The website for this book is located at www.maneeshsethi.com.

## Conventions Used in This Book

### Note

Notes provide additional information on a feature, extend an idea on how to do something, or illustrate a cool fact.

### Caution

Cautions warn you of potential problems and tell you what *not* to do.

### Tip

Tips give you some pertinent information on a better, faster, or easier way of doing something.

## Let's Get Ready to Rumble. . .

If you are still browsing this book in the bookstore, now would be the time to take it home. The bookstore would probably appreciate it if you buy it first (so would I!).

The first part quickly teaches you all of the intricacies of the BlitzMax programming language.

And so we begin. . .

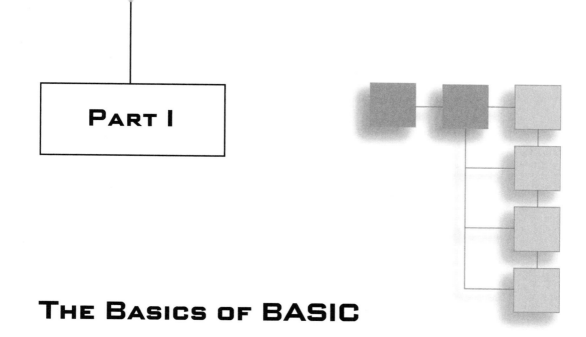

# PART I

# THE BASICS OF BASIC

# CHAPTER 1

# GETTING STARTED

Welcome to the amazing world of game programming! This book will teach you to develop your own video games. Game programming is a pretty big topic, however, and we are going to hurry through the boring material in order to get to the fun stuff. Let's get started right away!

One of the easiest languages for learning programming is BASIC. BASIC stands for **B**eginner's **A**ll-Purpose **S**ymbolic **I**nstruction **C**ode, but that's not really important. BASIC is very easy to write and understand and it's modeled after human language (it uses words instead of just numbers), so if you can speak English, you shouldn't have a hard time with BASIC.

We will be using a program called BlitzMax in this book. BlitzMax is built to use a modified version of BASIC in its programming, but the cool thing is that it lets you make video games that work on all operating systems (Windows, Mac, Linux). We begin with a short history of BASIC.

## A Brief History of BASIC

The language of BASIC was first developed in 1964 by J. Kemeny and T. Kurtz at Dartmouth College. It was designed to be a very easy language to understand, translate, and write. It was also meant to be the first step toward writing programs for tougher languages.

In the 1970s, Paul Allen and Bill Gates decided to develop a BASIC language for the new Altair personal computer. The developers of the Altair showed a lot of interest in the BASIC language, and Gates and Allen licensed it.

Bill Gates and Paul Allen put BASIC onto other types of computers. By 1980, BASIC was moved to Atari, Commodore, and Apple computers as well as the Altair. Bill Gates developed an operating system called DOS (Disk Operating System) with a BASIC interpreter. This allowed any user who owned DOS to write programs in BASIC.

Gates eventually became the head of Microsoft, and he and his company quickly realized how popular BASIC was. So, Microsoft decided to write a compiler for it that did not require DOS. QuickBasic, the first standalone BASIC compiler, was born. Soon after, Microsoft decided to focus on graphics, and developed Visual Basic, which created graphical programs using BASIC as a core language.

BlitzMax, the program we are using in this book, was developed by Mark Sibly, and is geared toward the game developer. BlitzMax is very easy to learn and understand due to its BASIC nature, and is a good way to learn game programming without having to worry about extra code that has almost nothing to do with the actual game itself.

## Installing BlitzMax

We need to get BlitzMax onto our computers so that we can start writing games as soon as possible. BlitzMax is a compiler, so it takes your code and turns it into a program that any computer can run. However, the demo version, included on the CD, does not include the compiler, but only the interpreter. Unlike a compiler, an interpreter does not create an executable file that can be run on any computer; instead, it only runs from within the compiler. In other words, the programs you write will only be able to be run from the program on your computer. If you want to compile the program into a standalone executable, you can purchase the full BlitzMax package from http://www.blitzbasic.com. In addition, you can download new versions of BlitzMax from http://www. maneeshsethi.com (this book's website).

### Installing on Windows

The BlitzMax installer is shown in Figure 1.1.

Okay, first things first. To install this program, put the CD into your CD-ROM drive, and run BlitzMaxDemo.exe. BlitzMax will ask you where you want to

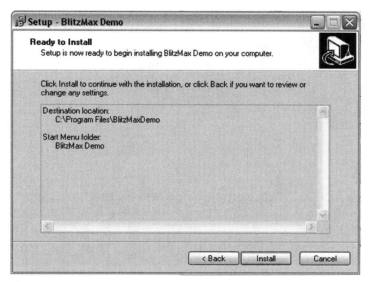

**Figure 1.1**
BlitzMax installer.

install the program. Choose a directory (the default one is a good choice), and click Install. When the installation finishes, click OK, launch the program, and you're done! You now have a full BASIC interpreter on your computer.

### Installing on a Mac

Installing BlitzMax on a Mac is even easier. On the CD is a directory called BlitzMaxDemo/. Simply drag that directory to your Applications directory, as shown in Figure 1.2, and open the file MaxIDE contained in the BlitzMaxDemo/ directory to open up BlitzMax. Easy peasy.

**Note**

In most of the screenshots in this book, I will be using a Mac. The screenshots might look a little different from your computer, but everything should be very similar—all your code will work on both Mac and Windows machines.

### Understanding the IDE

BlitzMax can seem a little daunting at first. The program has a lot of menus and icons, but you can master them with a little effort. The first thing you see when you open the program is the documentation window, pictured in Figure 1.3. If you need to find tutorials or sample programs, this is the place to do it. After you

**Figure 1.2**
BlitzMax installation on a Mac.

have read through anything that interests you, open a new document by selecting File > New or the New icon.

**Note**

The > (arrow) symbol means a selection from a menu. In other words, File > New instructs you to open the File menu and select New. You can access the menus at the top of the program, right above the main toolbar.

What you see in Figure 1.4 is considered the IDE. IDE means Integrated Development Environment, and it is an area in which you can write and compile your programs in the same workspace.

Each of the windows, toolbars, and menus is necessary for game programming, so a good explanation of each might be helpful.

## Windows and Panels

The main window takes up most of the program space and it is the most important part of BlitzMax. This window is where the actual code from the game is typed. The keywords and important parts of your program will be highlighted

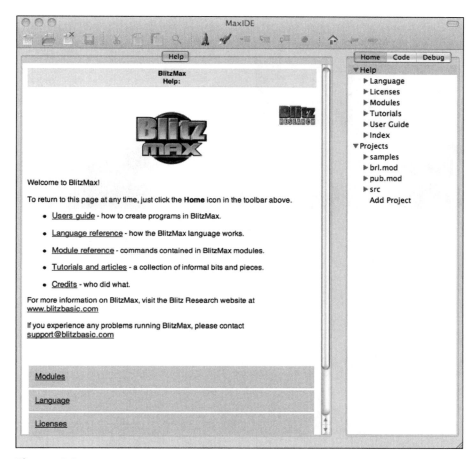

**Figure 1.3**
The Documentation window.

when you type in this area. If you want to see an example, type the word **End**, so that your screen looks like the one pictured in Figure 1.5. You will notice that as soon as you complete the word and press the spacebar, it becomes a different color. This highlight feature helps in reading and understanding your program.

Take a look to the right of the screen. Although not pictured in the previous figure, the only visible panel located on the right is under buttons labeled *Home*, *Code*, and *Debug*. Each of these buttons displays separate info on the panel. Home shows the documentation and files that you can open, Code shows information about the program you are currently editing, and Debug shows information as you run a program. These descriptions probably don't mean much to you now, but by the end of this book you will understand what they do.

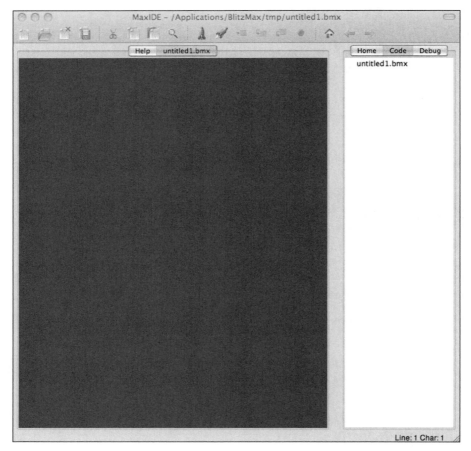

**Figure 1.4**
The BlitzMax IDE.

## Toolbars

The main toolbar (shown in Figure 1.6) is simply a set of shortcut icons. It allows you to perform actions quickly without searching through the menus for the command. Table 1.1 briefly describes each icon going from left to right.

## Menus

The menu toolbar allows you to exercise the full power of BlitzMax. The main menu bar looks like Figure 1.7. Buried within each menu are many helpful and useful commands. Table 1.2 shows the most important.

**Figure 1.5**
Highlighted vs not-highlighted code.

**Figure 1.6**
The main toolbar.

**Table 1.1**  Main Toolbar Shortcut Icons

| Icon | Description |
|------|-------------|
| New | Opens a new, blank BlitzMax document. |
| Open | Allows you to open an existing file from the disk. |
| Close | Closes a single document. |
| Save | If your program has been saved previously, the Save icon quick-saves the open document; if not, Save asks for a file name and a location to save the file to. |
| Cut, Copy, and Paste | The Cut command saves highlighted text to the clipboard but deletes the highlighted text, the Copy command saves the highlighted text to the clipboard but leaves the highlighted text untouched, and Paste places saved text in the clipboard in the document. |
| Find | Allows you to search for a certain word or words in an opened document. |
| Build | Compiles but does not run the open document. |
| Run | Compiles and runs an open document. |
| Step, Step In, Step Out, Stop | Advanced debug tools. |
| Home, Back, Forward | All three commands allow you to enter and navigate through the BlitzMax documentation. |

**Figure 1.7**
BlitzMax menus.

**Table 1.2** BlitzMax Menu Commands

| Command | Description |
|---|---|
| Edit > Block Indent/Outdent | This command will indent or outdent a highlighted portion of text. Useful for making your code easier to read. |
| Program > Build Options > Debug Enabled? | If this feature is enabled, Blitz will do error checking while your program is running, allowing you to detect errors. |

## The First Game: KONG

All right, now you will be able to see what a full game looks like. This is basically a simple *Pong* clone, and it is easy to control and play. The idea of this game is to score more points than your opponent by hitting the ball past his side of the table. To play, either run demo01-01.exe from the CD or compile the code.

To compile the code yourself, you need to find demo01-01.bmx on the CD. (It should be located in the Chapter1 source directory.) To open it, click the File menu on the top of the compiler and choose Open. Navigate to demo01-01.bmx, and press Enter. The code should now appear inside your compiler.

To actually compile, find the Program menu in BlitzMax. Select Program > Run Program, and the game will compile and run! If you get a window asking you to save the file, choose a directory to save it in or just click Cancel, and the program will run. You have just compiled your first program!

Feel free to examine the code; although it may seem very weird and hard to understand now, you will soon be able to figure out this code easily.

Table 1.3 lists the keys you will use for this game.

**Table 1.3** Keys Used in KONG

| Key | Action |
|---|---|
| Up Arrow | Move player up |
| Down Arrow | Move player down |
| Escape | Exit game |
| P | Pause and Unpause |

Okay, let's take a look at the code. Read it, but don't worry if some of it is hard to understand. This is the first program you have seen, and it isn't easy. You will learn how to actually write code like this throughout the book.

```
'demo01-01.bmx - A Complete game of KONG--A Pong Clone
'Author: Maneesh Sethi, http://www.maneeshsethi.com

'Set up graphics mode
Graphics 800,600

'Seed the random generator (make random numbers actually random)
SeedRnd(MilliSecs())

'Create a back buffer
'SetBuffer BackBuffer()
'Set the handle to the center of images
AutoMidHandle True


Const HUMAN_SPEED = 7 'The human's max speed
Const COMPUTER_SPEED = 6 'The computer's max speed
Const X_RANDOM_FACTOR = 2 'The variance of the x speed after colliding with
something
Const Y_RANDOM_FACTOR = 1 'The variance of the y speed after colliding with
something
'The ball's speed at the beginning of a level
Const LEVEL_START_XV_MIN = 3
Const LEVEL_START_XV_MAX = 6
Const LEVEL_START_YV_MIN = -8
Const LEVEL_START_YV_MAX = 8

'TYPES
'The player type: both the human and the opponent
Type Tplayer
 Field y:Int 'The vertical position of the player
 Field score:Int
End Type

'The ball type: for the ball
Type Tball
 Field x:Int
 Field y:Int
'xv and yv are the velocity variables
```

```
 Field xv:Int
 Field yv:Int
End Type

'IMAGES
'The picture of the human player
Global player1image = LoadImage("player1.bmp")

'The picture of the computer player
Global player2image = LoadImage("player2.bmp")

'The picture of the ball
Global ballimage = LoadImage("ball.bmp") 'Load the ball image

'TYPE INITIALIZATION

'Create a ball
Global ball:Tball = New Tball
'Create the human
Global player1:Tplayer = New Tplayer
'Create the computer
Global player2:Tplayer = New Tplayer
```

This is the end of the declaration section of the code. This part sets up the important variables for the program as well as the types and images. (Don't worry; you will be introduced to all of this as the book progresses.)

After the declaration, we begin the initialization. Initialization is the process of setting up everything that will be used in the program—in this section, the initialization section sets up the beginning score values and the players' position on the screen.

```
'INITIALIZATION

DrawText "Ready...Set",400,300
'Wait for one second
Delay(1000)
DrawText "GO!!!", 420,330
Flip
'Delay for 1/5 of a second
Delay(200)

'Initialize the level
```

```
InitializeLevel()

'Set initial scores
player1.score = 0
player2.score = 0
```

The initialization section sets up some important variables for the game, such as the score and the player variables. These variables keep track of how the player is doing and where he or she is located.

After initialization, the actual loop begins:

```
'MAIN LOOP
While Not KeyHit(KEY_ESCAPE)

'Clear the screen
Cls

'Draw the ball
DrawImage (ballimage,ball.x,ball.y)
'Draw the human
DrawImage (player1image, 60, player1.y)
'Draw the computer
DrawImage (player2image, 740, player2.y)

'Test what user pressed
TestKeyboard()
'What should AI do?
TestAI()
'Draw the HUD
DrawScore()

Flip

Delay 20

Wend 'END OF MAIN LOOP
```

### What Is a Frame?

I am about to reference the word *frame* a bunch of times in a second. What does "frame" mean? A frame is the screen at any given moment. A game can be compared to an animated film—both are made up of a bunch of different pictures that, when put together, create animation. The frames blend together so quickly that the objects on the screen appear to be moving. An average game runs at 30 frames per second, which means 30 pictures on the screen are blended together each and every second.

This is the end of the main loop. To put it bluntly, the main loop is the actual game. Every frame of a game is a single iteration of the main loop. By the way, a loop causes some code to be repeated over and over until some condition becomes false. Here, the condition is that the Esc key has not been pressed. Usually, the main loop is a `while` loop, shown here in the line

```
While Not KeyHit(KEY_ESCAPE)
```

At this point, the actual game loop has been completed, so we must now define the functions. A function is called with its name followed by parentheses; for example, InitializeLevel(). Functions are like little helpers that perform specific activities that we want to do over and over. If you look at the main loop, you will see that most of these functions are called from there, and some others are called from within other functions.

```
'INITIALIZELEVEL()
'Sets up starting values
Function InitializeLevel()

'Put ball in center of the screen
ball.x = 400
ball.y = 300

'Make the ball move in a random direction
ball.xv = Rand(LEVEL_START_XV_MIN, LEVEL_START_XV_MAX)
ball.yv = Rand(LEVEL_START_YV_MIN, LEVEL_START_YV_MAX)

'Place the players in their correct position
player2.y = 300
player1.y = 300
  End Function
```

This function sets up the starting values for the players and the ball. The ball is in the center of the screen and it is directed toward the right of the screen (to the computer player's side) with a small variation on how high or low it goes. The human player is near the left edge of the screen, and the computer player is near the right.

```
'DRAWSCORE()
'Draws the HUD in the top right
Function DrawScore()
'Write the human score
```

```
DrawText "Player 1: " + player1.score, 700, 0
'Write the computer's score
DrawText "Player 2: " + player2.score, 700, 30
 End Function
```

This is probably the simplest function in this program because all it does is draw the scores on the top right of the screen.

```
'TESTKEYBOARD()
'Moves player up and down based on keyboard
Function TestKeyboard()

'If player presses up, move him up
If KeyDown(KEY_UP)
 player1.y = player1.y - HUMAN_SPEED
EndIf

'If player presses down, move him down
If KeyDown(KEY_DOWN)
 player1.y = player1.y + HUMAN_SPEED
End If

'if player presses Pause, pause the game
If KeyHit(KEY_P)
 'make screen blank
 Cls

 DrawText "Press 'P' to Unpause Game",400,300

 Flip

 'wait for player to unpause
 While Not KeyHit(KEY_P)
 Wend

EndIf

End Function
```

This function determines what keys the user pressed, if any. If it doesn't make sense to you, try reading the following pseudocode.

### What Is Pseudocode?

Big word, huh? Pseudocode is a very helpful device in game programming, because it takes hard-to-understand concepts and turns them into human language. Pseudocode is the program code put into easier-to-understand terms. Basically, to convert code into pseudocode, simply change each line of code into human language. However, pseudocode does not have all the detail that real code does, so although it is good for understanding concepts, it isn't a good idea to try to put it back into a program. Within this book, pseudocode appears in italics. One thing to note is that psuedocode is NOT a computer language—it is only used by humans to understand code more easily. Don't try to type this in to BlitzMax—it won't work!

```
If (player presses up)
    Move player up


If (player presses down)
    Move player down


If (player presses 'P')
    Pause the game
```

Pretty easy to understand, don't you think? Refer back to the actual code to see how the sections match up.

The last function to understand is `TestAI()`. It won't make much sense if you read it without looking at the pseudocode first, so let's take a look at the pseudocode now.

```
If (ball is above computer)
    Move computer up

OR if (ball is below computer)
    Move computer down


If (ball hits player's paddle)
    Change direction of ball

OR if (ball hits computer's paddle)
    Change direction of ball

OR if (ball hits top wall)
    Change direction of ball
```

```
OR if (ball hits bottom wall)
      Change direction of ball

OR if (ball hits left wall)
      Score a point for computer
      Reset the level

OR if (ball hits right wall)
      Score a point for the player
       Reset the level
```

Next, look at the actual function TestAI().

```
'TESTAI()
'Updates ball and score and enemy
Function TestAI()

'If ball is above computer, move computer up
If ball.y > player2.y
 player2.y = player2.y + COMPUTER_SPEED

'if ball is lower than computer, move computer down
ElseIf ball.y < player2.y
 player2.y = player2.y - COMPUTER_SPEED
 EndIf

'If ball hits human player, reflect it away from him and vary its velocity and
direction
If ImagesCollide(ballimage,ball.x,ball.y,0,player1image,60,player1.y,0)
 ball.xv = -ball.xv + Rand(-X_RANDOM_FACTOR,X_RANDOM_FACTOR)
 ball.yv = ball.yv + Rand(-Y_RANDOM_FACTOR,Y_RANDOM_FACTOR)

'If ball hits computer, reflect it away from computer and vary its velocity and
direction
 ElseIf
ImagesCollide(ballimage,ball.x,ball.y,0,player2image,740,player2.y,0)
 ball.xv = -ball.xv + Rand(-X_RANDOM_FACTOR,X_RANDOM_FACTOR)
 ball.yv = ball.yv + Rand(-Y_RANDOM_FACTOR,Y_RANDOM_FACTOR)

'If ball hits top wall, reflect it downward
ElseIf ball.y <= 0
 ball.xv = ball.xv + Rand (-X_RANDOM_FACTOR,X_RANDOM_FACTOR)
 ball.yv = -ball.yv + Rand (-Y_RANDOM_FACTOR,Y_RANDOM_FACTOR)
```

```
'If ball hits bottom wall, reflect it upward
ElseIf ball.y >= 600
  ball.xv = ball.xv + Rand (-X_RANDOM_FACTOR,X_RANDOM_FACTOR)
  ball.yv = -ball.yv + Rand (-Y_RANDOM_FACTOR,Y_RANDOM_FACTOR)

'if ball hits left wall, computer has scored so computer gets one more point
ElseIf ball.x <= 0
  player2.score = player2.score + 1    'computer scores
  DrawText "Player 2 Scores!!!",400,300
  Flip
  'wait two seconds
  Delay(2000)

  'reset level
  InitializeLevel()

'If ball hits right wall, human scored so give him a point
ElseIf ball.x >= 800
  player1.score = player1.score + 1    'human scores
  DrawText "Player 1 Scores!!!", 400, 300
  Flip
  'wait 2 secs
  Delay(2000)
  'reset level
  InitializeLevel()
EndIf

  'update ball's position on screen
  ball.x = ball.x + ball.xv
  ball.y = ball.y + ball.yv

End Function
```

This one is a lot harder to understand. TestAI() changes the position of the ball based on its direction variables and changes the position of the computer's paddle based on the position of the ball. It also increments the score if either team hits the ball past the opposing paddle. If you are having trouble understanding this function, look back at the pseudocode.

Once again, if you want to have a better perspective of this game, run demo01-01.bmx off the CD.

**Caution**

Because of margin constraints, some of the lines of code may have spread over two lines or more. In a real game, all the code must be on one line, or else it won't run. For example, if I had written something like the following line

```
ElseIf ImagesCollide(ballimage,ball.x,ball.y,0,player2image,740,player2.y,0);
This tests to see if the ball has collided with player 2's image.
```

Typing it into the compiler with the line break would not work. It must be on the same line, even though the margins in the book made it appear broken up.

Figures 1.8 and 1.9 show the KONG title screen and main screen.

## Compiling the Code

Compiling the code is a very simple procedure. Just open the file (demo01-01.bmx) off the CD in BlitzMax (or type it into the workspace), save the file (File > Save) onto your computer, and select Program > Build and Run, as shown in Figure 1.10.

**Figure 1.8**
KONG title screen.

**Figure 1.9**
KONG main screen.

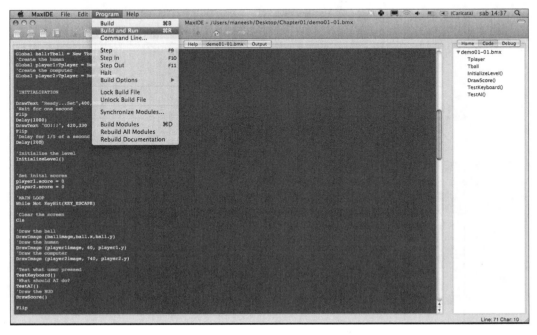

**Figure 1.10**
Compiling the game.

Well, that isn't what you would call a full game. I did not add any special effects or sounds, because they aren't very important at this point. The idea is to get a feel for what code looks like and how it is written. You will notice that the meanings of most of the functions are easy to understand because of the function names. This helps in understanding the program.

Let me summarize the main parts of a game. The game consists of:

- The initialization section

- The main loop

- The shutdown

Initialization sets up variables and functions that are used throughout the game. Declaration is part of initialization and is used to set up variables that will be used later in the program. The game loop is what you see on the screen. Each *iteration* (an iteration is each time the program runs through the loop) of the loop is one frame of the game. Usually, there are at least 30 frames, or iterations, per second. See Figure 1.11 for a description of initialization, the game loop (also known as the main loop), and shutdown in KONG.

The shutdown sequence is the final part of the game, and it runs just before and during the end of the game. It closes all open files, deletes any running variables, and quits the game.

Of course, there are a few other important parts to any game, but I will go over them with you when learning about them is necessary. For now, read over the commented code (on the CD) and try to understand what is going on. If you follow the functions, it shouldn't be too hard.

### The Day That Maneesh Got Embarrassed

In March of 2004, I was on a show called "Call for Help" on *TechTV*. I decided to demonstrate this game, KONG, on the show, because it was an easy to understand and play game. Turns out I made a bad choice. During the game, some of the randomization code got messed up, so the ball bounced up and down and up and down repeatedly. My game actually crashed on TV!

You can see the segment on *TechTV* on my Web site, http://www.maneeshsethi.com. Just promise not to laugh!

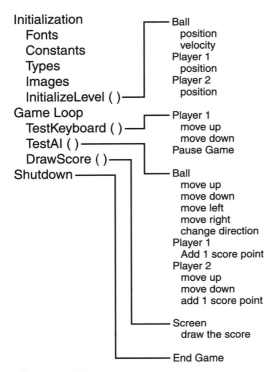

Initialization
   Fonts
   Constants
   Types
   Images
   InitializeLevel ( )
Game Loop
   TestKeyboard ( )
   TestAI ( )
   DrawScore ( )
Shutdown

   Ball
     position
     velocity
   Player 1
     position
   Player 2
     position

   Player 1
     move up
     move down
   Pause Game

   Ball
     move up
     move down
     move left
     move right
     change direction
   Player 1
     Add 1 score point
   Player 2
     move up
     move down
     add 1 score point

   Screen
     draw the score

   End Game

**Figure 1.11**
Initialization, game loop, and shutdown.

## Summary

We have certainly covered a lot of ground in this chapter! So far, we have learned about the history of BASIC; we have installed BlitzMax; we have learned the important features of the program; and we have written, read, and played our first game. One important thing: *Do not* be disheartened by the length or complexity of the sample code. This game is not a tough one, and although it seems long now, it will be relatively simple to write by the time you finish this book.

In this chapter, we went over the following concepts:

- The history of BASIC

- Installing the BlitzMax program

- Creating our first game

- Compiling our first game

The next chapter will introduce you to the fundamentals of BASIC; it will discuss common operators and operations. If you've made it this far, the next chapter should be a cinch.

Just sit back, relax, and enjoy the ride.

# CHAPTER 2

## GETTING TO KNOW BASIC

This chapter examines the simple and fundamental aspects of the BASIC language. We are going to start with text programs, so you won't see too many graphics in the programs in this chapter.

What is the best way to learn BASIC? I suggest taking what you learn from this chapter and writing your own programs. Although you will not be able to make graphical programs, you will be able to make simple text-based programs. Writing your own programs will help you really learn the ideas from this chapter. The next chapters build heavily on the concepts you learn here, so make sure you understand the fundamentals explained in this chapter before moving on to the next chapters.

In this chapter, you will learn how to use variables, input, and conditionals. Ready?

## Hello, World!

Okay, before you go any further, you're going to write your first program. This is a common one for first-time programmers to write in any computer programming language, most likely because it is so simple. This program simply displays the text Hello, World! on the screen. That's right, no graphics, no special effects, just pure, hardcore text.

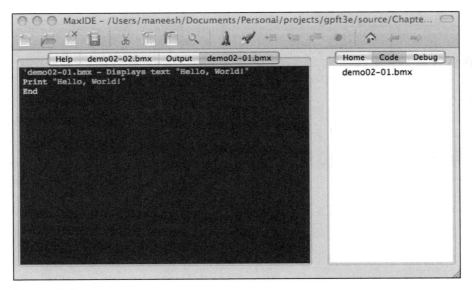

**Figure 2.1**
The Hello World program in BlitzMax.

Let's go over how to compile the following code. Type what follows into your BlitzMax compiler or open demo02-01.bmx (see Figure 2.1). Next, select Program > Build and Run and watch the magic.

If you decide to type the code into the compiler, make sure that the workspace into which you are typing is blank first. Only the code should be displayed in the main window of the BlitzMax compiler.

If you don't want to compile the code, you can also run this program from the CD. Figure 2.2 shows the executed Hello World program.

```
'demo02-01.bmx - Displays text "Hello, World!"
Print "Hello, World!"
 End
```

Although this program may seem very simple, it is a big hurdle you have just crossed. You just created a file, typed in the code, compiled it, and ran it as a program. Congratulations!

Let's analyze this program a bit (although there isn't much to analyze). First of all, the line

```
'demo02-01.bmx - Displays text "Hello, World!"
```

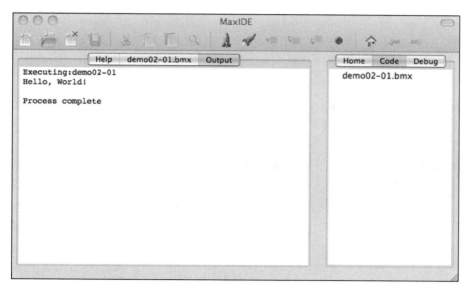

**Figure 2.2**
The executed Hello World program.

is a comment. A comment is any text that is written after an apostrophe ('). The comment ends at the end of the line. A comment does not have to occupy its own line; it can be written after some actual program code. For example, this line

```
Print "This is code" 'this is a comment
```

consists of two parts: a line of code and a comment. Comments are used to help you understand the code; the compiler does not understand or care about information in comments. The compiler automatically ignores any comments. Figure 2.3 demonstrates how comments look inside a compiler.

**Tip**

> You might be wondering, "If it is my code, why would I need a comment to understand it? I wrote it, so I understand it!" The problem with this assumption is twofold: one, you may decide to share the code with someone after you write the program, and two, you could forget how your program works and spend a lot of time trying to figure out what some parts do. I remember once, at an old coding job, I had to rewrite some old code. "Who wrote this crappy code?!" I asked my boss, because it was taking hours to rewrite. He looked up the logs—guess who wrote it? Me, a few months before. I had forgotten not only what the code did, but that I had written it in the first place. Anyway, the moral of the story is *always comment your code*.

The next line of code is the meat of the program.

```
Print "Hello, World!"
```

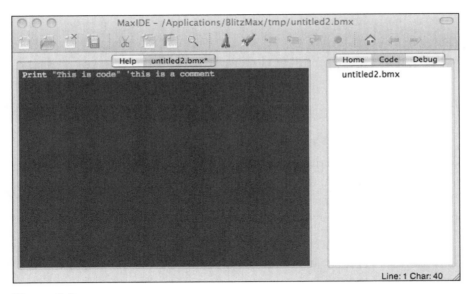

**Figure 2.3**
Comments in a compiler.

This line prints the text string "Hello, World!" on the screen (a text string is simply a set of characters) and begins a new line. To see what I mean by new line, add another Print command to the code. You will see that the new text is written below the old text.

Note the quotation marks around "Hello, World!". Quotation marks, or simply quotes, are necessary around any part of a string. The quotes identify to the program that what is being typed is a set of letters and numbers, not a variable name. If you leave off the quotes, you will get an error.

I usually like to provide the function declaration for easy reference when calling functions. A *function declaration* describes any parameters taken in by the function as well as the function name. The function declaration for Print is:

```
Print [string:String]
```

**Note**

Notice the square brackets ([]) on the left and right of the [string] variable. These brackets mean that the variable is optional and not required. (If you use Print without a string after it, it will simply print a blank line.) If the variable is required but omitted, you will receive an error and not be able to compile your code.

**Table 2.1** Parameters for Print

| Parameter | Description |
| --- | --- |
| string:String | A text string followed by a new line that will be displayed onscreen. If string is omitted, only a new line will be printed. |

As you can see, the function's name is Print and the only parameter is [string]. A string is simply a series of characters put together; you can think of a sentence as a string. The string would be the entire sentence lined up together, including the spaces and punctuation.

First of all, Print is a function. Functions (which are described in more detail later) come in two flavors: user-defined and compiler-defined. User-defined functions are written by the programmer (TestKeyboard() from the Chapter 1 game is an example) and compiler-defined functions are embedded in the compiler and are available for use in a program. Print is an example of a compiler-defined function.

See Table 2.1 for a description of the Print parameters.

One question remains: What is that colon doing on the variable name? That brings us to the next topic, variables.

## Variables

Variables are used in almost every program. A variable is just that: "variable." This means that the value of a variable can change. For example, say you were running a program that uses a high score that is stored in a variable. When the high score changes, the high score variable changes to reflect the new score.

## Declaring Variables

Variables are very easy to use, because they can be used as regular numbers. However, unlike numbers, variables must first be declared. When a variable is declared, the program knows that the variable exists, and you can use it in your program.

Three types of variables exist in BASIC: integer variables, floating-point variables, and string variables. See Table 2.2 for a description of the types of variables.

**Table 2.2** Description of Variable Types

| Variable | Description |
| --- | --- |
| int_var:Int | Fixed-point variables with no decimal places. This type is the default type, so you can omit the :Int if you want to. |
| float_var:Float | Floating-point variables with decimal places allowed. |
| str_var:String | A text string. |

**Note**

When variables are created, they are automatically assumed to be integers, or whole numbers in other words. Therefore, the percent sign on all integer variables is unnecessary and from now on, they will mostly be omitted from the code.

Each type of variable is defined in a similar way. Simply type the name of the variable you want to define followed by the type name (:Int, :Float, or :String). For example,

```
highscore:Int = 100
pi:Float = 3.14159
myname:String = "Maneesh Sethi"
```

## Using Variables

You are now ready to write a few programs using variables. These programs should demonstrate a few important points about variables.

```
'demo02-02.bmx - Adds two cool numbers

'VARIABLES
favnum:Int = 314
coolnum:Int = 13

'Print the two variables
Print "I like " + favnum + " And I like " + coolnum
'Print the variables added together
 Print "These numbers added together are " + (favnum + coolnum)
```

The output is shown in Figure 2.4.

Well, this is certainly interesting. Let's check it out. First, a comment is written to describe the program. This is good practice and should be used on most

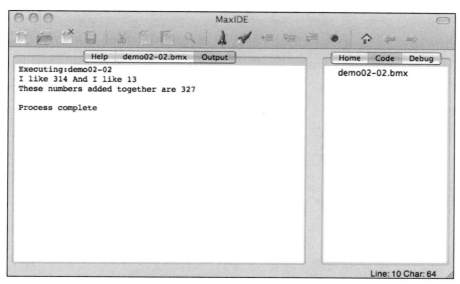

**Figure 2.4**
The demo02-02.bmx program.

programs. Next, I initialized two variables: `favnum:Int` and `coolnum:Int`. Then, I called the `Print` function. The string variable begins with the static text `"I like"` and then displays `favnum`. To display `favnum`, you use the concatenation operator (+). The concatenation operator links separate strings together; in this case, it displays the variable `favnum`. It finishes out the first `Print` statement by displaying `"And I like"` + the variable `coolnum`.

The next `Print` statement displays `"These numbers added together are"` and shows 327, which is equal to 314 + 13. However, try removing the parentheses around `favnum` and `coolnum`, like in Figure 2.5. A strange answer comes up when these parentheses are removed: 31413!

The reason for this strange answer is that without the parentheses, the addition operator (+) is interpreted as the concatenation operator due to the context in which it is used. It tries to add the integer, 314, to the string "These numbers added together are". Because there are no parentheses, the program tries to add a string to an integer—something that doesn't make sense. So, to fix the situation, the program converts the number to a string and adds the string "13" to the end of the string "314" and displays it as a string rather than an integer. The only way to fix this problem is to use parentheses.

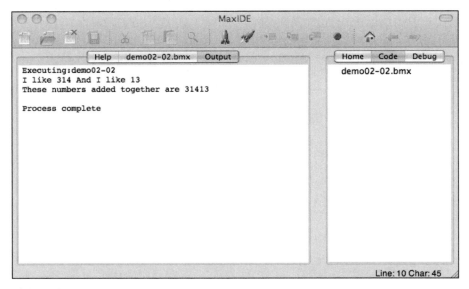

**Figure 2.5**
Demo02-02.bmx without parentheses.

Here is an example of concatenation using only string variables.

```
'demo02-03.bmx - adds strings together
string1:String = "I "
string2:String = "like "
string3:String = "programming!"
'concatenate the strings
completestring:String = string1 + string2 + string3
'Print 'em out
Print completestring
```

In this program, a set of single words are created and joined together in the completestring:String variable using the concatenation operator. As you can see in Figure 2.6, "I " + "like " + "programming!" becomes "I like programming!".

**Note**

So far, when declaring integers, I declared them as such: int_var:Int. However, by default, Blitz assumes that a new variable is an integer. So, from now on, integers will not be defined with the Int identifier.

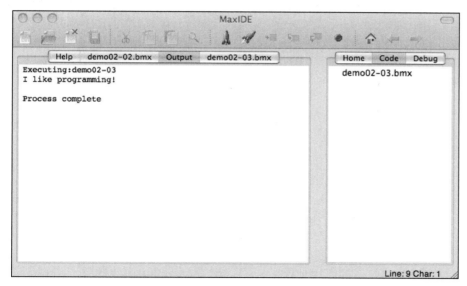

**Figure 2.6**
The demo02-03.bmx program.

# Input

Finally, you understand how variables work. Now, let's use those variables to get input from the user of the program. Using input, you can recognize what keys the user presses, or you might have the user answer a question. Either way, most input is stored in a variable. Figure 2.7 shows the output of this program.

```
'demo02-04.bmx asks user's name and shows it
'get the user's name
name:String = Input("Hi! May I know your name please?")
Print "Hi " + name + "."
```

The first line is a comment that tells what the program does. The second line takes in the input, and the third and final line displays what the user entered.

Input is declared as this:

```
Input:String([prompt:String])
```

**Caution**

Notice that the function name, Input:String, has :String attached to the end. This symbol signifies the return type of the function. Because it is a string, the function only returns strings. What this means is that if you request the user to put in numbers to add together, such as 2 + 2, the value returned will be "2 + 2", NOT 4. Of course, if the user typed in 4, the function would return 4.

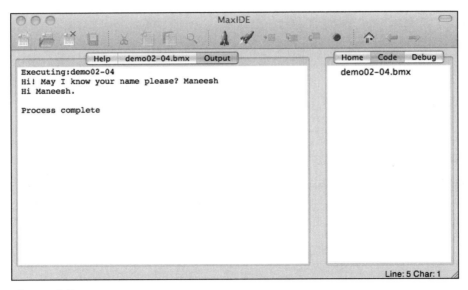

**Figure 2.7**
The demo02-04.bmx program.

Input is the name of the function. Table 2.3 explains that prompt is a string that is displayed to the computer before taking the input value. prompt is usually used to ask the user to provide you with the info you want so that the user will know what to tell the program. Notice that there are parentheses around prompt in the function. Parentheses are required; if you fail to place them in the program, the program will not compile.

In the previous program, name is set equal to the Input command. When the Input command receives an answer from the user, it is stored in the name variable. If you left this line looking like this:

```
Input("Hi! May I know your name please? ")
```

without including a variable, the response that the user made would be simply thrown away. Using Input without a variable is not a good idea.

Input only returns strings. Thus, you will get an error if you try to assign the results of the Input function to an integer variable.

Okay, you now have the basics of input down. However, this input function isn't very useful so far. Who wants a program that tells them their own name? This brings us to the next topic: conditionals.

| Table 2.3 Input()'s Parameter | |
|---|---|
| **Parameter** | **Description** |
| `prompt:String` | The string displayed to the user before allowing the user to enter an input value. |

## Conditionals

Conditionals are a very important part of any program. Conditionals allow your program to think. With them, any program can make choices and decisions. Before you can fully understand conditionals, however, you must first learn about the BlitzMax idea of truth and falsehood.

## Truth and Falsehood

BlitzMax has a different idea about what is true and what is false than we humans do. To a human, some things may be partly true, but to a computer, any expression is either true or false. Although parts of an expression can be different than the rest, the entire expression is only evaluated as one or the other.

BlitzMax (and computers in general) believes that zero is false and any other value (nonzero value) is true, although the true value is usually one. This makes programming a much easier job.

To determine whether something is true or false, you use the relational and logical operators. These operators check one statement against another to see whether the aspect of their relationship that is being checked is true or false. Table 2.4 lists all the relational and logical operators.

Using Table 2.4 as a guide, you can see that if, say, variable A is equal to 14 and variable B is equal to 12, A>B will return True, because 14 is a larger number than 12.

## If...Then

The first conditional you will learn is the `If` statement. The `If` statement has a very basic declaration:

```
If
```

**Table 2.4**  Relational and Logical Operators

**Relational Operators**

| | |
|---|---|
| > | Greater than |
| >= | Greater than or equal to |
| < | Less than |
| <= | Less than or equal to |
| = | Equal to |
| <> | Not equal to |

**Logical Operators**

And
Or
Not

The idea of an `If` statement is that it allows your program to make choices. You pass an expression into the `If` statement by following the `If` command with the expression:

```
If expression is true Then
;Do something
 Endif
```

As you can see, the `If` statement is followed by an expression. If the expression is true, the code between the `If` and `EndIf` commands is executed. If not, nothing happens.

```
'demo02-05.bmx - Tests if you are old enough to vote

'Find out how old the user is
age_str:String = Input("How old are you? ")
'Cast the string to an integer
age:Int = Int(age_str)

'If older Or equal To 18, Print out confirmation that user is allowed To vote.
If age >= 18 Then
 Print "You are legally allowed to vote!"
 EndIf
```

This program simply asks how old you are, tests it against the age 18, and then prints `"You are legally allowed to vote!"` if you are 18 years or older. But what if you want to tell the user something else, even if they aren't over 18? As you can

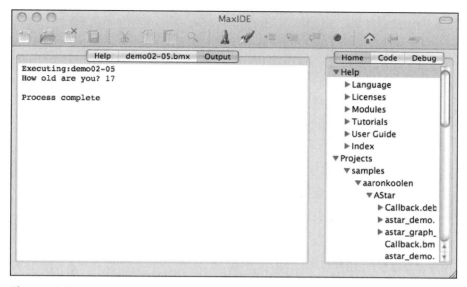

**Figure 2.8**
The demo02-05.bmx program.

see in Figure 2.8, this program does nothing if the user is younger than 18. The program then waits for the user to press a key for the program to exit.

The EndIf command signifies the end of the If...Then test. When the program reaches EndIf, it resumes normal processing of commands instead of only executing the commands when the condition tested in the If statement is met.

Did you notice something strange about the conditional test? We did something weird with the line after the Input. Check it out:

```
'Cast the string to an integer
age:Int = Int(age_str)
```

What is this Int(age_str) doing? It's actually called a cast—that is, it converts the string variable age_str into the integer variable age. This is done by putting the name of the new type (Int, in this case, although it could be String or Float) around the name of the old variable. The string is now converted into an integer, and we can test the value of the integer against the integer 18.

## If...Then...Else

Perhaps you want the program to test if the user is younger than 18. You could rewrite the program by adding another If statement to check if the user is younger than 18, but there is an easier (and better) way: Use the Else statement.

```
'demo02-06.bmx - Tests if you are old enough to vote

'Ask how old the user is
age_str:String = Input("How old are you? ")
age = Int(age_str)

'If older or equal to 18 then let them vote
If age >= 18 Then
  Print "You are legally allowed to vote!"

'If younger than 18, do Not let them vote
Else
  Print "Sorry, you need to be a few years older."
  EndIf
```

Figure 2.9 shows the output.

This time, the program tests the user's age, but if it is less than 18, it prints out the sentence under the Else statement.

There is also one other effective use of the If...Else conditional. You can combine the two to create Else If.

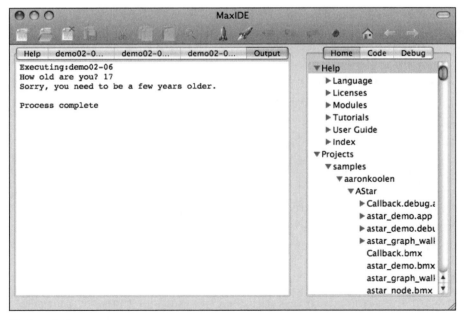

**Figure 2.9**
The demo02-06.bmx program.

```
'demo02-07.bmx - Tests if you are old enough to vote

'find out how old the user is
age_str:String = Input("How old are you? ")
age = Int(age_str)

'If exactly 18, write that voting is legal
If age = 18 Then
  Print "You can now vote."
'If older than 18, write out that voting has been legal For a While
Else If age > 18
  Print "You've been able to vote for a while."
'If younger than 18, write out that voting is illegal.
Else If age < 18
  Print "Sorry, you will have to wait a few years to vote."
  EndIf
```

Figure 2.10 shows the output.

## Caution

This program will only work if the user enters an integer, but if the user enters a string (such as `"hello"` or `"eighteen"`), the variable will always be assigned zero. This is because it is impossible to convert a string to a number, so Blitz automatically assigns a string not made of numbers to zero. You can fix this problem using a loop or `Goto`, which will be explained soon.

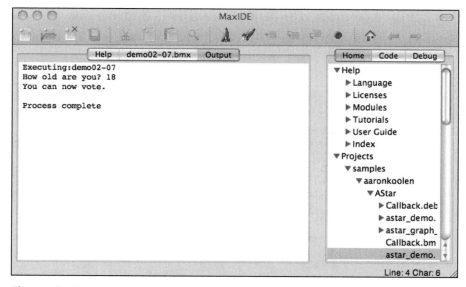

**Figure 2.10**
The demo02-07.bmx program.

This program tests all three user possibilities.

Sometimes, you might want to test a large number of possibilities, and using If...Then can be awkward. A conditional statement was made to fix this problem: Select...Case

## Select. . .Case

Select...Case makes working with a large number of values much easier. The best way to demonstrate is with an example.

```
'demo02-08.bmx - tests the keys pressed

x_str:String = Input("Enter 1 to say hi, or 0 to quit. ")
x = Int(x_str)
Select x
 Case 1
        Print "Hi!"
 Case 0
        End
 Default
        Print "Huh?"
 End Select
```

In this listing, the program asks the user to enter either one or zero. It then either writes "Hi!" or quits the program. The default case is a catch-all command; if the user enters neither one nor zero, the default code is displayed.

### Note

If you haven't observed it already, notice that I have been indenting my code in a very easy to understand and logical manner. This makes reading and understanding code much easier, and I highly recommend that you do the same. We'll talk more about style in Chapter 4.

In this case, Select...Case isn't very necessary. Because there are only two cases, it is just as easy to use an If...Else. However, when the programs get more complex, Select...Case becomes a more useful tool.

By the way, the declaration for Select...Case is

```
Select variable
```

Easy enough, huh?

# Logical Operators

Logical operators are a base for expressions and conditional statements. You can view all of the BlitzMax logical operators in Table 2.5. It lists all the conditions that make the logical operators true and false.

The AND operator is true only if both its parameters are true; the OR operator is true if one or more of its parameters are true; and the NOT operator is true only if its parameter is false. Here is an example of the AND operator.

```
'demo02-09.bmx - Shows use of the And operator

'Find out how old the user is
age_str:String = Input("How old are you? ")
age = Int(age_str)
'find out if the user lives in America
location_str:String = Input("Do you live in America? (1 For yes, 2 For no) ")
location = Int(location_str)

'Write out the proper string depending on the user's age and location
If age >= 18 And location = 1 Then
  Print "Congrats, you are eligible to vote!"
Else
  Print "Sorry, you can't vote."
  EndIf
```

The output is shown in Figure 2.11. For me, I'm 20 years old, but I currently live in Italy. Can I vote? Legally, I think so (I'm an American citizen!), but it's difficult when I'm outside the country. Let's see what the program has to say about it.

## The NOT Operator

The NOT operator is a little bit different than the other two logical operators. Instead of two operands, it only takes one. And instead of returning a value based

**Table 2.5** Logical Operator Truth Table

| P | Q | P AND Q | P OR Q | NOT P |
| --- | --- | --- | --- | --- |
| 0 | 0 | 0 | 0 | 1 |
| 0 | 1 | 0 | 1 | 1 |
| 1 | 1 | 1 | 1 | 0 |
| 1 | 0 | 0 | 1 | 0 |

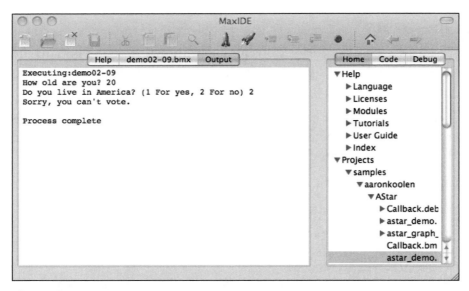

**Figure 2.11**
The demo02-09.bmx program.

on the other two operands, it only returns the opposite of the operand it is working on.

Remember that because false is zero and true is one, the only value NOT will return is one or zero. If you write

    Not 0

your answer will be one, and conversely if you write

    Not 1

your answer will be 0.

## The Goto Command

Before writing a full-fledged game, I want to introduce you to the concept of Goto. Goto is a simple command, but it can be misused very easily, so I recommend using Goto as sparingly as possible. Almost always, if something can be done by using Goto, it can be done in another way.

Goto works like this: you add a label somewhere in your code, and Goto jumps to that label. (See Figure 2.12.)

```
   .label
   Print "Hello"
   Selection = Input ("Enter 1...")
   If (selection = 1)
   Goto label
   End
```

**Figure 2.12**
Using Goto.

The best illustration of this is a sample program.

```
'demo02-10.bmx - Demonstrates the use of Goto
'Place a label
#label
Print "Hello"

'Does user want to repeat?
selection_str:String = Input("Enter 1 if you want me to repeat 'Hello' ==> ")
selection = Int(selection_str)

If (selection = 1)

  'Go to the top and print "Hello" again
  Goto label
EndIf
 End
```

The output is shown in Figure 2.13.

As you can see in Figure 2.12, calling Goto starts the program back at the top. This is accomplished by putting #label at the top of the program. You can make Goto move anywhere by simply moving the line #label. Notice that when you define the label, you put a hash sign (#) before it. When you call it from Goto, however, you discard the hash sign.

## A Text-Based Guessing Game

Now, let's apply all of what you learned in this chapter to create your first guessing game! Basically, the users enter a number, and you will tell them if they are too high or too low. You will allow the users to guess until they figure it out. In order to make this game work, you will be using a loop. If you cannot understand what the loop's function is, it is explained in the next chapter.

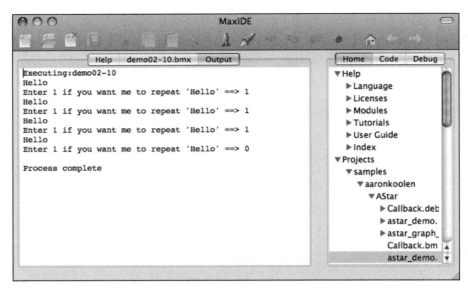

**Figure 2.13**
The demo02-10.bmx program.

First you need to create an initialization section. It will look something like this.

```
'demo02-11.bmx - Try to guess the number
Print "Welcome to the Guessing Game!"
'Seed the random generator...don't worry, what this means will be explained later
SeedRnd MilliSecs()

'Pick a number between 1 and 100
numbertoguess = Rand(1,100)
'The num of guesses the user has used
 numofguesses = 0
```

The randomizer works like this: numbertoguess is assigned to a random number, which is returned by Rand. Rand returns a number between what is given; here, it returns a number between 1 and 100. This section prints out introduction text, sets up the guessing number, and declares some variables.

Next you set up the loop and the test to make sure the player guessed a number between 1 and 100.

```
'set the beginning of loop label
#loopbegin
  'Print a blank line
```

```
Print
'Find out the user's guess
guess_str:String = Input("Guess a number ")
guess = Int(guess_str)

'If player guesses outside of range, tell him to guess again
If guess > 100 Or guess < 1
      Print "Pick a number between 1 and 100, silly!"
      'Go back to the beginning
      Goto loopbegin

      EndIf
```

The first line of this code sets up a label to go back to the loop later. Next, the loop begins, the player is asked for input, and the number is tested to see if it is within the correct range. If not, the player is sent back to the beginning of the loop.

Now, you insert the code to test and see if the player has guessed correctly.

```
'Add a guess to the guess counter
numofguesses = numofguesses + 1

'If the guess is too low, go back to beginning
If guess < numbertoguess Then
      Print "The number was too low."
      Goto loopbegin
'If guess is too high, go back to the beginning
Else If guess > numbertoguess Then
      Print "The number was too high."
      Goto loopbegin
      EndIf
```

The first line adds one to the user's number of guesses. Then, the code is tested to see if the user has guessed too high, too low, or just right. If the player has guessed just right, the code just continues through to the end of the program without going back to the beginning of the loop.

Finally, you enter the last section of code.

```
Print "You guessed the number " + numbertoguess + " in " + numofguesses   + " tries!"
```

This program can be run off the CD. It is named demo02-11.bmx. Figure 2.14 shows the output of the complete Guessing Game.

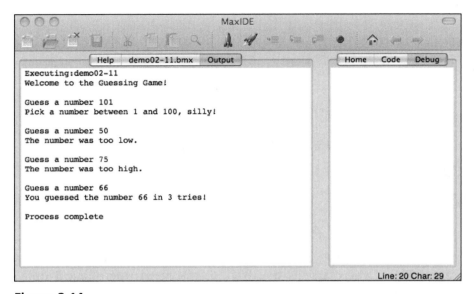

**Figure 2.14**
The complete Guessing Game.

## Summary

This has been a tough chapter for you as well as me. I hope that you remember most of what I have told you so far. I suggest you write a few sample programs using everything taught in this program before you head on to the next chapter; it will help solidify the information in your head.

This chapter covered the following concepts:

- The Hello, World! program

- Variables

- Input

- Conditionals

The next chapter discusses loops, functions, arrays, and types. I hope you're ready!

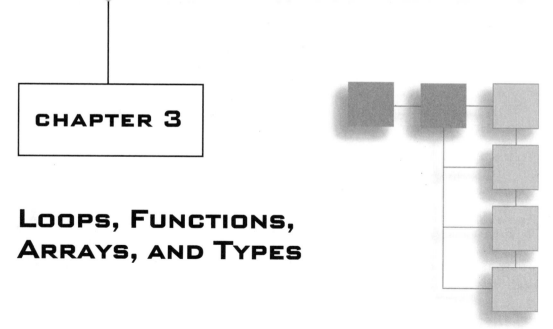

# CHAPTER 3

# Loops, Functions, Arrays, and Types

We are finally moving up to the tough stuff. This chapter introduces the important and interesting subjects of loops, functions, arrays, and types. All of these are essential to any computer game program.

In this chapter, I'm going to explain each of the processes separately, and then we will create a simple game that incorporates them all. By the time you get there, you will know how to use loops, functions, arrays, and types.

## Understanding Loops

A *loop* is a block of code that is repeated over and over until a condition is met. For example, the main game loop is repeated over and over until the player quits or wins the game. We can use Goto, a command that we learned in the previous chapter, as a loop. If you remember the demo02-10.bmx program, a set of commands was repeated until the user wanted them to stop. Loops work exactly like this: a set of commands is repeated over, and over, and over, until a condition is met—either the user wants to exit the loop or the loop is executed a specific number of times. Figure 3.1 shows a sketch of a loop.

Loops are used for many repetitive tasks in computer programs. In a space shooter game, for example, we have to use a loop to check every bullet against the enemy ships. We will also use loops to update the artificial intelligence (AI) for each of the ships.

x = 0

Loop until x = 10
   Do Whatever

Return to top or exit
;once loop exits, x equals 10, and
;Do whatever has happened 10 times

**Figure 3.1**
The loop.

There are three types of loops, and although they are somewhat interchangeable, each has a specific style and it is best if they are used in the proper situation. The three types of loops are

- `For...Next`

- `While...Wend`

- `Repeat...Until`

## For...Next

The `For...Next` loop steps through a block of code a set number of times. In other words, you use it when you know how many times the loop should iterate. You might use this loop when you want the player to move up exactly 10 spaces. Because you know the number of times you want the player to move up, you might have each iteration of the loop move the player up one space and have the loop go through its commands ten times. This loop also can update the info of a set of types (types are explained later in this chapter).

**Note**

Before we move on, I want to discuss the concept of iterations. As you know, a loop processes a number of commands over and over again, starting at the top, going to the bottom, and moving back to the top again. An *iteration* occurs when all of the commands have been processed one full time. When the loop finishes the last statement of the loop, but has not returned to the top of the loop, it has completed one iteration. When it returns to the top, the second iteration begins, and so on.

`For...Next` loops are always used as follows:

```
For variable = beginning_number To ending_number [Step step_amount]
      'Perform actions
   Next
```

As you can see, a For...Next loop begins with For and ends with Next. The To command defines how many times the loop performs its actions. Step_amount, which is optional, defines how much is added to beginning_number each time. If you omit Step, beginning_number is incremented by 1 each time the loop is traversed.

Let's examine a code example:

```
'demo03-01.bmx - counts from 1 to 10
'start counter at one and loop till 10
For counter = 1 To 10
'Print whatever counter is equal to
Print counter
Next
```

Figure 3.2 shows the output.

This program simply prints the numbers 1 through 10 on the screen. The first line after the entry comment begins the For...Next loop. It declares counter and initializes it to 1. The To command tells the compiler how many iterations the loop will go through. Here, it says it will count from one to ten.

The next line simply prints the value of counter, which adds one to its count every iteration of the loop. The final line of the loop returns the code to the beginning of the loop and raises counter by 1.

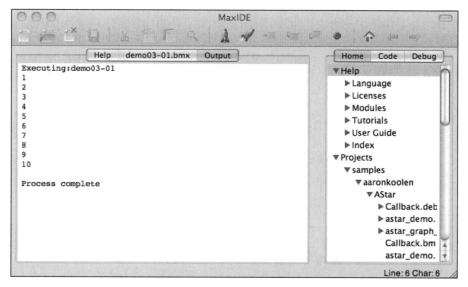

**Figure 3.2**
The demo03-01.bmx program.

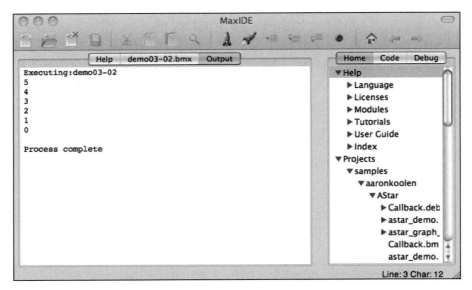

**Figure 3.3**
The demo03-02.bmx program.

You can change the step amount of the loop if you want. The step amount is how much is added to the variable on each iteration of the loop. By default, the step amount is 1.

To change the step amount, simply add the command Step after the To command like this:

```
'demo03-02.bmx - Counts backwards using step amounts
'start counter at 5 and loop till 0 by -1
For counter = 5 To 0 Step -1
 'Print value of counter
 Print counter
 Next
```

The output is shown in Figure 3.3.

**Caution**

Make sure to double-check your loops to ensure you did not make them never-ending. If this program had been written with the step value as 1 (as opposed to −1), the program would have looped forever and never ended. Figure 3.4 shows the output if you change the −1 to a positive 1. Why don't you see an infinite list of numbers? Fortunately, BlitzMax normally catches this error and simply skips the loop.

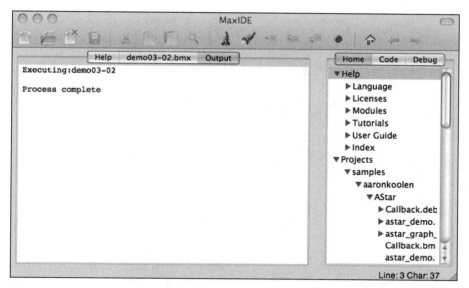

**Figure 3.4**
The demo03-02.bmx program with an infinite loop.

## While...Wend

The next type of loop is the While...Wend loop. This loop is very much like the For...Next loop, but it is normally used to test variable conditions. In other words, the While...Wend loop is normally used when you aren't sure when to exit the loop.

While loops are the most common main loops in games. The main loop (also known as the *game* loop) is a loop that runs over and over until the game is over. Because it cannot be determined *exactly* when to end a game, the While...Wend loop is a perfect choice.

```
'demo03-03.bmx - Waits for a key and then exits
Graphics 640,480
DrawText "This program is worthless.",0,0
DrawText "Press escape to exit.",0,12
Flip
'Wait until user presses 1 to Escape
While Not KeyDown(KEY_ESCAPE)
Wend
 End
```

**Figure 3.5**
The demo03-03.bmx program.

---

**Note**

You might notice some strange functions in this program, such as Flip and Graphics. To check for KeyDown(), you have to be in graphics mode, and the Graphics command does that. You will learn more about this in Part 2; for now, just pretend it isn't there.

---

Figure 3.5 shows the output of this program.

This program simply displays some text and asks you to quit. Almost a waste of time, huh? Well, at least it demonstrates While...Wend, and it introduces a new function, KeyDown().

The While...Wend loop begins like this:

```
While Not KeyDown(KEY_ESCAPE)
```

This line of code sets up a While loop that exits only when the user presses the Esc key. The loop continues until the user presses the Esc key. KeyDown(), which is declared as

```
KeyDown(keycode)
```

determines whether Esc has been pressed.

Here, the keycode KEY_ESCAPE is used as the scan code. A *scan code* is a code generated by pressing any key on a keyboard. Each key has its own separate key code. Esc has the scan code of KEY_ESCAPE. You can see a list of all of the scan codes in Appendix A.

KeyDown returns 1 (true) if the key has been pressed and 0 (false) if the key has not been pressed. Because we want the While...Wend loop to continue until the key has been pressed, we invert the return value by including NOT. Therefore, if the player does not press Esc, the KeyDown returns 0. The NOT command inverts this to a 1, and the While...Wend loop continues to the next iteration.

Now is a good time to introduce the basic game loop. This loop only ends when the user presses Esc. If the user loses, a function is called that will end the program. Note that this code *will not* work. It will only call functions that don't exist (functions are introduced later in this chapter).

```
'Basic Game loop
While Not KeyDown(1)
    PerformLogic()
    Animation()
    If playerlost Then
        GameOver()
    EndIf
Wend
```

This game loop is basically the most simplified version possible. Unless the player loses or presses Esc, the loop continues to iterate. The PerformLogic() function probably updates the AI for the game, and Animation() probably draws and animates everything onscreen. If the playerlost variable is set to 1 (most likely by the PerformLogic() function), the GameOver() function is called and the game is over.

You should always strive to keep your main loop as simple as possible. It should not perform more operations than necessary. You will learn how to delegate operations to smaller and more efficient functions soon in this chapter.

## Repeat...Until

The final BlitzMax loop is the Repeat...Until loop. This loop is almost exactly like the While...Wend loop, except that the condition is written after the closing statement (Until) instead of the opening statement (Repeat).

Doesn't seem like a big difference, huh? The only time you use this type of loop is when you know for sure that the loop should be executed at least once. This is common in situations that involve displaying menus and testing for keys.

```
'demo03-04.bmx   - Closes program after player presses ESC.
Graphics 640,480
DrawText "Why did you open this program?",0,0
Flip
'y is the variable that judges the location of the text
y=12
Repeat
 'Print text
 DrawText "Press Esc to exit.",0,y
 'wait a sec
 Delay 1000
 Flip

 'Move next line of text down
 y=y+12

'repeat until user hits esc
Until KeyHit(KEY_ESCAPE)
DrawText "Program is ending.",0,y
 Flip
```

The output is shown in Figure 3.6.

This program simply writes "Press Esc to exit." to the screen until the user presses Esc. It introduces two main functions: Delay() and KeyHit().

Delay() pauses the program's execution for a set number of milliseconds. Delay is declared as

```
Delay(milliseconds)
```

where milliseconds is the number of milliseconds you want to delay the program for. This program delays the execution for one second (1000 milliseconds).

The other new function introduced is KeyHit().

```
KeyHit(keycode)
```

keycode is the code for the key that might be pressed. This function determines whether the key was pressed. If the key was pressed, it returns true; if not, it returns false.

**Figure 3.6**
The demo03-04.bmx program.

The y variable tracks the location of the Text command. Each time, the y variable is incremented by 12, moving the text down one line.

The reason that the text is moved down 12 pixels is because the font size of the text is size 12. Moving the text down 12 pixels is equivalent to making a new line in the program. The condition for exiting the Repeat...Until loop is the opposite of While...Wend and For...Next loops. Instead of continuing to iterate the loop only as long as the condition is true, the Repeat...Until loop continues only when the condition is false. Take extra precautions to make sure you do not create a never-ending loop.

**Note**

You might wonder about the difference between the new function KeyHit() and the previously introduced function KeyDown(). The fact is, there is very little difference. KeyDown() determines whether the button is down at the time of the test, whereas KeyHit() determines whether it has been down since the last KeyHit() was checked. You can see the difference in any game. If you use KeyDown(), you can hold down a key to make it work repeatedly; if you use KeyHit(), you have to press the button every time you use it.

Because the program used Repeat...Until, the "Press Esc to exit." line will always be shown, even if you press Esc before the loop begins. If you ever write a program that utilizes menus (most RPG [*Role-Playing Game*] games do), you should use a Repeat...Until loop.

Okay, I have thoroughly discussed each of the loops. I hope that you are now an expert on how, as well as when, to use all three types of loops. Now on to an extremely important subject: functions.

## Understanding Functions

Functions are integral to any program. Even in the programs you have been writing so far, you have used functions such as Print() and Delay(), and you have even written your own implicit main function. This section teaches you how to write your own functions that will make understanding and writing your program much easier and simpler.

Functions are small snippets of code that usually perform a single task. All programs consist of at least one function: main. Although main isn't actually defined, it still exists within the program.

Every line of code written so far (with the exception of the ones in Chapter 1) has been written in the function main. This function is the starting point and ending point of every BlitzMax program. Figure 3.7 shows an example of the main function in action. Because the main function is never formally declared, I always write a comment telling myself where it begins. I suggest you do the same.

Main calls two types of programs to do its work: user-defined and program-defined functions. *User-defined functions* are those that are written by the programmer, such as TestAI() in the Chapter 1 game. All of these functions must be

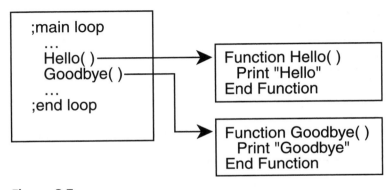

**Figure 3.7**
A function example.

defined before they are used. *Program-defined functions* are defined within the compiler, like the function `Print`. All of these have already been written; all you have to do is call them with the proper parameters.

A parameter is a piece of information sent to the function to tell it what to do. For example, the `string` variable is a parameter to the `Print` function. This variable tells `Print` what you want printed to the screen.

You can send parameters to your own functions as well, but make sure that you declare the parameters in advance. If your function is called with an extra parameter, your code will not compile.

To use any function, you first must declare it. The function declaration is usually written directly before the function code.

```
Function functionname([parameter variable,...])
```

Looks kind of complex, huh? Let's make this easy. First, type **Function**. This is required for every function declaration. Now, pick a function name (make sure it describes what the function does; for example, if it counts, call it *Count*). Now, add an open parenthesis. Add as many parameter variables as you need, each separated by a comma. Finally, add an ending parenthesis.

Here is an example.

```
Function ConvertFtoC (fvalue:Float)
```

This function most likely converts a Fahrenheit value to a Celsius value. You can see that by looking at the function's name. Make sure yours are easy to understand, too.

Next, you write the actual function code.

```
Return (5.0/9.0 * (fvalue:Float - 32))
```

Remember that the * sign means multiplication and the / sign means division. This code returns the Celsius value of the variable sent. A return value is any number or string returned by a called function. For example, on the `KeyHit()` function, either a one or a zero is returned. Here, the returned value is the Celsius equivalent to the Fahrenheit number.

Finally, we end the function.

```
End Function
```

We now need a main function call to actually use this function.

```
Print "Welcome to our FtoC converter"
fvalue_str:string = Input("What Fahrenheit value do you wish to convert?")
fvalue = Float(fvalue_str)
cvalue:Float = ConvertFtoC(fvalue )
 Print fvalue + " Fahrenheit = " + cvalue + " Celsius."
```

This section of code is the actual main program. It starts off by introducing the program and receiving the Fahrenheit value to convert. Next it calls ConvertFtoC() and stores its value in the variable cvalue. Finally, it prints the results.

Let's put all these parts together now.

```
'demo03-05.bmx - Converts Fahrenheit to Celsius

'MAIN PROGRAM
Print "Welcome to our FtoC converter"
'get fahrenheit and put it in fvalue
fvalue_str:String = Input("What Fahrenheit value do you wish to convert? ")
fvalue = Int(fvalue_str)

'Convert fvalue to Celsius
cvalue = ConvertFtoC(fvalue)

'print results
Print fvalue + " Fahrenheit = " + cvalue + " Celsius."

'END OF MAIN PROGRAM

Function ConvertFtoC(fvalue)
 'convert value and return it
 Return 5.0/9.0 * (fvalue - 32.0)
 End Function
```

Figure 3.8 shows the output of this program.

And that's all there is to functions. Well, almost...

## Scope Considerations

There are two possible scopes in Blitz Basic: global and local. (There is one more type, for Field variables, but we will talk about those when we get to Types.) *Global variables* are visible throughout the program, in every function and every line of code. *Local variables* are valid only in the function in which they are

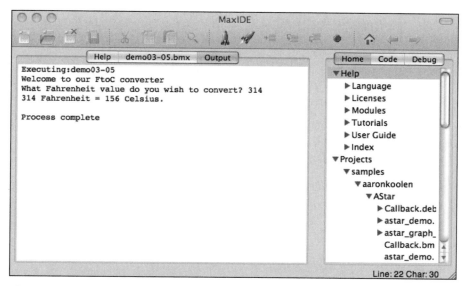

**Figure 3.8**
The demo03-05.bmx program.

defined. This means that a variable defined within one function is not valid in another.

## What Is Scope?

Scope is kind of hard to understand, so to help, I went to http://www.dictionary.com and looked up scope. Here is what it said:

"The scope of an identifier is the region of a program source within which it represents a certain thing. This usually extends from the place where it is declared to the end of the smallest enclosing block (begin/end or procedure/function body). An inner block may contain a redeclaration of the same identifier, in which case the scope of the outer declaration does not include (is "shadowed" or "occluded" by) the scope of the inner."

What? If you finished reading that (20 bucks says you gave up after "program source within which it represents a certain thing"), you are probably as lost as you were before.

Scope is a range of operation from where variables can be referenced. The fact that there are two kinds of scopes allows programmers to create programs that have two or more variables with the same name. You can have one variable with the name variablex in the global scope (otherwise known as the main program) and another variable named variablex in the function HiIAmAFunction(). Even though every other part of the program, including other functions, will use the global scope's version of variablex, HiIAmAFunction() will use its separate, more specialized, version of variablex.

By the way, Scope is also a mouthwash.

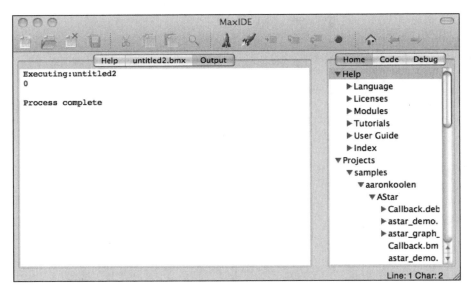

**Figure 3.9**
The broken `CallMe()` program.

Let me show you an example of scoping. Note that this code will not work. It is only used to demonstrate scope problems.

```
'CallMe() - Broken
CallMe()
Print x

Function CallMe()
      x = 314
End Function
```

The example output is shown in Figure 3.9.

As you can see, this program calls `CallMe()` and x is assigned to 314. Then it tries to print x, but it ends up printing 0! What gives?

You guessed it—scope. This function calls `CallMe()` and has x assigned to 314. But when it returns back to main, the 314 has been flushed from memory. Although x is equal to 314 in `CallMe()`, it is equal to 0 in main.

There are a few ways to fix this. One way is to have `CallMe()` return a value like this:

```
CallMe()
Print "x is equal to " + CallMe()
```

```
Function CallMe()
      x = 314
      Return x
End Function
```

In this example, `CallMe()` returns the `x` value, which is printed by `main`.

The other way to solve this problem is to use global variables. Global variables have global scope and are visible throughout the program. This means that the scope of `x` in `CallMe()` will be the same as the scope of `x` in `main`.

To create a global variable, simply precede the variable with the `Global` identifier.

```
'demo03-06.bmx - Fixed CallMe()
Global x
'call CallMe() function
CallMe()

'concatenate "x is equal to" and the variable x
Print "x is equal to " + x

'FUNCTION CALLME()
'sets x to 314
Function CallMe()
 x = 314
 End Function
```

The example output is shown in Figure 3.10.

**Note**

Notice that I wrote `Global x` in the `main` program rather than the function `CallMe()`. This is because you can only create global variables in the main program. If you want to use global scope, you must create the variable in the main program. By the way, the act of creating a variable without actually setting the variable is called *declaring*. Making the variable equal to something is called *defining* it.

This time, we make `x` global. Then, when we assign 314 to `x`, `x` is equal to 314 in every function, and not just in `CallMe()`.

**What Is Portable Code?**

Porting is an important concept, because in the long run, it can save you a lot of time. In English, for something to be portable, it must be able to easily move around. Think of that *Game Boy Advance* you saw at Wal-Mart a few days ago. Portable code is easy to move around. Portable code is independent code that doesn't rely upon global variables for information. This allows you to cut and paste functions from one program to another. Take the demo03-05.bmx, the Fahrenheit-to-Celsius calculator. That is a very portable function because you can rip that program right out and use it in another program, if the need ever arises. Because the function does not rely on any global variables, you have nothing more to set up. When the function does rely on global variables, it is extremely hard to cut and paste code from one program to another, simply because global variables usually do not exist in two different programs.

Global variables are common in games, but you should try to use them as little as possible for a few reasons. First, because every function has access to them, it is very easy to change the variable by accident. Second, using global variables makes functions less portable. If a function only uses parameters and local variables, it can be ported to other programs by just copying and pasting. If it uses global variables, you have to go through the code and change any references to global variables that don't exist in the new program. Although it doesn't seem like a big deal now, it can be a big pain to have to search through functions when you decide to add them to a new program.

By the way, another way to create a local variable is to add the keyword `Local` before a variable, such as:

```
Local x
```

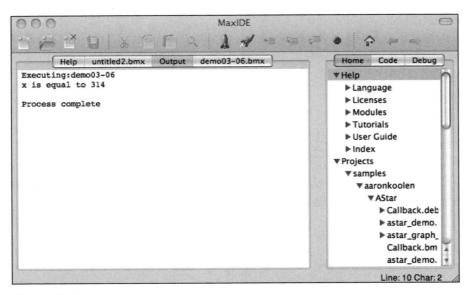

**Figure 3.10**
The fixed `CallMe()` program.

If you add the `Local` keyword to x in the previous program

```
x = 314
```

the x variable in `main` will once again equal zero. This is because the local scope takes precedence over the global scope. Therefore, the local version of x is initialized to 314, while the global version is left unaffected.

There is no difference between

```
Local variable
```

and

```
variable
```

if there is no declared global variable. In other words, when you declare a local variable, you can omit the `Local` keyword (although you might want to keep it just for clarity and style).

## When to Use Functions

Functions are necessary to programming. You know that you have to use them, but when should you do so?

Use functions whenever you have to perform a task. I know that this is a vague statement to make, but you should have at least a few functions for anything but the most trivial of programs.

Usually, the main function should do little, if any, work. The tasks should be handed to functions. If the task can be subdivided into two or more tasks, be sure to create the extra functions. You can always call functions from within another function.

Here is an example: say you are creating a spaceship game and you have a function to draw everything onscreen. You should probably make separate functions for drawing each part of the game: a separate function for drawing the ships and the bullets. It is possible to subdivide those even more. If you wanted to, you could create separate functions for drawing the bullets from the player and bullets from the enemy. Two more functions would draw the player and the enemy ships.

Basically, if you see a place where a function could be useful, write it. It takes hardly any more code than just putting the task in the `main` function and it makes your code much more portable, not to mention readable.

## Understanding Arrays

One large problem in programming is the creation of a large number of variables. Think about how long it would take to create 10 variables of the same type right now. It might look something like this:

```
variable0 = 314
variable1 = 314
variable2 = 314
variable3 = 314
variable4 = 314
variable5 = 314
variable6 = 314
variable7 = 314
variable8 = 314
variable9 = 314
```

Seems like a waste of time, huh? But imagine if you had to create a thousand variables. That might take forever!

As you might have guessed, BlitzMax has a way to remedy this problem. The solution is to use a feature called an *array*. Arrays are basically sets of variables with almost the same name. An array looks like any other variable, except it appends a subscript (a number within parentheses) to the end of the variable name.

Imagine an array as a single-column box that contains separate places to place jars (see Figure 3.11). Each jar contains a number. In this case, each jar contains the number 314, but you can change these numbers. You can access the number through the array counter, which looks like `variable[0]` or `variable[1]`. Basically, each jar is independent of the other jars, but they are all packaged in the same box. In arrays, the box represents the array, the jars are the individual array variables, and the numbers are the variable data.

Any variable that is part of an array is written something like this:

```
variablename[subscript#]
```

Here, the name of the array is `variablename` and the `subscript#` (it is always an integer, never a string) is equal to the number of array variables you want to generate.

Now we actually have to create the array. Let's use the variables from the previous example.

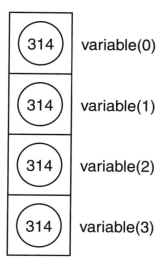

variable(0)

variable(1)

variable(2)

variable(3)

variable array

**Figure 3.11**
Box to array comparison.

```
Local variable : Int[10] 'Declare array

variable[0] = 314
variable[1] = 314
variable[2] = 314
variable[3] = 314
variable[4] = 314
variable[5] = 314
variable[6] = 314
variable[7] = 314
variable[8] = 314
variable[9] = 314
```

Doesn't seem any simpler, does it? That's because I created the array in the longer way. However, using a For...Next loop, we can condense this into a much shorter procedure.

**Note**

Note that I did use the keyword Local before the name of the array. You do need to use Local before arrays—it's required. Or Global, if you want a global array.

```
'demo03-07.bmx - initializes 10 vars to 314

'Declare array
```

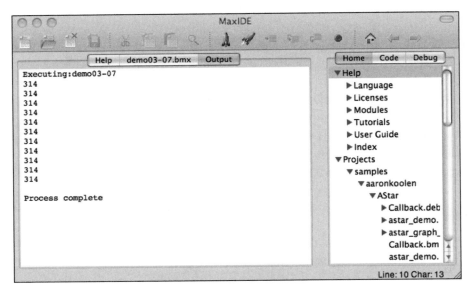

**Figure 3.12**
The demo03-07.bmx program.

```
Local variable : Int[10]

For i=0 To 10

  'set array to 314
  variable[i] = 314
  Print variable[i]
Next
```

The output is shown in Figure 3.12.

This does the same thing and more (it prints out the variable as well), but it is a heck of a lot shorter! This time, the array is declared just as in the previous example. Next, a For...Next loop iterates through each variable and sets it equal to 314! Easy, huh?

**N o t e**

Make sure you notice that all of the variables begin with 0. Computers count differently than humans because they start counting with 0 rather than 1. In other words, the 10th variable in declaration of array[10] is array[9]. In other words, when you declare an array, you are telling the computer how many elements the array should have, plus one. However, because computers always count from 0, you access the array elements beginning with 0 and ending with n, where n is equal to the size of the array. For example, if you take an array declared as array[5], the array would contain the elements array[0], array[1], array[2], array[3], array[4], and array[5]. So an array that had five elements would be accessed with the numbers; 0, 1, 2, 3, 4, and 5—no more, no less. I often use less than the maximum amount of units, however, so I use 0-4 on an array[5] declaration.

---

To see how the box and jar example fits in with this program, see Figure 3.13.

All right, how about one more example of functions? This program will set a series of variables to an increasing number. From there, the user can choose to add, subtract, multiply, or divide two of the numbers. It's sort of like a mini-calculator.

```
'demo03-08.bmx - Allows user to perform math operations of 1-100

'op1 and op2 are global so they can be accessed from all functions
'op1 contains first operand, op2 contains second
Global op1
Global op2
Global array : Int[101] '0 - 100
InitializeArray()

'continue is 1 as long as program is running
cont = 1
```

**Figure 3.13**
Demo03-07.bmx box and jar example.

```
While cont 'as long as the computer wants to play
 'Get the first operand
 op1_str:String = Input("What is the first number? ")
 op1 = Int(op1_str)

 'Get the second operand
 op2_str:String = Input("And the second? ")
 op2 = Int(op2_str)

 ' what does the user want to do?
 operator:String = Input("Enter +, -, *, or / ")

 'Print the answer
 PrintAnswer(operator)

 'Find out if user wants to continue
cont_str:String = Input("Enter 1 to continue or 0 to quit. ")
        cont = Int(cont_str)

  'Insert a new line
  Print ""
Wend
End



'This function sets up the array
Function InitializeArray()
For i=0 To 100
 array[i] = i
Next
End Function



'This function prints the answer to the expression
Function PrintAnswer(operator:String)
Print op1 + " " + operator + " " + op2 + " is equal to " + FindAnswer(operator)
End Function


'This function performs the math based on the user input
Function FindAnswer(operator:String)
```

```
Select operator
     Case "+"
          Return array[op1] + array[op2]
     Case "-"
          Return array[op1] - array[op2]
     Case "*"
          Return array[op1] * array[op2]
     Case "/"
          Return array[op1] / array[op2]

End Select
End Function
```

This ends the initialization and the main loop sections of the calculator program. The program begins by creating two global variables: op1 and op2. These are the two numbers that will be added together. For example, in the expression 3 + 14, 3 represents op1 and 14 represents op2.

Next, it creates the array. The array has 101 elements, and therefore, it goes from array[0] to array[100] (remember that arrays begin counting from 0). After the array declaration, InitializeArray() is called.

The continue variable is then created. This variable determines whether the program is still running. As long as continue is not equal to 0, the game loop continues to run.

The main loop begins next. First, it receives the variables op1 and op2 from the user. After that, it asks for operator. operator gives the users a choice of what operation they want to perform (addition, subtraction, multiplication, or division).

The loop then calls PrintAnswer() to print the answer. Finally, the loop asks the users if they would like to go through the program again. If the user chooses yes, continue remains as 1 and the game loop starts from the top. If not, the program exits.

This program has two user-defined functions: PrintAnswer() and InitializeArray(). Let's take a look at each of them.

```
'This function sets up the array
Function InitializeArray()
For i=0 To 100
 array[i] = i
Next
 End Function
```

This function simply creates the array that is used in the following calculations. Each array element contains its respective number. Therefore, the 14th element (array(13)) is equal to 13. After the numbers 0 through 100 have been initialized, they are all sent back to the main loop to go through the rest of the input.

The next user-defined function is PrintAnswer().

```
'This function prints the answer to the expression
Function PrintAnswer(operator:String)
Print op1 + " " + operator + " " + op2 + " is equal to " + FindAnswer(operator)
End Function
```

This function simply writes out what the user wants to do. If the user wants to add 13 and 31, this function writes out "13 + 31 is equal to 44." You might be wondering how it gets the answer. That is accomplished by the final user-defined function: FindAnswer().

```
'This function performs the math based on the user input
Function FindAnswer(operator:String)
Select operator
     Case "+"
          Return array[op1] + array[op2]
     Case "-"
          Return array[op1] - array[op2]
     Case "*"
          Return array[op1] * array[op2]
     Case "/"
          Return array[op1] / array[op2]

End Select
End Function
```

Note that if op1 or op2 is larger than 100 or less than 0, the program will not function.

The output is shown in Figure 3.14.

By the way, one thing about this program. The program will crash if op2 is set to 0 and operator is division. This is because it is impossible to divide any number by 0. As you can see, this function begins with a Select statement. The Select command chooses an action based on which operator is being used. If the user chooses to multiply something, the function returns op1 times op2. The return value is then printed to the screen in the PrintAnswer() function.

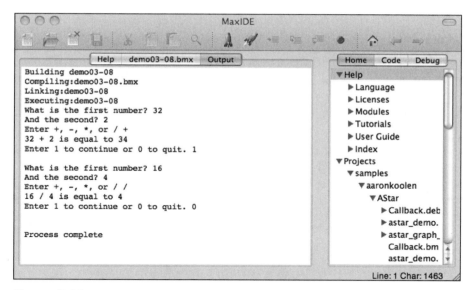

**Figure 3.14**
The demo03-08.bmx calculator program.

**Note**

If you happen to try dividing two numbers that aren't evenly divisible, you will get the correct number, but the decimal place will be missing. That is because this program uses integers. Try modifying this program so that it uses floating-point variables instead. (Remember, a floating point variable uses a decimal—like 1.002.)

Figures 3.15 and 3.16 portray the array as a box and demonstrate how two numbers are added.

## Multi-Dimensional Arrays

Multi-dimensional arrays are very similar to regular arrays, except that, well, they have more than one dimension. In essence, the main difference is that a multi-dimensional array has more than one subscript. An easy way to visualize a multi-dimensional array is to use the box example again. However, instead of only having one column, it has two or more, as shown in Figure 3.17.

Multi-dimensional arrays are used in situations in which you need sets of variables within the array set. For example, you might create an array of bullets. You could then create an array with two dimensions, and place the bullets shot by the player in one dimension, and the bullets shot by the enemy in the other. This is demonstrated in Figure 3.18.

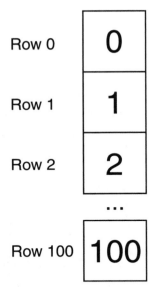

**Figure 3.15**
The array box.

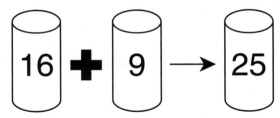

**Figure 3.16**
Adding two jars.

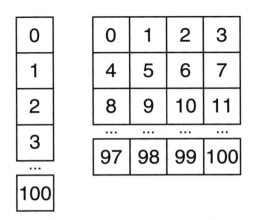

**Figure 3.17**
Single and multi-dimensional arrays.

**Figure 3.18**
The two-dimensional bullet array.

Okay, let's make a multi-dimensional array. This process is very similar to making a single-dimensional array; you only have to add another subscript into the declaration.

```
Local bullets : Int[2,100]
```

This command creates an array of bullets with two parts. The first part determines who shot the bullet and the second part determines which bullet it was. Each column contains 100 bullets.

Now, to actually use the array, you only have to add the second subscript to the variable call like this:

```
Local bullets[0,23]
```

This command calls the 24th bullet from the player. Remember, because the computer begins counting at 0, the subscript 23 is the 24th element of the array.

All right, let's make a program. This simply draws out 25 asterisks (*) and 25 plus signs (+). It doesn't do much, but you will understand how you can use arrays when you learn about types in the next section. Figure 3.19 portrays the info in a table.

```
'demo03-09.bmx - Draws out 25 '*'s and 25 '+'s
'create the array
Local starsplusses:String[2,25]

'initialize the array. The first dimension will contain *'s and the second will
contain +'s
For rows = 0 To 1
  For columns = 0 To 24
        'Assign either + or *, depending on the return value of FindChar$()
        starsplusses[rows,columns] = FindChar(rows)
  Next
Next
```

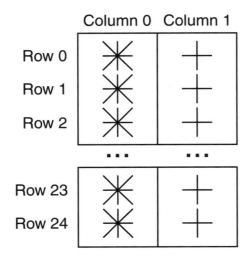

**Figure 3.19**
The `starsplusses[]` array.

This first fragment begins by creating the `starsplusses[]` array. Because its subscript is [2,25], it will contain a total of 50 objects. How did I get this number? I simply multiplied the first subscript by the second subscript: 2*25 = 50.

The next section of the code initializes the array. It runs two `for` loops within each other. In multi-dimensional arrays, two `for` loops are commonly used. The first loop runs throughout the first subscript and the second loop runs throughout the second subscript. The outer loop, `For i = 0 To 1`, counts from 0 to 1. The second `for` loop counts from 0 to 24. The line

```
starsplusses[rows,columns] = FindChar(rows)
```

determines what each element is set equal to with the help of the `FindChar()` function.

`FindChar()` is a user-defined function. It looks like this:

```
'FUNCTION FINDCHAR$(i)
'returns * or +
Function FindChar:String(i)
  If i = 0
        Return "*"
  Else If i = 1
        Return "+"
  EndIf
  End Function
```

If the initialization loop calls this function with the row number being 0, the array element becomes an asterisk (star). If the function is called with the row being 1, the array element is a plus sign. Therefore, the array has two rows of 25 characters—one row is made up of stars, the other is made up of plusses.

Next, you need to display the array.

```
'display the array
For rows = 0 To 1
  toWrite:String = ""
  For columns = 0 To 24
        'Write each value to the screen
        toWrite = toWrite + starsplusses[rows,columns]
Next
'write a new line after each row
Print toWrite
Next
```

Once again, this function has two for loops running within each other. The outer loop counts by rows and the inner loop counts by columns. The string toWrite is set to blank at the beginning of the outer loop (the row loop) and a character is added to the row every iteration of the inner loop. At the end of the inner loop, the toWrite string is printed and set back to an empty string.

If you tried to print the string after every iteration of the inner loop, instead of adding it to the toWrite string and printing out everything at the end, the program wouldn't be so pretty. Figure 3.20 shows what demo03-09.bmx looks like when Print is substituted for the toWrite variable.

Figure 3.21 shows the demo03-09.bmx program.

## Using Types

The entire chapter has been leading up to *types*, because they are a very important and useful part of the Blitz Basic language. Types are simply a set of related data. That might sound a lot like the definition of an array, but with types, you can have different names for each of the variables, as well as different data types (string, integer, and floating point).

Here is an example. Imagine you have a player ship. The computer needs to know where to put the ship. For this example, we are going to put the ship at the

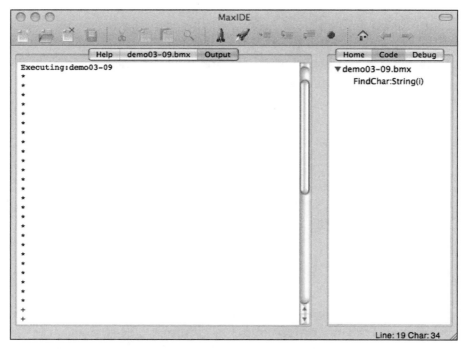

**Figure 3.20**
Demo03-09 without `Write`.

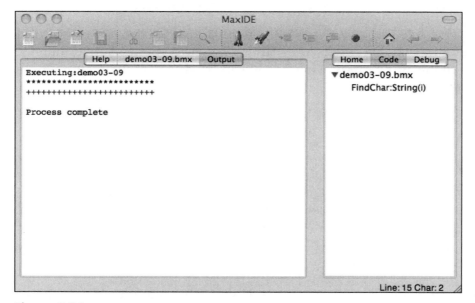

**Figure 3.21**
The demo03-09.bmx program.

coordinates 100, 100 (if you don't understand coordinates, they will be explained soon). You could do something like this:

```
playerx = 100
 playery = 100
```

Seems pretty easy, eh? What if you wanted to add a hit counter? You have to create another variable.

```
playerhits = 3
```

That's three variables. If you wanted to make it possible for the ship to move up and down, you would need two more variables. That's a total of five variables!

The best way to remedy this problem is to use types. A type can take all of these unorganized variables and attach them to a single type name, like in Figure 3.22. Here is the creation of a ship type:

```
Type ship
        Field x,y 'the ship's location
        Field hits';ship's hit points
End Type
```

To create a new type, add the keyword Type before the name of the type. Next, create the individual fields. Each field is a separate variable that is part of the type. Each Field variable can be an integer, a floating point, or a string.

Now you have declared the type, and you have to create a variable that can hold this new data type. The procedure to do this is a little different from defining a variable with one of the built-in types (strings, integers, and floats are the built-in types). To create this new variable, or *instance* as it is called, use the following syntax.

| Unattached | Attached Type player |
|---|---|
| Player x | x |
| Player y | y |
| Player hits | hits |

| | |
|---|---|
| Player x = 0 | Player\x = 0 |
| Player y = 0 | Player\y = 0 |
| Player hits = 0 | Player\hits = 0 |

**Figure 3.22**
Unattached and attached variables.

```
player:ship = New ship
```

Wow, that looks bizarre. Let's break it down piece by piece. The first thing that you see is the word `player` to the left of the colon. This word refers to the name of the variable you are creating. After the colon, you see the word `ship`. This is the type you want the variable associated with. This variable will now have all of the same fields as the `ship` type, declared previously. To finish the process, we provide the proper fields by setting `player:ship` equal to `New ship`.

This creates the new player ship. You could create an enemy ship by simply changing the name of `player` to `enemy`. Creation of a new type almost always uses this base:

```
instancename:typename = New typename
```

Now that we have organized all the loose variables by putting them in a type and creating an instance of the type, we can set the field variables.

```
player.x = 100
player.y = 100
 player.hits = 3
```

Not too bad, huh? To access one of the variables, just use this formula.

```
instancename.variablename
```

Now you can create, define, and access types. Let's get to an example and see how this baby works. To write this program, I am going to use the function `DrawText`, which is declared as

```
DrawText (str:String, x, y)
```

Refer to Table 3.1 to see what each parameter means. `DrawText` allows you to draw text on the screen, just like `Print`, but it also provides the capability for the programmer to choose the exact coordinate position that will appear.

This program uses `DrawText` to draw the players on the screen and to show their hit points. You will also be able to decrease the player's hit points and move them around. This is a pretty basic and simple game. Also, the ship will be represented by the characters <-*->. Table 3.2 describes the keys used in this game.

```
'demo03-10.bmx - Draws a ship which can be moved and killed

Graphics 400,300
```

**Table 3.1**  DrawText()'s Parameters

| Parameter | Description |
|---|---|
| string$ | The string you want printed |
| x | The x coordinate of the text |
| y | The y coordinate of the text |

**Table 3.2**  demo03-10.bmx's Keys

| Key | Function |
|---|---|
| Left arrow | Moves the ship left |
| Right arrow | Moves the ship right |
| Up arrow | Moves the ship up |
| Down arrow | Moves the ship down |
| Spacebar | Decreases the ship's hit points by one |
| Esc | Exits the game |

```
'CONSTANTS
'starting hitpoints, feel free to change
Const STARTHITPOINTS = 3
'What the ship looks like
Const SHIP:String = "<-*->"
' Where the player starts
Const STARTX = 200, STARTY = 150
```

This is the first part of the program. It begins by setting the graphics mode. Next, it designates which variables are constants. *Constants*, as you remember, are variables whose values don't change throughout the game. If you want to make a change to any of these variables, feel free to do so. The difference will be reflected throughout the entire program.

All of the constants are listed in Table 3.3.

Okay, let's keep going.

```
'TYPES
Type TShip
      Field x,y
      Field hitpoints
      Field shipstring:String
 End Type
```

**Table 3.3**  demo03-10.bmx's Constants

| Constant | Default Value | Description |
|---|---|---|
| STARTHITPOINTS | 3 | The number of times you can decrease the hit points (by pressing spacebar) before the game ends. |
| SHIP:String | "<-*->" | The characters that make up the player. Because there are no images, the player is simply a text string. Change this value to change how the player looks. |
| STARTX | 200 | The starting x position for the ship. |
| STARTY | 150 | The starting y position for the ship. |

**Table 3.4**  demo03-10.bmx's Types

| Field | Description |
|---|---|
| x | The x coordinate of the ship. The field is first initialized to the x value given in STARTX. |
| y | The y coordinate of the ship. The field is first initialized to the y value given in STARTY. |
| hitpoints | The number of hit points remaining on the ship. The field is first initialized to the hit point value given in STARTHITPOINTS. |
| shipstring:String | The actual look of the ship. This field is first initialized to the string value SHIP. |

This section defines all of the types used in the program. Here, only one is defined—TShip. The TShip type groups all of the variables necessary to draw the ship on the screen. Table 3.4 lists all of the fields of the TShip type.

**Note**

Notice that the type is called TShip. For styling purposes, whenever I create a type, I prefix the name of the type with a capital T. It's just an easy way to see which types were created by me. I recommend you use a similar style.

Next we move to the initialization of the program.

```
'INITIALIZATION SECTION
Global cont = 1 'continue?
Global player:TShip = New TShip
player.x = STARTX
player.y = STARTY
```

```
player.hitpoints = STARTHITPOINTS
player.shipstring = SHIP
```

The initialization section defines all of the variables that will be used in the program. It also initializes the fields of the TShip type. The first variable, cont, is used in the game loop as the variable that determines whether the game continues playing. As long as the user wants to continue, cont is equal to 1.

The line

```
Global player:TShip = New TShip
```

creates an instance of the TShip type with the name player. Therefore, any fields that are in the ship type can now be accessed via player. The rest of the initialization section sets up the player type by assigning its fields to their respective constants.

Next, move on to the game loop.

```
'Game loop
While cont = 1
 Cls
 DrawText player.shipstring$, player.x, player.y

 TestInput()
 DrawHUD()
 Flip
Wend
 'End of loop
```

The game loop is short, as it should be. It begins by testing the cont variable. If cont is equal to 1, the game runs; if not, the game exits. After that, the loop clears the screen by calling Cls. Without calling Cls, the screen would exhibit streaks, like in Figure 3.23. After that, the player is drawn to the screen at the given position. The loop then tests the input by calling TestInput() and draws the HUD by calling DrawHUD(). The HUD is the *heads-up display*, or the area of the screen that explains some values that are being used in the game.

```
'TestInput() changes the direction or hitpoints of the player
Function TestInput()

'If player presses left, move him left.
```

**Figure 3.23**
The main loop without Cls.

```
If KeyHit(KEY_LEFT)

 player.x = player.x - 3
 If player.x <= 0
        player.x = 10
 EndIf
EndIf


'If player presses right, move him right.
If KeyHit(KEY_RIGHT)
 player.x = player.x + 3

 If player.x >= 385
        player.x = 380
 EndIf
EndIf


'If player presses up, move him up.
If KeyHit(KEY_UP)

 player.y = player.y - 3
 If player.y <= 0
        player.y = 10
 EndIf
EndIf
```

```
'If player presses down, move him down.
If KeyHit(KEY_DOWN)

  player.y = player.y + 3
  If player.y >= 285
        player.y = 280
  EndIf
EndIf

'If player presses spacebar, remove a hitpoint

If KeyHit(KEY_SPACE)

  player.hitpoints = player.hitpoints - 1
  If player.hitpoints <= 0
        cont = 0
  EndIf

EndIf

'If player presses Esc, set cont to 0, and exit the game
If KeyHit(KEY_ESCAPE)
  cont = 0
EndIf

End Function
```

The TestInput() function is very long, but also very simple. It simply tests the keys that the user has pressed and updates the variables based on the input. Starting from the top, if the player presses the left arrow, the player moves three pixels to the left. If the player happens to move the character too far (off the screen), the ship's position is moved back to the right. If the user presses the right arrow, he moves left a little. The same happens if the user moves the ship too far up or down—the ship is repositioned back on the screen.

If the player presses the spacebar, the hitpoint counter decreases by one. The program then tests the counter to determine whether the player has 0 hit points. If so, cont is set to 0, and the game is exited on the next frame.

The last test determines whether the user pressed Esc. If so, cont is set to 0, and the game exits on the next frame.

```
'DrawHUD() draws user's info in top right of screen
Function DrawHUD()
 DrawText "X position: " + player.x, 260, 10
 DrawText "Y position: " + player.y, 260, 20
 DrawText "Hitpoints:   " + player.hitpoints, 260, 30
 End Function
```

The final function in the program, DrawHUD(), simply writes out the ship's information to the screen. The x and y coordinate positions and remaining hit points are drawn in the top-right section of the screen.

Figure 3.24 shows how the loop works, and Figure 3.25 is a screenshot of the actual program.

### What Else Can I Do with Types?

I just showed you how to create types that allow you to have variables associated with your own type name. Not bad, but there is actually a lot more you can do with types. With the creation of BlitzMax, you can actually put functions inside your types so that only variables of your type can use your functions. Additionally, you can do lots of advanced programming things with BlitzMax's types. However, most of them are outside the scope of this book. If you want to learn more about the power of types, check out the documentation in the BlitzMax program.

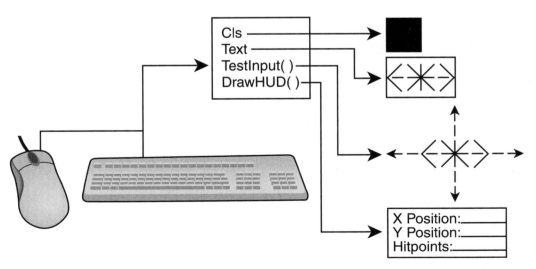

**Figure 3.24**
The main game loop.

**Figure 3.25**
The demo03-10.bmx program.

## Coordinate Systems

I'm going to leave the concept of types for a moment to talk about coordinate points. Coordinates explain where on the screen something is. They are shown in the format of x, y. For example, something that is at coordinate 314, 13 has an x position of 314 and a y position of 13. The coordinate plane looks like Figure 3.26. The origin, or 0 value of both the x and y direction, is at the top-left part of the screen. X increases from the origin right, and y increases from the origin down. When you want to get to coordinate position 314, 13, for example, you move from the origin 314 spaces to the right and 13 spaces down.

Each position is a single pixel on the screen. A *pixel* is the smallest measurement of a computer screen. Each pixel is a different color, and the pixels fitted together create an image. To see the size of a single pixel on your machine, run demo03-11.bmx (see Figure 3.27). The tiny white dot in the center is a single pixel. Small, huh?

When you want to plot an object to the screen, you plot it to a certain pixel position. Usually the top-left corner of the object is drawn to that pixel position. So, as in Figure 3.28, if you want to write some text to a certain position, the top left of the text is at the selected pixel.

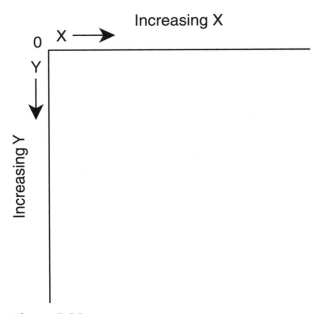

**Figure 3.26**
A coordinate system.

**Figure 3.27**
A single pixel.

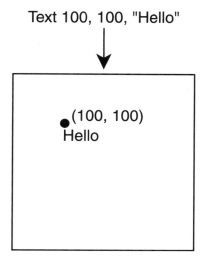

Text 100, 100, "Hello"

(100, 100)
Hello

**Figure 3.28**
Drawing objects at pixel locations.

## Putting It All Together: Textanoid!

Okay, now, using all we have learned, you can put it together and make a game. This game is a simple text-based copy of *Arkanoid* that uses all of the processes discussed in this long chapter.

Because we will be using text, the basic game commands are run by the DrawText() and KeyDown() commands. Basically, the idea of the game is to get rid of all the blocks by hitting them with the ball. The players control a paddle, which can move left or right. The player attempts to keep the ball from hitting the bottom wall of the game board. Each time the player clears the field of blocks, the player will reach a new level. Theoretically, you can go on to an infinite level (because the difficulty never increases), but I'm betting the player will get bored before then.

The full source of the game can be found on the CD under the name demo03-11.bmx. This game might be hard to understand for a beginning programmer; however, I am going to help you through the tough parts of the code. Let's start off with the defined types.

```
'TYPES
'the player type
Type TPaddle
  Field x,y    'coordinates
```

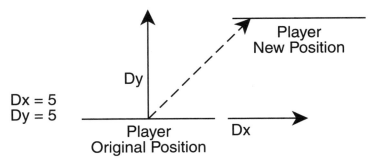

**Figure 3.29**
How `directionx` and `directiony` work.

```
End Type

'The ball type
Type TBall
  Field x,y    'the coordinate
  Field directionx, directiony    'the velocities of the ball
  End Type
```

`directionx` and `directiony` are described in Figure 3.29.

These types define the player and the ball in the game. The x and y coordinates are simply the position of each object on the screen, but the `directionx` and `directiony` variables might seem strange.

**Note**
> Notice that I decided not to make a block type. I felt that it would be easier to create it as an array. For an exercise, try to make and use a block type in the program.

The *direction* variables define how the ball moves—the `directionx` defines the left and right movement and the `directiony` variable defines the up and down movement. Referring to Figure 3.29, you can see that as `directionx` moves the paddle left, `directiony` moves the paddle up. The end result is a new position that is above and to the left of the original position.

Next up is the constants section:

```
'Constants
Const BLOCKSTRING:String = "XXXXXXX"
Const PADDLESTRING:String = "--------"
Const BALLSTRING:String = "O"
```

```
Const BLOCKROWS = 3
Const BLOCKCOLUMNS = 7
Const BLOCKXGAP = 85
Const BLOCKYGAP = 32
Const BLOCKXORIGIN = 16
Const BLOCKYORIGIN = 8
Global BLOCKHEIGHT = TextHeight(BLOCKSTRING)
Global BLOCKWIDTH = TextWidth(BLOCKSTRING)
Global PADDLEWIDTH = TextWidth(PADDLESTRING)
Global PADDLEHEIGHT = TextHeight(PADDLESTRING)
Global BALLWIDTH = TextWidth(BALLSTRING)
Global BALLHEIGHT = TextHeight(BALLSTRING)
Const STARTX = 300
 Const STARTY= 340
```

Refer to Table 3.5 to see what each constant means. By the way, the function `TextHeight()` (which is used in each of the height variables) returns the height in pixels of the selected text. The `TextWidth()` function returns the width of the string.

**Table 3.5** Textanoid!'s Constants

| Variable | Description |
| --- | --- |
| BLOCKSTRING | Defines what each block looks like |
| PADDLESTRING | Defines what the paddle looks like |
| BALLSTRING | Defines what the ball looks like |
| BLOCKROWS | The number of rows of blocks |
| BLOCKCOLUMNS | The number of columns of blocks |
| BLOCKXGAP | The number of pixels between each column |
| BLOCKYGAP | The number of pixels between each row |
| BLOCKXORIGIN | The number of pixels from the top-left corner of the window to the first column |
| BLOCKYORIGIN | The number of pixels from the top-left corner of the window to the first row |
| BLOCKHEIGHT | The height of each block |
| BLOCKWIDTH | The width of each block |
| PADDLEHEIGHT | The height of the paddle |
| PADDLEWIDTH | The width of the paddle |
| BALLHEIGHT | The height of the ball |
| BALLWIDTH | The width of the ball |
| STARTX | The starting x coordinate of the player |
| STARTY | The starting y coordinate of the player |

**Note**

You might be wondering why the HEIGHT and WIDTH variables are global and not constant. The reason is that a constant value can never be variable. The FontHeight() function can return a different value, and therefore it is variable. Because I need to use the HEIGHT and WIDTH variables throughout the program, I made them global.

Okay, next is the initialization section.

```
'Initialization
'Seed the random Generator
SeedRnd MilliSecs()
'Initialize the score
Global score = 0
'The number of total block hits
Global blockhits = 0
'The level the player is on
Global level = 1

'Create an array of blocks
Global blocks[BLOCKROWS, BLOCKCOLUMNS]

'Create a new ball
Global ball:TBall = New TBall
'Create a new paddle
Global player:TPaddle = New TPaddle

'Initialize the new level
NewLevel()
```

Let's discuss this section. First the SeedRnd() command seeds the random generator. Next, this section creates the score, blockhits, and level variables. score is the points the player has accumulated, blockhits tells how many times the player has hit a block, and level shows the players what level they are on. All of these variables are used in the function DrawHUD().

**What Is SeedRnd()?**

You might wonder why I always use the command SeedRnd Millisecs() before using the Rand() function. The fact is no computer is random. Because it was created to do certain tasks correctly each time, it cannot truly create random numbers. Because of this fact, using Rand() by itself in a program would cause the same number to be generated over and over. The program uses SeedRnd() to change the starting point of the random generator each time, so it does not generate the same numbers over and over. MilliSecs() is a good function to use to seed the generator because MilliSecs() is never the same twice.

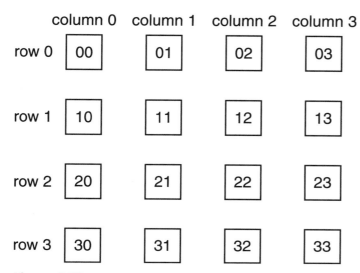

**Figure 3.30**
Rows and columns.

The command

```
Global blocks[BLOCKROWS, BLOCKCOLUMNS]
```

creates a multidimensional array called blocks. If you recall, a multidimensional array is just like a regular array, but it has rows as well as columns. This fits in easily with the block setup.

Refer to Figure 3.30 to see the block rows and columns, complete with subscripts. You can see that the columns extend from the top to the bottom, and the rows extend from the left to the right.

The next two variables created are ball and player. These two variables create the ball and player from the ball and paddle types.

Finally, you initialize the level by calling NewLevel(). This user-defined function creates all of the blocks and sets up the ball and paddle. The function is defined as:

```
Function NewLevel()
For rows=0 To BLOCKROWS-1
 For cols=0 To BLOCKCOLUMNS-1
       'Set block to existing (1)
       blocks[rows,cols] = 1
 Next
Next
ResetLevel()
 End Function
```

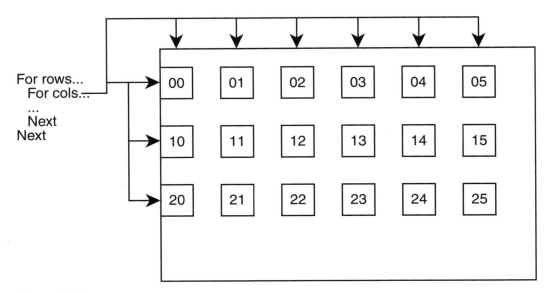

**Figure 3.31**
The for loops.

The first for loop counts each of the rows and the second for loop counts each of the columns. Notice that I make the for loops count to the number of rows and columns minus 1. This subtraction offsets the fact that the starting number in an array is 0. Referring to Figure 3.31, you can see that this counter goes through each of the columns in the first row before moving to the next row and starting again. Whenever you see dual for loops to count through the blocks, all of the columns in the first row are counted before moving to the next row. Each of the blocks is set to one, which means they will be drawn (if they are destroyed, the blocks are set to zero).

The next line calls the function ResetLevel(). ResetLevel() is defined as this:

```
Function ResetLevel()
  ball.x = 320
  ball.y = 150
  ball.directiony = 4
  ball.directionx = Rand(-5,5)
  player.x = STARTX
  player.y = STARTY
  Delay 500
End Function
```

This function sets up the starting variables for the player and ball. The ball appears at the top-center corner of the screen and the player appears at the constant starting position. The ball is set to move toward the paddle at 12 pixels per frame and left or right randomly. The randomness of the ball's movement can sometimes cause a problem, however. There is always a chance that directionx will be equal to 0, and the ball will move straight up and down, without moving left or right at all. I left this problem in the program to illustrate a problem with random functions, and to give you an exercise. Try to fix this problem so a directionx of 0 can never occur!

Well, that was initialization. Next up, the game loop:

```
'Game Loop
While Not KeyDown(KEY_ESCAPE)
 Cls

 DrawHUD()
 TestInput()
 DrawBlocks()
 DrawPaddle()
 CheckBall()

 Flip
 Wend
```

As you can see, the loop does almost nothing other than calling other functions. If you look at Figure 3.32, you will see the function layout for this program—which functions call which other functions, and so on.

**N o t e**

You might wonder what the Flip command does. This command switches the background buffer with the foreground buffer. Don't worry what this means—it is explained in Chapter 5.

The first call the loop makes is to DrawHUD(). Referring to Figure 3.33, you can see that DrawHUD() simply shows the players what level they are on, what their score is, and how many blocks they have hit.

```
Function DrawHUD()
 DrawText "Level: " + level, 0,440 'write the level
 DrawText "Score: " + score, 0, 450 'write the score
 DrawText "Block Hits: " + blockhits, 0, 460 'write the block hits
 End Function
```

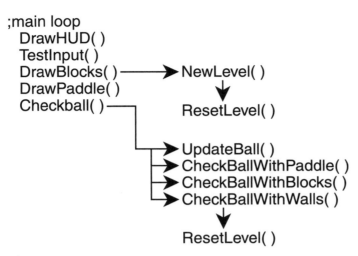

**Figure 3.32**
Textanoid!'s function outline.

**Figure 3.33**
The DrawHUD() function.

Not too bad, huh? The only thing you might want to notice are the coordinates. The x coordinate is 0, which means it is on the left side of the screen, and the y coordinate is 440, 450, and 460, which is pretty close to the bottom (the total height of this window is 480, as seen in the Graphics call at the beginning of the program).

The next call from the loop is to `TestInput()`. `TestInput()` determines whether the player moves her paddle or quits the game.

```
Function TestInput()

 'hit Esc
 If KeyDown(KEY_ESCAPE)
        'quit the game
        End

 'hit left arrow
ElseIf KeyDown(KEY_LEFT)
     'move paddle left
     player.x = player.x - 10

 'hit right arrow
ElseIf KeyDown(KEY_RIGHT)
     'move paddle right
     player.x = player.x + 10
EndIf
End Function
```

Just for review, the `KeyDown(`*keycode*`)` function determines whether the selected key was pressed. This function tests the Esc key, the left arrow, and the right arrow. If the player pressed Esc, the game ends. The left and right arrows move the paddle around the board.

The next function is `DrawBlocks()`. This function loops through each block and draws it if it is equal to 1. If a block is set to 0 (a block is set to 0 when it is hit by the ball), it is not drawn.

```
Function DrawBlocks()

 x = BLOCKXORIGIN
 y = BLOCKYORIGIN
'This variable creates a new level if there are no blocks
 Local moveToNewLevel = 0

'For all the rows
 For rows = 0 To BLOCKROWS - 1
'reset rows position
        x = BLOCKXORIGIN
```

```
    For cols = 0 To BLOCKCOLUMNS - 1

            'If the block exists, draw it on screen
            If (blocks[rows,cols] = 1) Then
                    DrawText BLOCKSTRING, x, y
                    moveToNewLevel = moveToNewLevel + 1
            EndIf
        'Move over to the next block
        x = x + BLOCKXGAP

    Next
    'Move to the next column
    y = y + BLOCKYGAP
Next
If moveToNewLevel = 0
        level = level + 1
        NewLevel()
EndIf

End Function
```

This might be tough to understand, but I'm here to help! The function starts with setting x and y to BLOCKXORIGIN and BLOCKYORIGIN. Refer to Figure 3.34 to see how the origin variables define how far from the top-left corner the first block is.

**BLOCKXORIGIN = 16**
**BLOCKYORIGIN = 8**

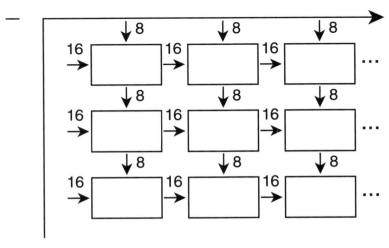

**Figure 3.34**
The x and y origins.

The moveToNewLevel variable determines whether there are any blocks left. Every time a block is found, NewLevel is incremented. At the end of the function, if moveToNewLevel equals 0, a new level is created.

The function now creates two for loops to iterate through the rows and columns of blocks (just like in NewLevel()). The only line between the two for loops is

```
x = BLOCKXORIGIN
```

This line resets the x value to BLOCKXORIGIN after all of the columns in one row have been tested. This line is necessary; if it were not included, the program would believe that the second row started offscreen. This is shown in Figure 3.35.

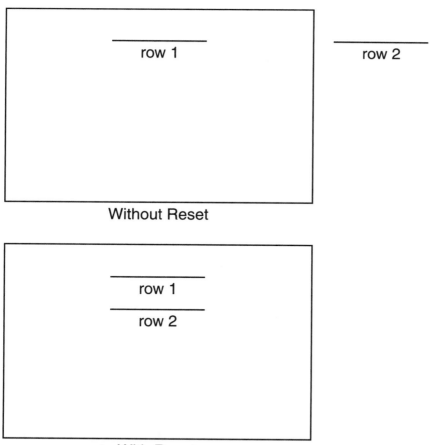

**Figure 3.35**
DrawBlocks() with and without resetting the x value.

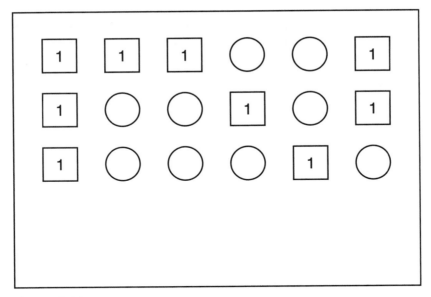

**Figure 3.36**
The block test.

The next few lines test each block:

```
'If the block exists, draw it on screen
If (blocks[rows,cols] = 1) Then
  DrawText BLOCKSTRING, x, y
moveToNewLevel = moveToNewLevel + 1
  EndIf
```

Figure 3.36 shows how each block is tested. If the current block is equal to 1, the block is drawn; if not, it is not drawn. At least one block must be drawn to continue the level; if no blocks are drawn, the moveToNewLevel variable never increases and stays at zero.

The final line before the column loop's Next command is

```
x = x + BLOCKXGAP
```

This line advances the x variable to the next block. The BLOCKXGAP constant contains the number of pixels between each block in a single row (otherwise known as every column).

After all the columns in the first row have been tested, the loop moves to the next row. This is achieved by adding a gap to the y variable:

```
y = y + BLOCKYGAP
```

Just like BLOCKXGAP, BLOCKYGAP is the number of pixels between each row. After all the boxes in one row are tested, the y value moves down a few pixels to begin drawing a new row.

The final lines of the function test the moveToNewLevel variable to determine whether any blocks were hit. If none were (and moveToNewLevel equals 0), the level is increased and NewLevel() is called. This call begins the next level and redraws all the blocks.

Back to the game loop, the next function called is DrawPaddle(). DrawPaddle() is very simple.

```
Function DrawPaddle()
 'Draw the paddle
 DrawText PADDLESTRING, player.x, player.y
 End Function
```

The only action this function performs is drawing the players at their x and y positions.

Finally, the game loop makes its final call—CheckBall().

```
Function CheckBall()
 'Move and draw ball
 UpdateBall()

 'Check and see if ball hit anything
 CheckBallWithPaddle()
 CheckBallWithBlocks()
 CheckBallWithWalls()
 End Function
```

This function is the biggest one in the program. First off, it updates the position of the ball.

```
Function UpdateBall()
 'Move the ball to the left or right
 ball.x = ball.x + ball.directionx

 'Move the ball up or down
 ball.y = ball.y + ball.directiony

 'Draw the ball
 DrawText BALLSTRING, ball.x, ball.y
 End Function
```

This function begins by moving the ball based on its directionx and directiony variables. Then it draws the ball on the screen.

Next, the CheckBall() function calls CheckBallWithPaddle().

```
Function CheckBallWithPaddle()
        If ball.x >= player.x And ball.x <= player.x + PADDLEWIDTH
            And ball.y + BALLHEIGHT >= player.y
            And ball.y + BALLHEIGHT <= player.y + PADDLEHEIGHT

            ball.directiony = -ball.directiony + Rand(-3,3)
            EndIf
End Function
```

This function is pretty simple. The If statement determines whether the ball hit the paddle. You might have trouble understanding the If test, so I'll explain it to you.

See Figure 3.37 to understand how the test works. The line tests the ball and determines whether its x value falls between the left side of the paddle and the right side and whether its y value falls between the top and the bottom of the paddle.

If the ball has collided with the paddle, the directiony variable is flipped. This makes the direction move upward instead of downward. Also, if it hits the

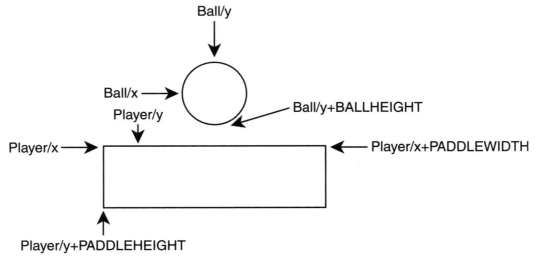

**Figure 3.37**
The ball-paddle collision.

paddle, the speed of the ball increases by a value between −3 and 3 (if it increases by a negative value, the ball slows down).

Next, the CheckBall() function calls CheckBallWithBlocks(). This function tests the ball to determine whether it has hit any blocks.

```
Function CheckBallWithBlocks()
'y is the first row
y = BLOCKYORIGIN

For rows=0 To BLOCKROWS - 1

 'Reset x to first block of column
 x = BLOCKXORIGIN

 'For every column of blocks
For cols = 0 To BLOCKCOLUMNS - 1'

      'If it exists
      If blocks[rows,cols]

            'If the ball hit the block, delete the block
            If ball.x >= x And ball.x <=  x + BLOCKWIDTH
                    And ball.y >= y And ball.y <= y + BLOCKHEIGHT

              blocks[rows,cols] = 0   'Delete block

              ball.directiony = -ball.directiony + Rand(-2,2)   'Reverse
its direction and add randomizer

              score = score + 75

              blockhits = blockhits + 1

              'It can't hit more than one block, so leave function
              Return
        EndIf
      EndIf

      'move to next column
      x = x + BLOCKXGAP
Next
```

```
'move to next row
y = y + BLOCKYGAP
Next

End Function
```

This function might seem tough, but it is a lot like DrawBlocks(). The first thing the function does is set up the origins. Then it begins the rows loop and resets the x value, just as in DrawBlocks(). Now, in the column loop, the block is tested to see whether it exists. If it does, the ball is tested with the block. If the ball does hit the block, the block is deleted (by setting it to 0), and the direction is reversed along with a random speed increase. Finally, the score is updated, the blockhits variable is increased, and the function returns (because the ball can't hit two blocks in one frame).

The last action the CheckBall() function performs is to check the ball with the walls.

```
Function CheckBallWithWalls()
'If ball hits the left wall, reverse its direction and add randomizer
If ball.x <= 0
 ball.directionx = -ball.directionx + Rand(-2,2)

'If ball hits top wall, reverse its direction and add randomizer
ElseIf ball.y <= 0
 ball.directiony = -ball.directiony + Rand(-2,2)

' If it hits right wall, reverse its direction and add randomizer
ElseIf ball.x >= 640 - BALLWIDTH
 ball.directionx = -ball.directionx + Rand(-2,2) '

'If ball hits lower wall, dock points for missing ball
ElseIf ball.y >= 480
 score = score - 200

 'Reset the level
 ResetLevel()
EndIf
 End Function
```

If the ball hits the top, left, or right wall, it is reversed. If it hits the bottom wall (if the paddle fails to hit it), 200 points are subtracted from the score, and the level is reset.

**Figure 3.38**
Textanoid!

Hey, take a look at Figure 3.38. It's the final version of Textanoid!

## Lists

Before we finish this (already enormous) chapter, I want to talk about one final topic: Lists. What is a list? A list is a collection of objects, usually objects of the same type, that are all related in some way. By using a list, you can keep track of all items of a specific type, iterate through all of them using a special loop, and update and keep track of all of them.

When is this useful? Imagine you are creating a game with thousands of random flies on the screen. You want the flies to each randomly move around, each having its own speed and position. By creating a list of flies, you can control each one, and iterate through that list, updating the speed of each fly during the game.

How do you create a list? Very simply. You do the following.

```
listvar:TList = CreateList()
```

**Table 3.6**  ListAddLast()'s Parameters

| Variable | Description |
| --- | --- |
| list:TList | The list to which you want to add a value. |
| value | An object of any type (including a user-defined type) which is added to the end of the list. |

Simple, eh? Notice that the variable is of the type TList. Now, when you want to add something to the list, simply use the function ListAddLast() (which adds an element to the end of the list).

The function declaration for ListAddLast() is this:

```
ListAddLast:TLink(list:TList, value)
```

Table 3.6 lists all of the parameters for ListAddLast().

After doing this, you've got a list of objects! Now, what if you want to go through all of the elements of the list and update the items? Simply use an EachIn loop. An EachIn loop is similar to a For...Next loop, but it simply iterates through every element in a list.

Imagine you have a type TFly and a list flies. To loop through all the flies, you simply do this:

```
For fly:TFly = EachIn flies
    'do something with variable fly
Next
```

When this loop is executed, the variable fly is assigned to each element inside flies, and the code in between the For and Next is executed for every value of fly.

Let's create a short program that uses lists. This program creates a list of flies, prints out their speeds, then doubles their speeds and prints out the list of flies again.

The first thing the program does is create the type and the list of flies.

```
'demo03-13.bmx - A demo of lists

'TYPES
Type TFly
```

```
    Field name:String
    Field speed
End Type
```

```
flies:TList = CreateList()
```

Notice that each fly has a name, which is a string, and an integer speed. Next, the list of flies is created. The list, flies is currently empty.

Next, the program creates three flies and gives them names and speeds.

```
'individual flies
fly1:TFly = New TFly
fly2:TFly = New TFly
fly3:Tfly = New TFly

'set speeds
fly1.name = "1. Clay Bavinger"
fly1.speed = 1
fly2.name = "2. Gus Jewell"
fly2.speed = 2
fly3.name = "3. Shawn Gogia"
fly3.speed = 3
```

As you can see, there are three flies with speeds of 1, 2, and 3. Now, we can actually add these flies to the list!

```
'Add flies to the list
ListAddLast(flies, fly1)
ListAddLast(flies, fly2)
ListAddLast(flies, fly3)
```

The three flies are now associated with the list of flies. Now, we print out the speeds of all of these original flies. I wrote a function to do this.

```
Function PrintSpeeds(list:TList)
    'Print out all the speeds
    Print "There are " + CountList(list) + " flies."
    For fly:TFly = EachIn list
      Print "Name: " + fly.name + " Speed: " + fly.speed
    Next
 End Function
```

As you can see, this loop uses an EachIn loop. The first thing it does is print out how many flies there are using the CountList() function. This function is simple

| **Table 3.7** CountList()'s Parameters | |
| --- | --- |
| **Variable** | **Description** |
| list:TList | The list in which you want to know how many elements exist. |

and is provided by BlitzMax—it simply tells you the number of elements in a list. The declaration for CountList() is as follows:

```
CountList(list:TList)
```

Table 3.7 details the parameter.

Simple, eh? Now, look closely at the EachIn loop.

```
For fly:TFly = EachIn list
  Print "Name: " + fly.name + " Speed: " + fly.speed
 Next
```

The variable fly is assigned consecutively to each of the elements inside of the list. The name and speed are then printed to the screen.

After printing the speeds, we then double the speeds of each fly. This is done with another EachIn loop, as follows.

```
Print "All the flies just doubled their speed!"
For fly:TFly = EachIn flies
  fly.speed = 2 * fly.speed
Next
```

### Note

You might be wondering why the list is called list in the previous loop where we printed the names and speeds, but flies when we double the speeds. The reason why is because the function I created, PrintSpeeds() has the declaration

```
PrintSpeeds(list:TList)
```

When we print the speeds, a copy of the list flies is made and it is renamed to be list. We call PrintSpeeds() as follows

```
PrintSpeeds(flies)
```

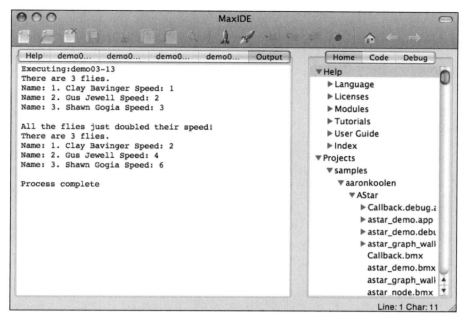

**Figure 3.39**
The demo03-13.bmx program.

Simple, eh? Finally, we finish up by printing the speeds of the list of flies again.

That's how you use lists! Figure 3.39 shows the output.

## Summary

Well, this has been one heck of a chapter. We learned about loops, functions, arrays, and types, and created our first animated game! This chapter is probably one of the most important in the book. You learned the basics of any BlitzMax program, and you are now able to write any text-based program you can think of. I suggest you take a break now, and try to digest and understand what you have read. You might want to reread the parts you don't understand, and go through the listings again. Also, read and try to understand the full game from Chapter 1. It uses everything you have learned here with a small bit of graphics code added. Again, you can access help online at www.maneeshsethi.com or by e-mailing me at maneesh@maneeshsethi.com if you have any questions.

I have an exercise for you, if you feel like expanding on your learning. When you play the final game from this chapter, you might notice that every once in a while, the ball moves only straight up and down, or slows to a complete stop. Try to fix this issue so that the ball cannot slow down too much or stop moving left and right. (Hint: try randomizing `directionx` to make sure it does not move straight up and down.)

This chapter covered the following concepts:

- Loops

- Functions

- Arrays

- Types

- Creating Textanoid!

Okay, this chapter is now officially over. Get some rest and have some fun, or whatever. I'll be waiting for you whenever you feel like learning some more.

# CHAPTER 4

# THE STYLE FACTOR

I intend to make this chapter short and sweet, so that we can get on to the graphics stuff as soon as possible. A question you may be asking yourself right now is "What is style?" Well, my computer dictionary says that style is "Distinctive and stylish elegance."

In my eyes, style is not just how something looks. Style is how something *feels*. I have looked at one piece of code with contempt and another with understanding, simply because of the way it feels. But, of course, to achieve the feeling, you have to create the look.

Style in computer programming is creating code that is understandable and readable. It is code that you can see day after day and not detest. Style is one of the most overlooked and underappreciated parts of computer programming. This chapter quickly introduces you to the foundations of style, and leads you to create your own.

Another thing to note is that a lot of times, ugly code is also poorly written. It is illogical and tough to understand, and that usually leads to unnecessary bad coding. Try to keep the code neat and your programs will be better.

## Developing Style

Everyone has his or her own style of coding; it's an inevitable fact. No two people enjoy their code the same way. Basically, to create a style for yourself, you just have to discover what is right for you and stick with it. Lesson one in the style primer: *Be Consistent.*

Let's start out with the most basic form of style: white space. Examples of white space are tabs, spaces, and new lines. Under most circumstances, you can add as much white space as you like to the beginning and end of most lines. White space can also be included between test commands (such as < and >) and what is being tested, as in Figure 4.1.

## White Space and Indentation

The easiest way to see the use of white space is with examples. The first code snippet I will show you is a block of code using white space. This is what your code should look like. You can ignore what the program actually does and just see how it looks.

```
For x = 0 To 10
    If x > 5
            Print "x is greater than 5; it's equal to " + x + "."

            If x > 7
                Print "Wow, x is really high, it's " + x   + "."
            EndIf

    Else
            Print "Too bad, x is less than or equal to 5."
    EndIf
Next
```

Not a bad looking format, eh? It's pretty easy to figure out which If statement goes with which EndIf statement, right? Well, the next example is the same code with absolutely no white space. Try understanding it now!

**Figure 4.1**
White space.

```
For x = 0 To 10
If x > 5
Print "x is greater than 5; it's equal to " + x + "."
If x > 7
Print "Wow, x is really high, it's " + x + "."
EndIf
Else
Print "Too bad, x is less than or equal to 5."
EndIf
 Next
```

This code is much harder to understand. If you wanted to actually comprehend its meaning, you would have to look closely and try to follow through the If commands. Now, imagine this code block was 10 or 15 times the length of the one I just showed you (programs can commonly grow that large in big games). It would be terribly difficult and a waste of time trying to understand all that code!

One thing you should know: adding white space does not affect the output of the program at all. There will be neither extra spaces nor new lines anywhere in the output of your program. See Figures 4.2 and 4.3 to see the outputs of both programs: white space and no white space.

## Comments

I may have talked a little about comments previously, but I am going to explain them in depth now. Comments, as you know, are simply statements you write within your program to explain what you are doing. In a program, comments look like this:

```
Print "This is a statement." ;this is a comment
```

Make sure you notice the semicolon before the comment. The semicolon is required for every comment; in fact, it is how a comment is identified to the compiler. Comments are used to explain how a part of a program works: it may define what a single statement does, or it may tell what a whole block of statements does. I use almost one comment every other line in my programs; it helps because I often forget what I was trying to do after I finish a program. When I come back a few days or weeks later, the comments are still there to help guide me through my code.

Comments aren't only used to offer help for a single statement. I usually create a block of comments at the beginning of my programs to tell me what the program

**Figures 4.2 and 4.3**
Output of programs with white space (top) and without white space (bottom).

does. I often use a large box to draw my eyes toward it like this (the full listing for this program is named demo04-01.bb on the CD):

```
'''''''''''''''''''''''''''''''''''''''''''''''''''''''''''''''
' HelloWorld.bmx''''''''''''''''''''''''''''''''''''''''''''''''
```

```
' By Maneesh Sethi'' ''''''''''''''''''''''''''''''
' This program prints "Hello World to the screen.'''''
' There are no input variables required'''''''''''''
'''''''''''''''''''''''''''''''''''''''''''''''''''''''
```

As you can see, this box of comments is the intro to a Hello World program. I put a box like this at the top of most programs. It tells the reader four things: what the filename is, who the author is, what the purpose of the program is, and any extra info the user needs to use it.

There are some extra rows of information that you can add to the box. Maybe you want to tell the reader what version of the program this is, and you might want to reference others who helped you with it. Perhaps you have some special restrictions on the program ("this program does not run on Windows XP"), or something of that nature.

The next part of the program is that actual code. With comments, it might look something like this:

**Note**

This program is way more complex than it needs to be. There isn't much sense in using functions and variables in a simple Hello World program. The only reason I used functions and variables in this program is to demonstrate the use of comments.

```
'VARIABLES
'The hello string to be printed on the screen
hellostr:String = "Hello World!"
'END VARIABLES

'MAIN PROGRAM
'Pass "hellostr" to PrintString function
PrintString(hellostr)
'END MAIN PROGRAM

'FUNCTIONS
''''''''''''''''''''''''''''''''''''''''''
'Function PrintString(str:String)''''''
'This function prints the variable str
'Parameters: str - the string to be printed
''''''''''''''''''''''''''''''''''''''''''
Function PrintString(str:String)
'Print str on screen
```

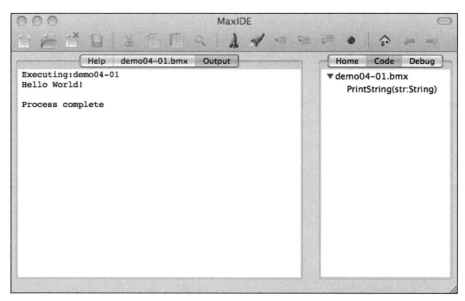

**Figure 4.4**
Hello World!

```
Print str
End Function
'END FUNCTIONS
```

And there you have it! A fully commented version of Hello World, as shown in Figure 4.4. Let's take a look at some of these comments.

## Pre-Program Comments

Before the actual main program, I create a few commented sections that I call the pre-program comments. This usually includes local variables, global variables, constants, array dimensions, and anything else that you declare before the program starts. For each section, I write a line of code that explains what is following. For example, in demo04-01.bmx, I created a section for variables. At the end of the declarations, I add a line of code that tells the reader that it is the end of the section (END VARIABLES in the Hello World example).

I also comment each variable individually to explain what they do specifically. Adding these simple lines of code makes it much easier to find out what a variable is named and what its value is simply by searching the top of a program.

## Main Program Comments

I add some simple comments to the beginning of and inside the actual main program. At the beginning, I add a comment detailing the starting point of the actual program. I also add comments after statements, just as in the rest of the program.

Main program comments also tell where the main game loop begins and ends. I add those comments at the top and bottom of the `While...Wend` loop. Comments are usually included near function calls, such as the call to `PrintScreen(str:-String)` in demo04-01.bb. The comments detail which function it calls and what the function does.

## Function Comments

The function comments are written at the beginning of each and every function. I usually begin the function definitions after the end of the main program; consequently, I comment the `'FUNCTIONS` header directly after `'END MAIN PROGRAM`.

---

**Refresher: The Difference between a Declaration and a Definition**

I use the terms definition and declaration a lot in this chapter, and now is as good a time as any to go over the difference again. A *declaration* simply refers to or states a function or variable, and a *definition* actually defines it. For example, the declaration of `PrintString` is `Print-String(str:String)`. The actual definition, however, is

```
Function PrintString(str:String)
        Print str 'Print str$ on screen
            End Function
```

In summary, when I refer to the declaration of a function, I am talking about the call to it in code or the title of the function. When I refer to the definition of a function, I am talking about the actual code inside the function.

---

Before I define any functions, I always create a box that explains the function. On demo04-01.bmx the `PrintString(str:String)` function is commented like this:

```
''''''''''''''''''''''''''''''''''''''
'Function PrintString(str:String)''''''
'This function prints the variable str
'Parameters: str - the string to be printed
''''''''''''''''''''''''''''''''''''''
```

As you can see, this block states the name of the function, its purpose, and its parameters. Make sure you add a block like this to the beginning of every function—it makes understanding them a heck of a lot easier.

## Function and Variable Names

Naming your variables correctly can help solve a lot of problems in programs. Every once in a while you might come across the problem of not knowing what a variable does. You will need to backtrack and follow your program from the beginning. A way to solve this problem, however, is to name your variables a very easy-to-understand name. This can help reduce, if not eliminate, later forgetfulness.

## Names

When declaring and defining variables, make sure you come up with a name that easily describes what the variable does. For example, when writing the Hello World program, I could have easily named the variable anything. I could have chosen names like

```
i:String

row:String

howareyou:String

_123:String

hellostr:String
```

but there is a reason I didn't. For most of them, they don't make sense. For example, what does `howareyou` have to do with a string? (Unless of course, I am asking how the user is feeling.) You may be wondering, though, why I didn't pick `hellostr`. In this program, it would have been fine; however, in most programs, the contents of a variable change. Because they usually do change, creating a variable that tells exactly what is inside the variable rather than what kind of data it contains can create the exact same problem it is supposed to fix. If you changed the program so that `hellostr` was equivalent to `''Today is my birthday,''` the `hellostr` no longer makes sense in the context, and you might have to change all of the variable names in the program.

## Naming Format

The format of your variable names is largely up to you. No rules are set in stone as to how to name your functions and variables. The only thing that is required is that your format remains consistent throughout the program.

Here are some different ways to format the same variable.

```
hellostr:String

Hello_Str:String

helloStr:String

HelloStr:String

Hellostr:String
```

As you can see, these variables are all the same. However, each name is slightly changed.

The first variable is my choice for regular variables. I keep it simple: both words are in lowercase. Some people use two words separated by an underscore (an underscore is a key achieved by pressing Shift+Dash). Others use the two words in different capitalization patterns.

Functions can also be named in similar ways. For example:

```
PrintString

printstring

Print_String

printString

Printstring
```

I usually choose the first method for functions: two joined words that are both capitalized. Once again, feel free to pick whichever you like, but make sure you stick with it.

Some other naming formats you might like to vary are constants, global variables, and array names.

I usually keep all the letters in a constant uppercase, like this:

```
Const CONSTANT = 1
```

My global variables are usually the same as regular variables, like this:

```
globalvar = 10
```

A lot of people prefer to add a g_ to the beginning of global variables. I choose not to, but feel free to try it.

For arrays, I keep it simple. I use one word if possible, and I keep it lowercase.

```
Int array[numofelements]
```

## Summary

Well, I hope you enjoyed this chapter. I tried to give the best explanation of style that I could, and hopefully I did a good job. I wrote this chapter because I believe style and clarity are important to every program, and also because it is tough to find any style primers out there.

Once again, nothing in the chapter must be followed *exactly*. Style is an individual thing; what appeals to one person might not appeal to the next. Try out all of the given styles and see which one fits you. The only thing I request of you is that you make your program simple and easy to understand. There is no need to use complex commands if you can get away with using a simpler block of code, even if it is a bit longer.

Try to get your programs to read like an essay—keep it organized and straightforward. Make sure you have your pre-program section listed, and try to comment any line of code that requires it. Make sure your style is consistent; if one function has an underscore between two words, make sure the next one does, too. Other than that, keep experimenting, and eventually you will develop your own style.

This chapter covered the following concepts:

- Developing style

- Comments

- Function and variable names

Hey, we just finished Part I. Take a break if you feel like it, or jump straight into Part II. We are finally getting into graphics; I guarantee it'll be more fun than you've ever had.

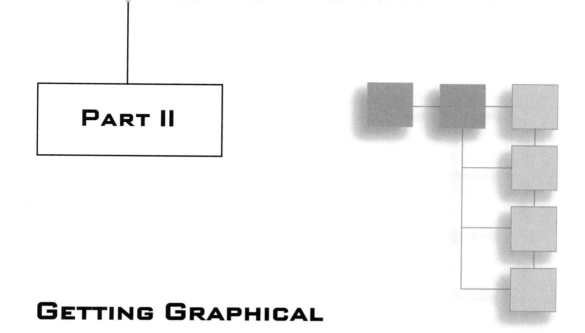

# PART II

# GETTING GRAPHICAL

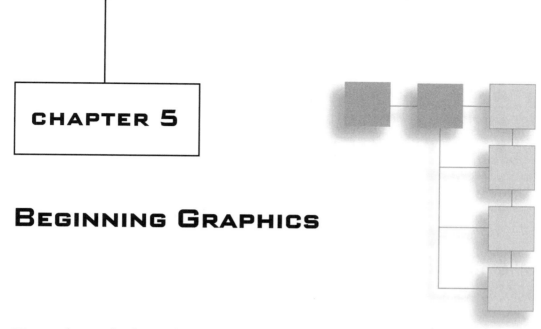

# CHAPTER 5

# BEGINNING GRAPHICS

Hey, welcome back! Today, we're gonna start using graphics in our program. This chapter will be a huge jump for you; it teaches you how to initialize the graphical window and how to perform image loads. It also shows you how to display and move your images on the screen.

Anyway, get ready. This chapter is simple, but it's packed with some serious stuff.

## Creating the Graphics Window

A graphics window is a little bit different from the text windows we have been using thus far. Unlike the programs we have been running to this point, which could only display text, graphical windows can also display graphics, such as images and pictures. They can also change colors of text.

Every BlitzMax graphical program contains a line of code that initializes the window. This process basically sets up the window for later use. To set up a graphical window, call the function `Graphics`. `Graphics` is declared as follows:

```
Graphics width, height, colordepth, [hertz]
```

Table 5.1 details each parameter.

### What Is Initialization?

I use the term *initialization* a lot in this chapter, and you might wonder what it means. To initialize a window is to set the window up, so, when you initialize the graphics in BlitzMax, you are setting it up. After initialization, you will be able to use graphics in the program.

| Table 5.1  Graphics Parameters | |
| --- | --- |
| **Parameter** | **Meaning** |
| width | The width of the window in pixels |
| height | The height of the window in pixels |
| [colordepth] | The colors per pixel (in bits), default leaves the game windowed |
| [hertz] | Advanced; generally leave blank |

## Width and Height

Let's discuss each parameter in depth. Take a look at width and height—they affect your program in a huge way, but only a few modes are commonly used. These modes are shown in the following list. You might be wondering why we only use these modes, and there certainly is a reason.

- 640 × 480

- 800 × 600

- 1024 × 768

- 1280 × 1024

- 1600 × 1200

If you were to take a ruler to your computer monitor and measure the height and width, you would always come out with a bigger width than height. But the cool part is, the numbers you come up with are always proportional to one another. For example, my monitor is 14.66 inches wide and 11 inches tall. If you divide 14.66 by 11, you get 1.33. This means that my computer monitor's width is 1.33 times its height. This proportion works for all monitors and most televisions as well. Try it out!

Because the monitor's width is longer than its height, all of the pixel values on the monitor must change. If you were to draw a box that was an exact square, it would end up looking like a rectangle on the monitor (its width would be longer than its height). To combat this problem, resolutions make the height pixels larger than the width pixels. The pixels are stretched out a bit, and the square actually looks like a square. Refer to Figure 5.1 to see the monitor's proportion.

14.66/11=1.33
1600/1200=1.33

Height →

Width                    11"

14.66"

**Figure 5.1**
The monitor's proportion.

| Table 5.2  Color Depth | |
| --- | --- |
| **Color Depth (Bits)** | **Colors** |
| 0 | The default option, makes the program a windowed application and sets the color depth to the default depth of the machine. |
| 8 | 256 |
| 16 | 65,536 |
| 24 | 16,777,216 |
| 32 | 4,294,967,296 |

## Color Depth

The next variable is color depth. The color depth is actually the number of colors that each pixel can be, and is numbered in bits. This parameter also enables you to choose between a windowed program and a fullscreen program. See Table 5.2 for the common color depths and their respective color counts.

**Note**

Take note that setting the color depth only makes a difference in full-screen mode. In windowed mode, the color depth of your game is limited to the color depth of the player's desktop; in full-screen mode, the color depth can be set to any one of the color depths from Table 5.2. To see your desktop's color depth in Windows, right-click on your desktop and then select Properties. Then find the Settings tab. Your color depth is under Color Quality.

Windowed

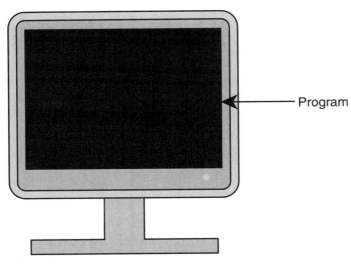

Full Screen

**Figure 5.2**
Full-screen and windowed modes.

**Note**

To determine how many colors each color depth provides, simply raise 2 to the power of the color depth. For example, if you want to find out how many colors a color depth of 8 gives, multiply 2 by itself 8 times ($2 \times 2 \times 2 \times 2 \times 2 \times 2 \times 2 \times 2$) or find 2 to the 8th power ($2\wedge8$).

**Note**

Although these are the only color depths used commonly today, other depths have been used in the past. For example, some very old games might have run in a color depth mode of 1, which provides only two colors—black and white.

**Caution**

Make sure you know which bit depth you should be using before you select it. If you use a color depth of 8, for example, but the colors in your game need at least a color depth of 16, the colors in your game won't show up.

If you do not set the color depth, or if you set it to 0, the game will run in windowed mode. If you set a specific depth, the game will be full screen. 0 is [color depth]'s default value; if you leave [color depth] blank, it is automatically set to 0. When your program runs in auto mode, it runs as a window. Figure 5.2 shows the difference in full-screen and windowed modes. Leaving it windowed is great for doing debugging.

## What Is Debug Mode?

I refer to debug mode a lot, and you might want to know what it means. When writing a game, you often come across hidden bugs that are extremely hard to find. Debugging allows you to step through a program line-by-line to discover where your program goes wrong. Debugging offers another reason for using functions—discovering bugs in a program where most of the code is located in functions separate from the main code is much easier than finding bugs in a program where all the code is thrown together in the main function.

When you plan to debug a game, you work in debug mode. This allows you to see the line you are debugging and find out what value each variable contains. When you have finished your game, you turn off debug and distribute the actual game. To turn debug mode on and off, check or uncheck Program > Build Options > Debug Build. See Figure 5.3 to see how to enable Debug Mode.

**Figure 5.3**
Debug mode.

**Figure 5.4**
KONG in full-screen mode.

Figures 5.4 and 5.5 show the difference between KONG in full-screen and windowed modes.

## Images

Whew, that was one big graphics call! Let's get into more specialized graphics stuff. This section explains how to load an image, how to draw it onscreen, and the like. Are you ready?

**Figure 5.5**
KONG in windowed mode.

| Table 5.3 | LoadImage()'s Parameter |
|---|---|
| **Parameter** | **Description** |
| filename | The path of the image |
| [flags] | Some optional flags, such as MASKEDIMAGE, which adjust the loading procedure of an image |

## LoadImage()

The first call we will be using is LoadImage(). This function loads the image of your choice into your program's memory. You must load an image before you can display it or manipulate it in your program. LoadImage is defined as this:

```
LoadImage(filename:String, [flags])
```

Table 5.3 examines each parameter. To load an image, just substitute the file name of the image for filename (make sure the file name is in quotation marks), and assign it to a variable, like this:

```
Global playerimage = LoadImage("playerimage.bmp")
```

The [flags] parameter is optional and advanced, but we will use it later in this chapter for loading an image with masking.

**N o t e**

Check out what I set the file name variable to. Making the file name just the name of the file (without adding any path info) works only if the image is in the same directory as the game. If not, you might need to include your drive information. It might look something like this:

```
Playerimage = LoadImage("c:\windows\desktop\playerimage.bmp")
```

Even so, I suggest you keep all your images in the same folder as the game, because if you ever decide to distribute your game, the game won't work on other computers unless the user puts the images in the *exact* same folder as yours.

I usually name my image variables in such a way that I can easily see that they are images. This means I begin my image names with its actual job (*player* in playerimage.bmp) and suffix it with *image*.

The name that you assign to the loaded image is called a *handle*. Basically, a handle is just an identifier that refers to an image in memory, like in Figure 5.6.

`LoadImage()`, by default, searches directly in the same folder as the location of the .bmx file. If you want to load an image from another directory, you must provide the full path to the image.

Okay, now that we've got this `LoadImage()` stuff down, it's time to actually draw it!

## DrawImage()

It is pretty easy to guess what this function does: it draws images! Table 5.4 examines each parameter. Let's start with the declaration.

```
DrawImage(handle,x,y,[frame])
```

`DrawImage()` has a couple of parameters, so let's move on to a discussion of the handle variables.

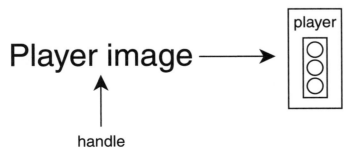

**Figure 5.6**
A handle to an image in memory.

**Table 5.4**  DrawImage()'s Parameters

| Name | Description |
| --- | --- |
| handle | The variable that holds the image |
| x | The drawn image's x coordinate |
| y | The drawn image's y coordinate |
| [frame] | Advanced; leave as 0 |

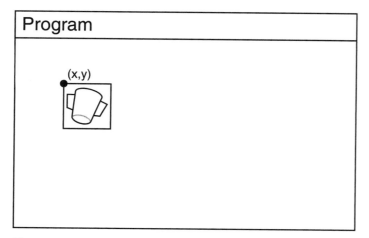

**Figure 5.7**
The image at x,y.

### Handle

This is a pretty easy-to-understand parameter. Remember when you loaded an image like this?

```
playerimage = LoadImage("player.bmp")
```

Well, the handle is playerimage. So, when you're sending parameters to Draw-Image(), use the same image handle that you loaded earlier as the DrawImage() handle parameter.

### X and Y

The x and y parameters work just like most x and y coordinates in BlitzMax. Using DrawImage(), your selected image is drawn at the x and y coordinates, as shown in Figure 5.7. Its top-left corner is located at the given x and y values. However, there is a way to center the image so that the image's center is located at x,y.

Very often, you will want to center the image. This is most useful when rotating images, because rotating images around the top-left corner looks bad (not to mention trippy) because you would expect images to rotate around their centers. Check out demo05-01.bmx to see how an image looks when it is rotated around the top-left corner.

Although actual rotation is a more advanced technique and is explained in a later chapter, I am using it to illustrate the use of placing the x and y values in the center of the image. The actual function is called `AutoMidHandle()` and is declared like this:

```
AutoMidHandle(true|false)
```

**Note**

What does "|" mean? | means *or*. When I say `AutoMidHandle(true|false)`, I mean `AutoMidHandle()` can use either `true` *or* `false`.

To use this function and place the x and y values in the center of the image, call `AutoMidHandle()` with the parameter `true`, like this:

```
AutoMidHandle(true)
```

Easy, huh? And to set the x and y location back to the top left, just call `Auto-MidHandle()`, like this:

```
AutoMidHandle(false)
```

It is a good idea to use `AutoMidHandle()`, because it helps you understand exactly where the images are located. Because your access point is directly in the center of the image, you won't need to worry about the image's width and height as much as if the access point was in the top left.

Table 5.5 details the parameters, and Figure 5.8 shows how demo05-02.bmx, which uses `AutoMidHandle(true)`, works. Look at the difference in Figures 5.7 and 5.8. In Figure 5.8, you can see how the x and y coordinates are located at the top-left corner of the image. In Figure 5.8, the x and y coordinates are in the center of the image. Try running demo05-02.bmx and watch how it rotates from the center instead of from the left corner, as in demo05-01.bmx.

Make absolutely sure that you place `AutoMidHandle(true)` before you load the image; otherwise, the function won't work.

**Table 5.5** AutoMidHandle()'s Parameters

| Name | Description |
| --- | --- |
| true | Places the x and y coordinates in the center of the image. |
| false | Places the coordinates at the top left of the image. |

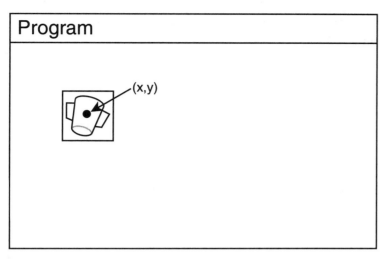

**Figure 5.8**
The image at x,y with `AutoMidHandle()` set to `true`.

### *[Frame]*

Okay, this command is very advanced. `[frame]` allows you to draw images that are animated. It is too advanced right now, but we will explore using animated images very soon!

## TileImage()

This function is pretty cool. It allows you to take an image and paste it along the background of the graphics window, creating a cool background image. Imagine, for example, a game that takes place in space. Using a starsystem as your background and tiling it is a good way to make it seem like the player is in space!

```
TileImage(handle, [x], [y], [frame])
```

x and y explain the starting coordinate of the tiled image and are usually set to 0,0 (the top left corner of the image); `[frame]` is used with animated images and should be set to 0 for now. To tile the image, call `TileImage()` like this:

```
TileImage(handle)
```

The following is the full source for the program, which can also be found on the CD as demo05-03.bmx:

```
'''''''''''''''''''''''''''''''''''
' demo05-03.bmx'''''''''''''''''''''
' By Maneesh Sethi'''''''''''''''''
```

```
' Creates a tiled image''''''''''
' No input parameters required'''''
'''''''''''''''''''''''''''''''''''
'INITIALIZATION

'Set up the graphics
Graphics 800,600

'IMAGES
'Create the dotfield image
dotfieldimage = LoadImage("stars.bmp")
'END IMAGES

'Tile the image
TileImage dotfieldimage
Flip

WaitKey
```

Figure 5.9 shows the dot field.

**Figure 5.9**
The dot field.

**Figure 5.10**
An individual tile.

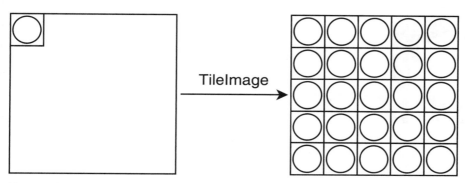

**Figure 5.11**
The TileImage function.

TileImage() works like this: it takes an image you give it and it places copies of it all across the programming board. Figure 5.10 shows an individual tile.

Think of it like a chessboard—there are only two images on a chessboard, black and white. But these two images are tiled over and over until the entire board is filled with black and white tiles. See Figure 5.11 for a visual aid to tiling, and Table 5.6 for a list of each parameter.

To tile an image, call TileImage() with the handle of an image you wish to tile. BlitzMax will take care of the rest. By the way, in later chapters, you will learn how to move the tiled field up and down to simulate movement.

The last part of the program calls the function WaitKey(). This function simply pauses the program until a key is pressed.

## SetMaskColor()

All right, the next function I want to go over is called SetMaskColor(). SetMaskColor() is defined like this.

```
SetMaskColor (red, green, blue)
```

**Table 5.6**  TileImage()'s Parameters

| Name | Description |
| --- | --- |
| handle | The image you wish to tile |
| [x] | The starting x coordinate of the tiled image; 0 by default |
| [y] | The starting y coordinate of the tiled image; 0 by default |
| [frame] | The chosen frame to tile; 0 by default |

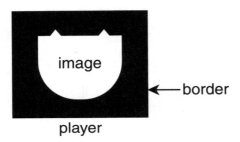

**Figure 5.12**
An unmasked image.

SetMaskColor() allows you to define a color of your image as transparent. What does that mean? Let me show you.

When you draw or create an image, you always have a border that is not part of the image. See Figure 5.12 for a description of the border. As you can see, the outer part of the image is not used, and it should be discarded. You don't want the border to be shown, like in Figure 5.13, do you?

**Note**

Because black is automatically masked by default, the image in Figure 5.13 does not have a purely black border. I added a tiny amount of blue to the image so that the background wouldn't be masked. The RGB value of this image's background is 0,0,10. We will talk more about what RGB means in a few pages.

Calling SetMaskColor() can get rid of that border for you. Table 5.7 explains each parameter. Because the RGB value of this background is 0,0,10, call the Set-MaskColor() function with the correct parameters.

After setting SetMaskColor(), you have to actually load the image. In addition to calling the standard LoadImage(), you have to add an extra parameter. The extra

**Figure 5.13**
A drawn image with a border.

| Table 5.7 SetMaskColor() Parameters | |
| --- | --- |
| **Name** | **Description** |
| red | The red value of the mask |
| green | The green value of the mask |
| blue | The blue value of the mask |

parameter is MASKEDIMAGE, and you simply add MASKEDIMAGE to the LoadImage() call as follows.

```
SetMaskColor red,green,blue
imagehandle = LoadImage("image.bmp", MASKEDIMAGE)
```

A full program that handles masking is detailed next:

```
''''''''''''''''''''''
'demo05-05.bmx
'By Maneesh Sethi
'Demonstrates the use of masking
''''''''''''''''''''''
'Initialize graphics
Graphics 640,480
```

```
'Load Background
lilliesimage = LoadImage("lillies.bmp")
'Draw background
DrawImage lilliesimage,0,0

'Set up masking
SetMaskColor 0,0,10

'Load the frog with masking
frogimage = LoadImage("frog.bmp", MASKEDIMAGE)
'Center the frog
MidHandleImage frogimage
'Draw it in the center
DrawImage frogimage,320,240

Flip

'Wait for user to press a button
WaitKey
```

Figure 5.14 is a picture of this program. Beautiful, isn't it? It looks as if the frog is actually part of the image! On the CD, demo05-04.bmx is a

**Figure 5.14**
An image drawn with a mask.

program without masking, and demo05-05.bmx is the same program with masking.

One thing to note: an RGB value of 0,0,0 is the default. 0,0,0 is the color black. This means that if your image is drawn with a black border, it will automatically be masked. In other words, try to make all your images have a black background so you don't need to worry about masking images.

You might have noticed the command Flip at the end of the program. By default, BlitzMax draws its information on the back buffer. By using Flip, you move the information from the buffer to the screen. We will learn more about this in later chapters.

## Colors

Before I end this chapter, I want to teach you how to work with color. Of course, color is an integral part of any program. When using page flipping (which is explained in the next chapter), color takes on an even greater importance.

You need to know some functions before you move on to the next chapter. These functions are SetColor(), Cls(), and SetClsColor(). You also need to understand RGB values.

## RGB

When working with color, you will often encounter RGB (red, green, blue) values. These numbers allow you to pick any one of 16 million different colors. That's a lot, huh?

**Why 16 Million?**

When you are using RGB values, you usually pick a number between 0 and 255 for each color. What does this have to do with the number of colors? Well, if you multiply 256 by itself three times because there are three colors (256 × 256 × 256), you get 16.7 million. This means that you have all 16.7 million values to choose from.

When color is used in functions, there are usually three fields for you to enter your choices—red, green, and blue. For each field, you can pick a number between 0 and 255 (256 choices total). The higher the number, the more of that color there will be. For example, if you set the red value to 255 and the green and blue values to zero (255,0,0), you will have a perfectly red color. 0,0,0 is black, and 255,255,255 is white.

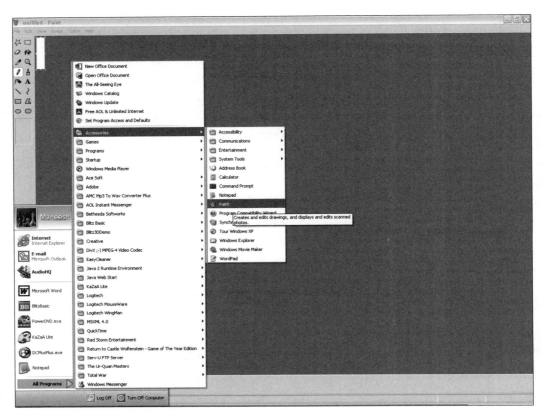

**Figure 5.15**
Opening Microsoft Paint.

Now, you may be wondering how you are supposed to find the exact values for the color you want. Well, there are two ways. You can use guess and check (by putting in guesses for the red, green, and blue fields), or you can use a program, such as Microsoft Paint.

With Windows, you can open Microsoft Paint by going to Start Menu > All Programs > Accessories > Paint. See Figure 5.15 for a visual image of Microsoft Paint and how to open it (the background is Paint, the foreground is the Start menu [your menu will probably be a little different]). Now choose Colors > Edit Colors. A window will pop up. Click where it says Define Custom Colors. Figure 5.16 shows you the custom colors box.

Now choose your color, and it should tell you the RGB value on the bottom. If it doesn't work at first, move the scrollbar on the far right, and then proceed to pick your color.

**Figure 5.16**
Defining custom colors.

That's pretty much all there is to RGB. You're ready to use color in your programs now.

## SetColor()

SetColor() is kind of a fun function. It defines what the default color of the program is. When you draw something, be it lines, shapes, or text (not images), it will be drawn with the defined color.

What can you do with SetColor()? If you want to make the text anything other than white, just use this. Or maybe you want to draw a green triangle. Just set the color to green and draw it! You can change the color at any time.

**Note**

The default color of any BlitzMax program (before you call SetColor()) is white (RGB 255,255,255).

You can start with the function declaration.

```
SetColor red, green, blue
```

See Table 5.8 for the parameters. You will most likely just put in the red, green, and blue values to get your color.

Now let's write a program that uses this function. This program will draw a bunch of ellipses with random sizes and colors.

**Table 5.8** SetColor()'s Parameters

| Name | Description |
| --- | --- |
| red | The color's red value |
| green | The color's green value |
| blue | The color's blue value |

```
''''''''''''''''''''''
'demo05-06.bmx
'By Maneesh Sethi
'Demonstrates the Color function, draws ellipses
'No Input Parameters required
''''''''''''''''''''''
Graphics 800,600

'Seed random generator
SeedRnd (MilliSecs())


'Max width of ellipse
Const MAXWIDTH = 200
'Max Height of ellipse
Const MAXHEIGHT = 200

'Main Loop
While Not KeyDown(KEY_ESCAPE)

'Clear the Screen
Cls

'Set the color to a random value
SetColor Rand(0,255), Rand(0,255), Rand(0,255)

'Draw a random oval
DrawOval Rand(0,800),Rand(0,600),Rand(0,MAXWIDTH),Rand(0,MAXHEIGHT)

'Slow down!
Delay 200
Flip
Wend
```

**Figure 5.17**
The demo05-06.bmx program.

Pretty cool, huh? Figure 5.17 shows a screenshot from the program. Let's look a little closer. The program first sets the graphics mode and seeds the random generator. Then it defines the maximum width and height of each ellipse. Feel free to change the values.

Next, the game enters the main loop. It first sets the color to a random value, using the line

```
SetColor(Rand(0,255), Rand(0,255), Rand(0,255))
```

This allows the next line to draw an ellipse with the random color. The ellipse function (notice that it is actually called DrawOval—I just like the word ellipse) is defined like this:

```
DrawOval(x,y,width,height)
```

Take a look at Table 5.9 for each parameter.

Well, that's pretty much it for the SetColor() function. Next up—the Cls and the SetClsColor() functions.

**Table 5.9**  DrawOval()'s Parameters

| Parameter | Description |
|---|---|
| x | The x coordinate of the ellipse |
| y | The y coordinate of the ellipse |
| width | The width in pixels of the ellipse |
| height | The height in pixels of the ellipse |

**Table 5.10**  SetClsColor()'s Parameters

| Name | Description |
|---|---|
| red | The color's red value |
| green | The color's green value |
| blue | The color's blue value |

## Cls and SetClsColor()

We are almost done with this chapter! Before I send you packing, though, I want you to have a bit of basis for the next chapter.

The function Cls's action is pretty simple. All it does is clear the screen. The next chapter goes over it in more depth. The SetClsColor() function works with Cls to allow you to change the background of your program.

SetClsColor() is defined like this:

```
SetClsColor(red,green,blue)
```

See Table 5.10 for a description of each parameter.

SetClsColor()'s job is to change the background color. This means that you can leave the default black behind and make the background anything you want it to be. To use this function, call SetClsColor() with the red, green, and blue values you want, and then call Cls to actually clear the screen with the background color.

Let's try a program. Demo05-07.bmx makes a bunch of colors appear on the screen (along with some advice you should follow). Try it out!

## Summary

Okay, you now have a working knowledge of graphics in video games. In this chapter, we learned about a lot of functions: `Graphics`, `LoadImage()`, `DrawImage()`, `SetColor()`, `Cls`, `SetClsColor()`, and `SetMaskImage()`. Believe me, you will find many uses for all these functions in your games.

This chapter studied the topics of:

- Creating a graphics window

- Loading, drawing, and using images

- Using colors

Next up, we learn about page flipping and basic input. The following chapter is important because you learn about basic animation.

# CHAPTER 6

# PAGE FLIPPING AND PIXEL PLOTTING

This chapter explains animation and pixel plotting. Animation is created through a process called *page flipping*, and it takes each frame of your game and seamlessly ties them together. *Pixel plotting* allows you to draw pixels, which are small dots, directly to the screen.

You have already been introduced to page flipping. Page flipping was discussed briefly in some of the earlier chapters. Page flipping is integral to most high-end games; it is the process that actually produces animation. So, why wait? Let's get started!

## Page Flipping

Page flipping is named for its similarities to a flipbook. Remember those? They were the small books that, when flipped through quickly, seemed to make an image move. In a video game, a similar process is used. A picture is drawn on an off-screen image called a *buffer*. The buffer is the page after the one you are currently looking at in the flipbook. When the pages are flipped, the off-screen image is flipped with the front screen image. It looks like Figure 6.1.

### What Is a Frame?

From what you have learned so far in this book, you should know that a frame is basically one scene of animation that is tied with other scenes so quickly that it creates an illusion of smooth animation. Essentially, a frame is a single iteration of the main loop. (In case you forgot, to iterate through a loop is to go through it once—in other words, to perform the instructions of the loop one time.) In a game, you iterate through the loop until the user quits the game. When a frame goes through the loop once, the game has achieved one frame of animation. This loop continues to iterate until the game is over.

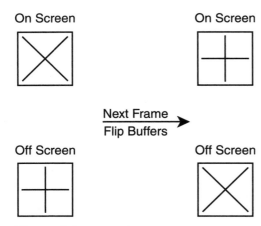

**Figure 6.1**
Page flipping.

Now, you might wonder how this would create animation. Well, this process happens at least 30 times a second. That means that in one second, at least 30 different frames are drawn on the screen. In a flipbook, a single page is the equivalent of a frame. It is impossible to see each individual page when the book is flipped, and the page-flipping procedure is no different. The frames flip quickly to create smooth animation: it is impossible to tell the difference between the individual frames.

Page flipping has been used in a lot of games in this book so far, but I really haven't explained how it works. Let's start with a sample of what a game looks like with decent page flipping. This file can be run from the CD; it is called demo06-01.bmx:

```
'demo06-01.bmx - An example of animation
'Initialize the Graphics
Graphics 800,600

'load the ship image
shipimage = LoadImage("ship.bmp")

'Seed the random generator
SeedRnd(MilliSecs())

'create a ship type
Type ship
     Field x,y    'the x and y coords
End Type
```

```
'create the ship
playerShip:ship = New ship

'position the ship randomly
playerShip.x = Rand(0,800)
playerShip.y = Rand(0,600)

While Not KeyDown(1)
        'Clear the screen
        Cls
        'move ship left and right
        playerShip.x = playerShip.x + Rand(-8,8)
        'Move ship up And down
        playerShip.y = playerShip.y + Rand(-8,8)

        'If ship goes off screen, move it back on
        If playerShip.x < 0
                playerShip.x = 15
        ElseIf playerShip.x > 800
                playerShip.x = 790
        ElseIf playerShip.y < 0
                playerShip.y = 10
        ElseIf playerShip.y > 600
                playerShip.y = 590
        EndIf

        'Draw the ship
        DrawImage(shipimage, playerShip.x, playerShip.y)
        Flip
Wend
```

Figure 6.2 shows three frames from demo06-01.bmx. Do you see how the ship moves smoothly?

Page flipping works because the next frame is drawn onto a back buffer so that the back buffer is flipped with the front buffer quickly and seamlessly.

Let's get started learning why this program works!

## Buffers

I know I've probably gone over this a hundred times, but I think it might be easier to create a section that explains what a general buffer is for future reference. Maybe it will also help you understand the idea.

**Figure 6.2**
Demo06-01.bmx running.

A buffer is an image. Each frame of your game is drawn onto a buffer; hence, each frame of your game is an image (frame = buffer, buffer = image, frame = image). Now, to create smooth animation (in other words, to make the game actually run), you usually need at least two buffers, although three buffers are used in many modern games.

The two buffers are known as the *front buffer* and the *back buffer*. The difference is that the front buffer is displayed on the screen, and the back buffer is drawn offscreen. Think of it like this: the front buffer is drawn on the top of a pad of paper, and the back buffer is drawn a sheet below, like in Figure 6.3.

By the way, there is another type of buffer called an *image buffer*. An image buffer is just like any other buffer, but it usually holds an image that you want to draw to manually. So, for example, assume you wanted to have a buffer where you want to draw two rectangles. Well, you can use the image buffer to create two drawn rectangles, and then move the image buffer into the actual game at any time. The cool thing about image buffers is that they can be any size, whereas the front and back buffers must be as large as the screen.

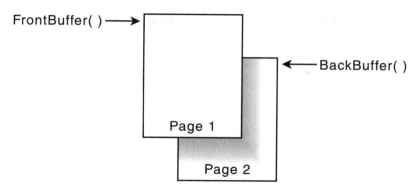

**Figure 6.3**
A buffer as a pad of paper.

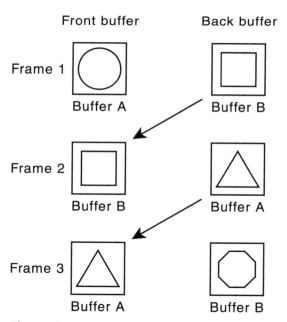

**Figure 6.4**
Buffers A and B.

Buffers are commonly used in page flipping. Because I have already explained the process, I'll go over it very quickly with respect to buffers. Basically, you have two buffers, buffer A and buffer B. Buffer A is the front buffer, and buffer B is the back buffer. While you are in the game, the image is drawn to buffer B. At the end of the frame, buffer A is swapped with buffer B, so the old frame, A, is now being drawn offscreen. Buffer B is now being displayed. See Figure 6.4 for a visual aid. Notice that the back buffer and front buffer never actually change locations.

This example brings up an interesting point: If the buffers are swapped each frame, shouldn't you have to alternate between drawing on the front buffer and drawing on the back buffer? The answer is no. Only the data is swapped between the two buffers, not the actual buffers themselves. This means that you only draw on the back buffer when producing animation.

BlitzMax has now made it impossible to draw to the front buffer. There really is no reason to, so having the ability to draw to the front buffer is unnecessary. Any drawing you do is automatically done on the back buffer.

### Swapping Buffers

So, if everything you draw is offscreen, how do you get it all on screen? This is the basis of page flipping; now, all you have to do is get that buffer to flip with the front buffer. To do this, use the Flip command. Flip looks like this:

```
Flip
```

This statement is very powerful—it exchanges all the data in the back buffer with all of the data in the front buffer.

#### Caution

Be careful where you place the Flip command. Flip should always be placed near the end of the main loop of your program. In the following example, you can see that Flip is located just after the DrawImage function. The reason for this is that if you add the Flip statement before drawing the image, your program will always flip the blank animation onto the screen. Because Cls is used at the beginning of every loop, your frame will delete the spaceship image from the previous frame and have nothing in the back buffer when the next Flip command arises. Of course, you can easily solve this problem by placing the DrawImage command near the top of your loop.

Now, let's go back to demo06-01.bmx in this chapter—the program with the smoothly animated ship. Let's look at the main loop again.

```
While Not KeyDown(1)
     'Clear the screen
     Cls
     'move ship left and right
     playerShip.x = playerShip.x + Rand(-8,8)
     'Move ship up And down
     playerShip.y = playerShip.y + Rand(-8,8)

     'If ship goes off screen, move it back on
     If playerShip.x < 0
          playerShip.x = 15
```

```
    ElseIf playerShip.x > 800
        playerShip.x = 790
    ElseIf playerShip.y < 0
        playerShip.y = 10
    ElseIf playerShip.y > 600
        playerShip.y = 590
    EndIf

    'Draw the ship
    DrawImage(shipimage, playerShip.x, playerShip.y)
    Flip
Wend
```

The first line after the opening test is:

```
Cls 'Clear the screen
```

This is a very important part of a page-flipping program. Basically, it just clears the screen of anything that was drawn on it in previous frames. It might seem unnecessary, but if you don't include it, the game will look like Figure 6.5.

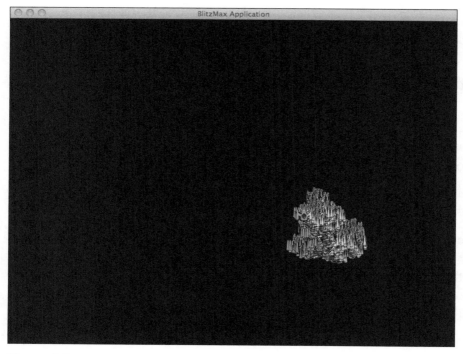

**Figure 6.5**
Demo06-01.bmx without `Cls`.

As you can see, without `Cls`, trails of the spaceship are very obvious. The `Cls` forces all of these trails to be deleted at the beginning of every frame, so it looks like the spaceship is actually moving. Figure 6.5 shows how the previous program would look without `Cls`.

Just for kicks, you might want to change the color of the background. You can do that using the command `ClsColor`, from the previous chapter.

Check out the last line before the `Wend`.

```
Flip
```

That's literally all the work it takes to create smooth animation!

So, that's a basic overview of page flipping. Now, let's move on to creating our own images.

## Transformations

Transformations are very important in game programming. They are used everywhere that you have movement; they change an image's position or direction. There are three types of transformations: translating, scaling, and rotating. Let's begin with translating.

## Translating

When you hear the word translation, you probably think of languages. Well, translating images is completely different! When using translations in game programming, you take an image at its current position and then "translate" it to another position, so translate is just a fancy way of saying move!

Translation is moving an image from one coordinate to another. When complete, translation looks something like Figure 6.6.

Translation is really simple. You are basically drawing an image at a different position. For example, say you have an enemy ship that moves from the top-left corner of the screen to the bottom-right corner of the screen, and you want the ship to move at five pixels per second. You might have an initialization section that looks like this:

```
shipx = 0
shipy = 0
```

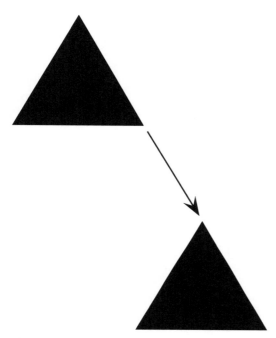

**Figure 6.6**
Translations.

## Refresher: Coordinate Position

Everybody forgets things after a while, huh? You might have forgotten how coordinate positions work, and because they are extremely important in this chapter, it might be a good idea to go over them.

The coordinate system has two axes: the x-axis and the y-axis. An axis is a named number line. The two axes on a computer screen look like Figure 6.7. (As you probably noticed, there are dash marks with numbers next to them. Of course, these dashes are not visible on the computer screen.) As you can see, the 0 point of both the x- and the y-axes is in the top-left point of the screen. If you travel farther across or down the monitor, the x- and y-axes are incremented. If you increment both, you can put the point anywhere you want on the screen. Figure 6.8 demonstrates a point that is 10 pixels to the right (on the x-axis) and 16 places down (on the y-axis).

Obviously, there must be a better way to explain this point than "10 pixels to the right (on the x-axis) and 16 pixels down (on the y-axis)." This way is inside parentheses; put the x coordinate first, and then a comma, and then the y coordinate. Thus, the point in Figure 6.8 is (10,16). The "10" means 10 pixels on the x-axis, and the "16" means 16 pixels on the y-axis.

This places the position of the ship at the top-left corner of the screen. You now begin the game loop. Because we are moving the ship diagonally down at five

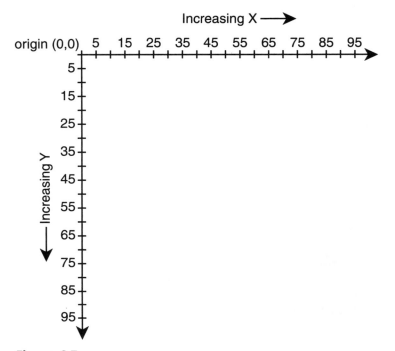

**Figure 6.7**
The coordinate system.

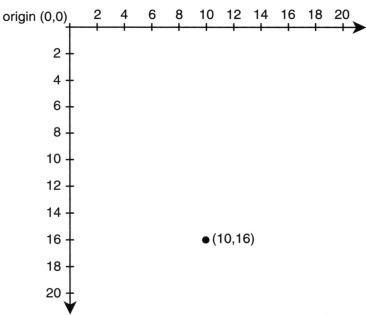

**Figure 6.8**
A point on the coordinate system.

| Frame # | x | y |
|---|---|---|
| 1 | 0 | 0 |
| 2 | 5 | 5 |
| 3 | 10 | 10 |
| 4 | 15 | 15 |
| 5 | 20 | 20 |

Equation
x=5 · framecount - 5
y=5 · framecount - 5

**Figure 6.9**
A table of coordinate values.

pixels per second, we will need to update the ship with some code like this:

```
While Not KeyDown(KEY_ESCAPE)
        Cls
        DrawImage shipimage, shipx, shipy
        shipx = shipx + 7
        shipy = shipy + 5
        Flip
Wend
```

Let's go through this. We start off with a loop, just like any other game. We first clear the screen so that we can use page flipping. Then, we draw the ship image. Note that you have a choice where to put your DrawImage command. I chose to put it at the beginning of the loop so that you can see the ship image at 0,0, but you can put it at the end of the loop. The DrawImage command draws the ship image at the set x and y coordinates. When the loop runs through the first time, shipx and shipy are both set equal to 0, but this changes with the next line of code. This line adds 7 to shipx and 5 to shipy. Because the additions occur each frame, the ship moves seven pixels to the right and five pixels down each frame. Figure 6.9 might help clear up the coordinate positions for you—it is a table of the values and the frame number. The equation, written next to the table in the figure, allows you to determine the position of x and y by plugging in a frame number. Of course, once the x and y values are off the screen, the image can't be seen anymore, but the image's coordinates are still updated.

### Why Do We Use Parentheses?

You might have noticed that some functions use parentheses and others don't. There is a pretty simple reason for this. Parentheses are required when the function returns a value. When the function does not return a value, the parentheses are optional. For example, LoadImage() requires parentheses because it returns the address of the loaded image like this:

```
image = LoadImage("image.bmp")
```

whereas `Text` doesn't require parentheses at all:

```
DrawText "No parentheses!", 0, 0
```

When you write functions, it is always good practice to include parentheses, even if they aren't required.

The rest of the main loop is a `Flip` command that works with page flipping. The full program is available on the CD as demo06-02.bmx. Figure 6.10 is a screenshot of the program.

Let's quickly come up with an equation for translation. This formula is very simple, but hey, so is translation!

```
x[1] = x + dx
y[1] = y + dy
```

**Note**

The `d` in `dx` and `dy` is there for a reason; it isn't just a random letter. In Greek, the letter delta, which is symbolized as a triangle ($\triangle$) means "change in." If you "read" the variable, you can see that `dx` and `dy` mean, "the change in x" and "the change in y."

**Figure 6.10**
The demo06-02.bmx program.

What does this mean? Well, if you input the proper coordinates (in this case, the x and/or y values) and add a number you would like to translate by (this number, dx or dy, can be negative or positive), you will get the new coordinate position for the variable. For example, in the lines of code:

```
shipx = shipx + 7
shipy = shipy + 5
```

shipx and shipy are x[1] and y[1], respectively. Shipx and shipy are x and y, and 7 is dx and 5 is dy. All of these variables are taking the place of the constants in the previous equation. Note that the x[1] and y[1] variables are the same as the x and y variables. This doesn't matter because you are updating them in order to move the image.

Are you ready to write a Translate function? Translate() translates any point you send it. Let's begin with a function declaration.

We are going to need an input coordinate and a transformation ("d") variable. So, the function might look something like this.

```
Function Translate(x,dx)
```

Easy, eh? And of course, the body of the function will be just as simple:

```
Return x + dx
```

Cool, huh? Table 6.1 describes each of the parameters for this function.

Let's rewrite the main loop with the new function.

```
While Not KeyDown(KEY_ESCAPE)
    Cls
    DrawImage shipimage,shipx,shipy
    shipx = Translate(shipx,7)
    shipy = Translate(shipy,5)
    Flip
```

**Table 6.1** Translate()'s Parameters

| Parameter | Description |
| --- | --- |
| x | The coordinate you want to translate |
| dx | The factor by which the x variable is translated |

```
Wend

Function Translate(x,dx)
      Return x+dx
End Function
```

And there we are! We now have a working translation function. Although it might seem trivial, it is probably a lot easier to understand the line

```
shipx = Translate(shipx,5)
```

rather than

```
shipx = shipx + 5
```

Don't you agree? Notice that the Translate() function does not use global variables, which makes this function extremely portable, because it can now be used in any other program. Copy the code and you can use Translate() as much as you want. By the way, the program using the Translate() function is available on the CD as demo06-03.bmx.

Okay, now that we've learned about translation, let's pump it up: next, we do scaling.

## Scaling

When you scale an object, you make the object bigger or smaller (or the same size, if you really want to). Scaling means making something a smaller or larger size but usually keeping the same proportions. Proportionality, though, is not required. Unlike translation, you cannot scale a point. This is because a point is a point—you cannot make a point a different size.

Let's start off by learning what a proportion is and how it is used.

### Proportion? What the Heck Is That?

A proportion is a ratio or a fraction. For example, the ratio of an object to another object that is two times bigger is 1:2 or 1/2. If the other object were three times as big, the ratio would be 1:3 (and the fraction would be 1/3). If you take a look at the fraction, you will notice that 1/3 is the same as 1 divided by 3. This is sort of interesting: the smaller object (the "1" in 1:3) is exactly 1/3 the size of the bigger object. If you flip the top and bottom of the fraction, you get 3/1, which is the size of the larger object compared to the smaller object (the bigger object is

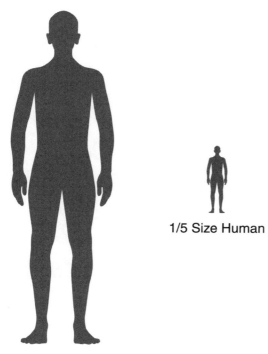

1/5 Size Human

Regular Size Human

**Figure 6.11**
A man and his 1/5 scaled counterpart.

three times the size of the smaller one). Take a look at Figure 6.11. In this figure, you can see the picture of a regular sized man on the left. The picture on the right is the same man, but he is scaled. He is 1/5 the size of the original man (the big man to small man ratio is 5:1).

You can also use ratios and fractions when an object becomes smaller. Say you have object A and object B. Object B is five times smaller than object A. The ratio in this example is 5:1, and the fraction is 5/1 (or just 5: any number divided by 1 is that number). As you can see, object A, which is the "5" in 5:1, is five times bigger than object B. If you flip the fraction 5/1, you get 1/5, which is the size of object B in comparison to object A.

A proportion can be thought of as a ratio or a fraction. You can also use percentages. When using BlitzMax, you typically use percentages. In other words, when you want to scale the size of an object, you multiply by a percentage number. For example, say you want to make something four times as large as it is. Just multiply each coordinate by 4. Referring to Figure 6.12, you can see a box

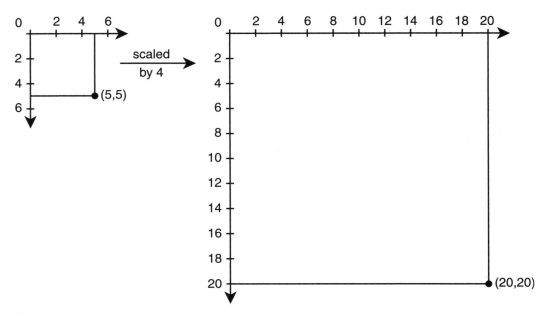

**Figure 6.12**
A scaled rectangle.

with coordinates 0,0, 0,5, 5,0, and 5,5. By multiplying each coordinate by 4 such that 0,0 remains 0,0; 0,5 becomes 0,20; 5,0 becomes 20,0; and 5,5 becomes 20,20, the box becomes four times as large. However, what if you want to make the object something like 5/8 as large? All you have to do is bust out a calculator and divide 5 by 8. Because 5/8 = .625, the multiplication factor will be .625.

So, now we have a basic outline for our scaling equation. The scaled equation looks a lot like the translation equation:

```
x[1] = x * sx
y[1] = y * sy
```

Notice the differences between translations and scaling. When translating, you add the d variable to the current x; however, when scaling, you multiply the s variable by the current x to scale it.

**Tip**

When scaling an object, you must use decimal percentages. If you want to make one object scaled to 50% of the previous one, don't multiply by 50. Your new object will be 50 times as large as the older one! Instead, think of it as a fraction. You want to make the new object 1/2 as large as the previous one. If you divide 1 by 2, you get .5. Multiply the object by .5 and your object is scaled to 50%.

### *Scaling Shapes*

Shape scaling is relatively simple. Just multiply the ending coordinate by the scaling factor, and you're done! The next step is to scale different kinds of shapes, such as rectangles and triangles. Ready to move?

### Scaling Rectangles

Let's write a few programs that utilize scaling within shapes. The first draws a rectangle, waits for the user to choose a ratio, and draws a new rectangle with a new size. On the CD, this file is named demo06-04.bmx.

We begin with a graphics call. After that, we initialize the variables:

```
'demo 06-04.bmx - Demonstrates Scaling

Graphics 800,600

'VARIABLES
'Create the variables that define the rectangle
rectbeginx = 25  'The x coordinate of the top left corner
rectbeginy = 25  'The y coordinate of the top left corner
rectwidth  = 256 'The x coordinate of the bottom right corner
rectheight = 256 'The y coordinate of the bottom right corner
sxy:Float  = .5  'The scaling factor
```

All that has happened so far is the creation of a few variables. I offset the box from 0,0 so that you can see the scaling more clearly. If you feel like it, change any of these variables.

Next, we move to the main section of the code. The first part deals with the first rectangle.

```
'MAIN SECTION
'Make sure the text goes near the bottom of the screen
DrawText "This is our first rectangle.", 0,500

'Draw the first rectangle, and make it not filled
DrawRect rectbeginx,rectbeginy,rectwidth,rectheight

'Show old rectangle
Flip

Delay 3000
```

We first start off with a call to Text. This forces the text, ''This is our first rectangle.'' to appear near the bottom of the screen, so it doesn't interfere with the rectangles. Next, we call the DrawRect function. This function, which is compiler defined, draws a rectangle from the starting coordinates (rectbeginx and rectbeginy) to the ending coordinates (rectwidth and rectheight). See Table 6.2 to see the DrawRect's parameters.

So, why did I put a Flip command in there? Remember, in BlitzMax, everything is drawn on the back buffer. Because we want to be able to see the rectangle that we just drew, we must use the Flip command to show it on screen.

**Note**

We haven't touched on variable types for a long time. In case you have forgotten, when :Float is appended to the end of a variable name, the variable is a floating-point variable. If a variable is floating point, it can hold decimal places. In other words, xyx can be 314, whereas xyx:Float can be 314.13. If you try to make a non-floating-point variable (an integer) include a decimal, the decimal portion will be removed. For example, the number 1.9 will become 1 because the .9 has been truncated or deleted. Be careful when doing this because if you truncate decimal numbers, you will lose information. And unless you intended to do this, it could be really bad. For example, if you were computing tax with the number 0.08 and got rid of the decimal part, you would end up with a tax rate of 0! In this program, the user can multiply the variable by any number, such as 1.5, .3, and so on. It would not be very good if the decimal was truncated, because the new variable would (most likely) end up being either 1 or 0. What a boring program it would be if the new rectangle was either deleted or kept the same size!

The scaling factor is stored in the variable sxy. This variable is used in the next section of code.

```
'Multiply the width and height by the scaling factor
rectwidth = rectwidth  * sxy
rectheight = rectheight * sxy
```

**Table 6.2** DrawRect's Parameters

| Parameter | Description |
| --- | --- |
| x | The x coordinate of the top left of the rectangle |
| y | The y coordinate of the top left of the rectangle |
| width | The width in pixels of the rectangle |
| height | The height in pixels of the rectangle |

```
'Show new input
Flip
```

To scale the new object, you must multiply each coordinate by the scaling factor. Here, both the x and y values are multiplied by the scaling factor.

The final section of the code draws the second rectangle and exits the program.

```
DrawText "The second rectangle is scaled to " + sxy * 100 + "% (" + sxy + ")." ,0,512
'Draw the new rectangle
SetColor 255,0,0
DrawRect rectbeginx,rectbeginy,rectwidth,rectheight
Flip

'Wait for the user to press a key before exiting.
WaitKey
```

The first line here draws a new rectangle with the scaled coordinates. Because the beginning x and y values remain the same, the rectangle is drawn over the old one.

Notice the SetColor function. This makes the new rectangle red, so it is clearly distinguishable from the old one.

The final two lines ask the user to press any key. Once the user presses a key, the program is over. Figure 6.13 shows a screenshot from the program.

This program teaches a lot of important ideas. Try this out: change the code to work with ellipses (using the DrawOval function).

You might have noticed something strange when using a scaling factor. When scaled by 1/2, as in Figure 6.13, the new rectangle is only 1/4 of the size of the original rectangle, even though you might expect it to be 1/2. The reason is that each coordinate is scaled by 2, not the rectangle as a whole. Therefore, the new rectangle is actually 1/4 the size of the original rectangle.

Now that I've shown you how to scale a rectangle manually, I want you to know that BlitzMax has a built-in method for scaling called SetScale. Table 6.3 lists the function's parameters.

If you wanted to, you could change the program from this:

```
'Multiply the width and height by the scaling factor
rectwidth = rectwidth  * sxy
rectheight = rectheight * sxy
```

to this:

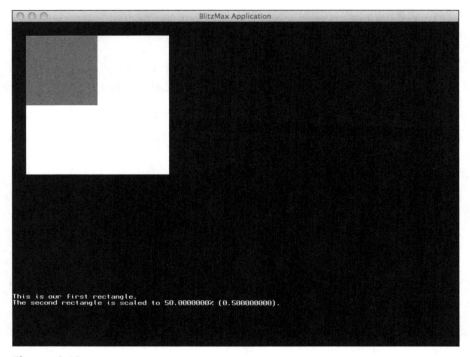

**Figure 6.13**
The demo06-04.bmx program.

| **Table 6.3** SetScale's Parameters | |
|---|---|
| **Parameter** | **Description** |
| scale_x | The scaling factor for the x dimension |
| scale_y | The scaling factor for the y dimension |

```
'Multiply the width and height by the scaling factor
SetScale sxy,sxy
```

Figure 6.14 shows the program with this change running.

Looks pretty much the same, right? Look closely. See the second row of text? It's super scrunched. The reason why is because SetScale sets the scale of every drawn object for the rest of the program, including DrawText, DrawRect, and DrawImage. Because the scaling code is put before the DrawText code, the text is also scaled.

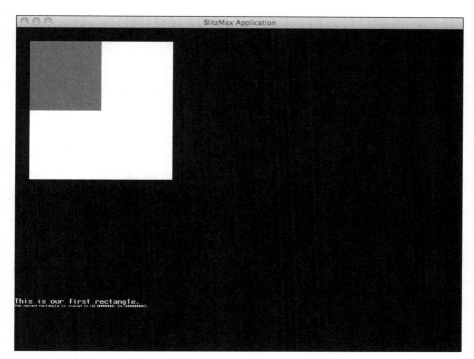

**Figure 6.14**
Using SetScale.

If you choose to use SetScale, make sure that you immediately set the scale back to the original values in the program. In demo06-05.bmx, I do so like the following.

```
'Draw the new rectangle
SetColor 255,0,0

'Multiply the width and height by the scaling factor
SetScale sxy,sxy

DrawRect rectbeginx,rectbeginy,rectwidth,rectheight

'Reset the colors and scale
SetColor 255,255,255
SetScale 1,1
DrawText "The second rectangle is scaled to " + sxy * 100 + "% (" + sxy + ")." ,0,512

Flip
```

I moved the `DrawText` line down below the `DrawRect` to demonstrate how to reset values. After using `SetColor` and `SetScale` and drawing the new rectangle, I reset the values to their original: white (255,255,255) for the text, and 1,1 for the scale. The output from this program is now identical to Figure 6.13.

## Scaling Triangles

We can now move on to something a bit more challenging: scaling a triangle. Unlike the rectangle, `DrawTriangle` doesn't exist. We have to draw each line manually.

Before we can begin discussing how to scale a triangle, we need to understand the difference between local and global coordinates.

There is a huge difference between global and local coordinates. A local coordinate, much like a local variable, is only visible from the object that is being drawn. Global coordinates, on the other hand, are the same for all objects.

Maybe an analogy will help to explain the difference. Take a human; for instance, let's take you. You are a person. There are many people. But you are the center of everything that you can see. To you, everything revolves around you. Therefore, your local coordinates stem from the top of you to the bottom of you. However, remember that this holds true for everyone else, as well. Each person has his or her own local coordinates.

Now, imagine a spaceship watching Earth from the sky. To the aliens, people are everywhere. Each person is not central to the spaceship; instead, the Earth as a whole is. So, to the aliens, the Earth is a coordinate plane (it isn't actually a plane, but nevermind that). Where you are now is located at some coordinate position (maybe 13,14), but that will change when you take a step to another area. Latitude and longitude perform the same actions as global coordinates—you can pinpoint a certain position anywhere in the world by indicating the latitude and longitude coordinates.

Look at Figure 6.15, which shows a map of the world with two people, Person A and Person B. Person A and Person B each believe they are the center of the world; that is, they think of themselves as located at 0,0. However, the spaceship that is watching them (you are the spaceship for now) sees them in two very different coordinate positions, shown by their latitude and longitude values.

When you move around, your global coordinates change. However, your local coordinates remain the same. Your viewpoint does not change, and therefore, your local coordinates stay with you no matter where you go.

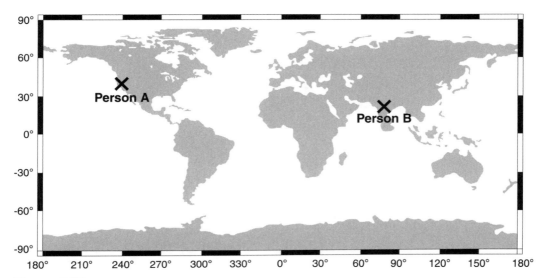

**Figure 6.15**
The spaceship and the world.

With objects in BlitzMax, this analogy works extremely well. To the triangle we are using in the following program, the center begins at coordinates 0,0. The object's global coordinates begin wherever it is displayed on the screen. Referring to Figure 6.16, you can see that the local coordinates of an object begin at the top-left corner and end at the bottom-right corner.

Now that we understand local and global coordinates, let's get into this program. We first set up the graphics mode.

```
Graphics 800,600
```

Now we are going to create a type called TPoint. TPoint will contain two fields: its x and y coordinates.

```
Type TPoint
      Field x,y
End Type
```

We need to have three points for this triangle: one for each vertex. A vertex (plural *vertices*) is a point where a line changes direction—in the case of a triangle, there are three vertices, one at each corner.

```
point1:TPoint = New point
point2:TPoint = New point
point3:TPoint = New point
```

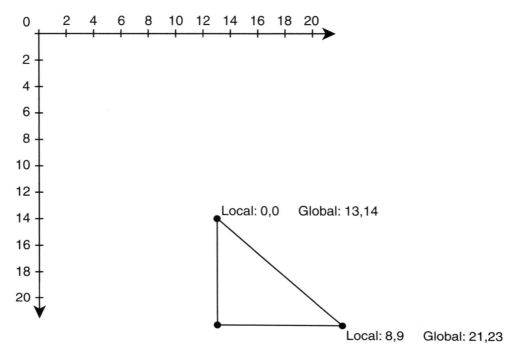

**Figure 6.16**
Global and local coordinates.

`point1`, `point2`, and `point3` are the three different vertices on the triangle. Referring to Figure 6.17, you can see that `point1` begins at the apex, or top, of the triangle, and `point2` and `point3` follow in a clockwise manner. The line that begins at `point1` extends to `point2`, the line from `point2` extends to `point3`, and the line from `point3` extends to `point1`.

Next, we need to define the local coordinates for our first triangle. In demo06-06.bmx, the vertices are defined like this:

```
'These variables define each vertex and are in local coordinates
point1.x= 0
point1.y= -100
point2.x= 100
point2.y= 100
point3.x= -100
point3.y = 100
```

These points are centered around 0,0. Note that all of these coordinates are local: obviously, you can never have negative values for global coordinates. Figure 6.18

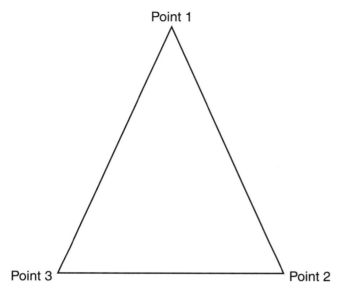

**Figure 6.17**
`point1`, `point2`, and `point3`.

shows the coordinates of each point on the triangle. As you can see, the origin point, 0,0, is in the exact center of the triangle.

As stated earlier, to obtain global coordinates, we will add a constant value to each local coordinate of the triangle. The constant section of this program has two variables.

```
'CONSTANTS
'The global indicators that are added to each local coordinate
'to place it on screen
Const xs = 400
Const ys = 300
Const sxy:Float = 2.0
```

I chose these two numbers because they center the triangle onscreen. Note that the program is 800 pixels by 600 pixels (these numbers are defined in the `Graphics` call), and 800 / 2 = 400 and 600 / 2 = 300. To achieve the correct global coordinates, the `xs` variable is added to each x coordinate and `ys` is added to each y coordinate.

Now that we have all of our initialization values defined and variables created, let's move on to the actual program. The program begins by printing out some info to the user.

Local

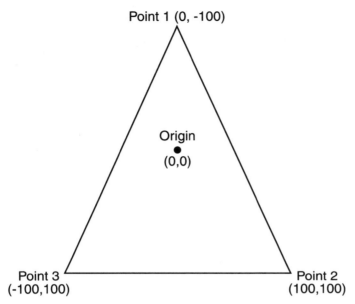

**Figure 6.18**
Local coordinates.

Next, the program draws the first triangle. This is accomplished with the Draw-Line function, which draws a line from one coordinate position to another. DrawLine is declared like this

```
Line x,y,x1,y1
```

Table 6.4 explains each parameter individually.

In essence, the DrawLine function draws a straight line from coordinates x,y to coordinates x1,y1. For this program, there are three DrawLine calls for each triangle.

```
'Draw out first triangle
DrawLine point1.x + xs, point1.y + ys, point2.x + xs, point2.y + ys
DrawLine point2.x + xs, point2.y + ys, point3.x + xs, point3.y + ys
DrawLine point3.x + xs, point3.y + ys, point1.x + xs, point1.y + ys
Flip
Delay 3000
```

As you can see, each DrawLine call draws a line from one of the vertices to another of the vertices. If you look closely, you can see that xs is added to each x coordinate and ys is added to each y coordinate. These numbers are added to the

**Table 6.4**  DrawLine's Parameters

| Parameter | Description |
|---|---|
| x | The x position of the starting coordinate |
| y | The y position of the starting coordinate |
| x1 | The x position of the ending coordinate |
| y1 | The y position of the ending coordinate |

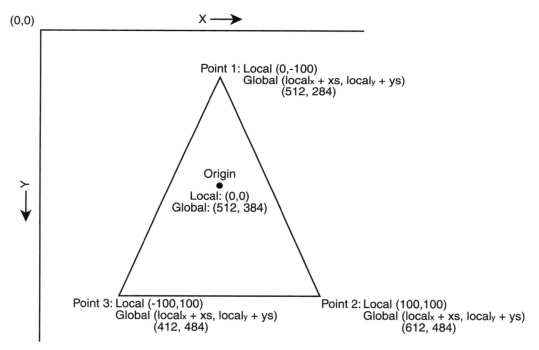

**Figure 6.19**
Local and global coordinates of the sample triangle.

triangle's local coordinates in order to move the triangle onscreen so they can be seen in the program. Figure 6.19 demonstrates the triangle's local and global coordinates. We then use Flip and Delay to show the triangle and pause the program for three seconds.

After the user has chosen a scaling factor, we scale each point. The following lines perform the scaling actions.

```
'Multiply all the coordinates by the scaling factor
point1.x = point1.x * sxy
```

```
point1.y = point1.y * sxy
point2.x = point2.x * sxy
point2.y = point2.y * sxy
point3.x = point3.x * sxy
point3.y = point3.y * sxy
```

Pretty easy, eh? All this block of code did was multiply each vertex's x and y position by sxy.

Okay, now we must get ready to draw out the new triangle. Since we want the new object to be easily seen, you need to change the color of the lines. This is easily accomplished using the SetColor function.

```
'Change the default color to green
SetColor 0,255,0
```

This makes all following DrawLine commands green.

Now, all we have to do is draw the new triangle. This is accomplished by calling DrawLine for each point, as we did for the original triangle.

```
'Change the default color to green
SetColor 0,255,0

'Draw final triangle (with scaled coordinates) in green
DrawLine point1.x + xs, point1.y + ys, point2.x + xs, point2.y + ys
DrawLine point2.x + xs, point2.y + ys, point3.x + xs, point3.y + ys
DrawLine point3.x + xs, point3.y + ys, point1.x + xs, point1.y + ys

Flip
```

Excellent! The program has now printed lines connecting each vertex, and therefore, drawn a new triangle.

Now all we do is finish the program.

```
'Wait for user to press a key before exiting
WaitKey
```

That's the complete program. Figures 6.20 and 6.21 demonstrate the program with scaling factors of 2 and .5. You won't be able to see that the new lines are drawn in green in the figures, but you can look at the program on the CD to see the new triangles drawn in green. If you notice, the new triangle is centered in respect to the original triangle. But, what if you don't want to keep it centered? All you have to do is change the local coordinates.

**Figure 6.20**
Demo06-06.bmx with a scaling factor of 2.

**Figure 6.21**
Demo06-06.bmx with a scaling factor of .5.

Wanna see something cool? When you are asked to input sxy#, enter a negative number. The new triangle is flipped. Check out Figure 6.22; it shows the program with an sxy# value of −1.

**Figure 6.22**
Demo06-06.bmx with a scaling factor of −1.

Figure 6.23 shows demo06-07.bmx. As you can see, the triangle grows downward, but it does not remain centered. Demo06-07.bmx is almost exactly the same as demo06-06.bmx, except the beginning variables have been changed. The variables are now initialized with different values.

```
'VARIABLES
'These variables define each vertex and are in local coordinates
point1.x= 0
point1.y= 0
point2.x= 100
point2.y= 100
point3.x= -100
point3.y = 100
```

**Figure 6.23**
The demo06-07.bmx program.

The big difference here is that point1.y has been changed to 0 from its value in demo06-06.bmx. Because any number multiplied by 0 equals 0, when sxy is multiplied in the line:

```
point1.x = point1.x * sxy
```

point1.x will always equal 0. Because the variable does not change, point1 will remain in the same position throughout the program. Thus, the triangle will grow from the top downward.

It comes out pretty nicely, don't you think? By the way, if you want it to grow upward, change the bottom points' y values to 0. Demo06-08.bmx shows the triangle growing upward.

The variables have been changed slightly; now they are

```
;VARIABLES
;These variables define each vertex and are in local coordinates
point1\x= 0
point1\y= -100
point2\x= 100
```

**Figure 6.24**
The demo06-08.bmx program.

```
point2\y= 0
point3\x= -100
point3\y = 0
```

As you can see, the two lower points are equivalent to 0. Now, when it is scaled by 2, it grows upward, as shown in Figure 6.24.

One thing you should know about this program: because changing the y values for the bottom two points moves the figure up a little, I changed the ys variable a little. The constants section now reads:

```
'CONSTANTS
'The global indicators that are added to each local coordinate to place it on
screen
Const xs = 400
Const ys = 400
Const sxy:Float = 2
```

The ys variable in demo06-08.bmx was changed from 300 to 400 to offset the 100-pixel difference between the original triangle in demo06-06.bmx and the new triangle in demo06-08.bmx.

Now let's create a scale function.

```
Function Scale(x,sx)
      Return x*sx
End Function
```

Table 6.5 examines each parameter. If you wanted to scale the x coordinate of point1, just call it like this:

```
Scale(point1.x,sxy)
```

assuming that sxy is the scaling factor.

### Scaling Images

BlitzMax makes scaling images extremely easy by providing the function SetScale. We talked about SetScale earlier when I described a simple way to scale rectangles. Table 6.3 described the function's parameters. The function declaration is as follows.

```
SetScale scale_x, scale_y
```

As an example, we will scale an image of a spaceship. The original spaceship looks like Figure 6.25.

Demo06-09.bmx is pretty short, so I am just going to show the entire program and explain it at the end.

```
'demo06-09.bmx - Demonstrates the use of SetScale for scaling images
Graphics 800,600

'Set AutoMidHandle to true
AutoMidHandle True
```

| Table 6.5 | Scale()'s Parameters |
|---|---|
| **Parameter** | **Description** |
| x | The value you want to scale |

**Figure 6.25**
The original spaceship image.

```
'CONSTANTS
sxy:Float = 4.0

'IMAGES
'Load the spaceship that will be drawn on screen
spaceshipimage = LoadImage("spaceship.bmp")

DrawText "First, we'll display the original image and then one that is " + sxy +"
times as big.",0,500

'Draw the spaceship directly in the center of the screen
DrawImage spaceshipimage, 400,300

Flip
Delay 3000
'Prepare the screen for the scaled spaceship by clearing it
Cls
'Scale the image
SetScale sxy, sxy

'Draw the new scaled spaceship
DrawImage spaceshipimage, 400,300
Flip

'Reset scale
SetScale 1,1

'Wait for user to press a key before exiting
WaitKey
```

Figures 6.26 and 6.27 show the program running with a scale factor of 4.

The first thing the program does is initialize the graphics and set `AutoMidHandle` to true, so that the images are centered. It then loads the spaceship and draws it onscreen.

Using the `sxy` constant, the image is scaled and then drawn to the screen.

```
'Prepare the screen for the scaled spaceship by clearing it
Cls
'Scale the image
SetScale sxy, sxy

'Draw the new scaled spaceship
```

**Figure 6.26**
The demo06-09.bmx program.

**Figure 6.27**
The demo06-09.bmx program four times as big.

```
DrawImage spaceshipimage, 400,300
Flip

'Reset scale
SetScale 1,1
```

The newly scaled spaceship is drawn directly in the center of the screen, after being scaled by the `SetScale` function, which uses the scaling factors provided by the constant `sxy`.

These lines scale and draw the new image. After the user presses a key, the program exits.

Note that if you size the image to greater than 100 percent, the image looks a little blurry. The reason is that the scaling function stretches the image and makes each of its pixels a little bit larger.

Well, that's pretty much it for scaling. We can now move on to a really cool subject: rotation.

## Rotation

So far, you have learned two of the three types of transformations. Rotation is the final one that you will learn. Rotation is usually extremely hard to pull off, but BlitzMax makes it much easier.

Like scaling, BlitzMax provides a function for rotation—`SetRotation`. `SetRotation` is defined as this:

```
SetRotation rotation:Float
```

Table 6.6 examines the individual parameters. As you can see, `value#` rotates the given image in a clockwise manner.

Take a look at Figures 6.28 and 6.29. They demonstrate clockwise and counterclockwise directions, respectively. Oh yeah, a clock turns clockwise.

**Table 6.6**  RotateImage's Parameters

| Parameter | Description |
| --- | --- |
| `rotation:Float` | The number of degrees (between 0 and 360) you want to rotate image in a clockwise fashion |

**Figure 6.28**
Clockwise.

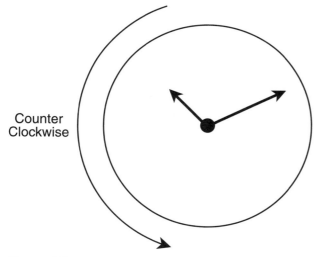

**Figure 6.29**
Counterclockwise.

Rotation might be equal to any number between 0 and 360. There are 360 degrees in a circle. Refer to Figure 6.30 to see the degrees in a circle.

As you can see, rotating an image is pretty simple. Let's write a program that rotates a shape. This program loads an image from the hard drive, and scales it arbitrarily.

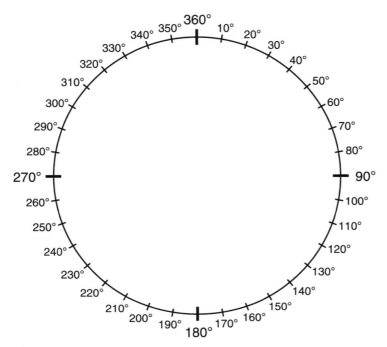

**Figure 6.30**
Degrees in a circle.

Following is the rotation section of the code in demo06-10.bmx.

```
'Draw the beginning image
DrawImage shipimage,400,300

Flip
Delay 3000

'Rotate the Image
SetRotation rotation

'Draw the new and rotated image on the screen
DrawImage shipimage, 440,300

SetRotation 0

Flip
'Wait for user to press a key before exiting
WaitKey
```

**Figure 6.31**
The demo06-10.bmx program.

This section draws the `shipimage` (which was loaded earlier in the program) at the center of the screen. The program then retrieves the `rotation` constant, and rotates the image using the command

```
SetRotation rotation
```

This line rotates the `shipimage` the number of degrees entered in `rotationvalue#`. The program then draws the new image to the right of the old image.

That's demo06-10.bmx. Figure 6.31 shows a screenshot from the program.

Asking a user for a rotation value is nice, but what about real-time rotation? Real-time rotation allows you to rotate an image at the spur of the moment. This effect is used in games such as *Asteroids*, where a spaceship is rotated onscreen.

Following is the main loop of demo06-11.bmx. Read through it and try to understand. An explanation follows.

```
'MAIN LOOP
While Not KeyDown(KEY_ESCAPE)
```

```
'Clear the Screen
Cls

'Add Text
DrawText"Press left to rotate counter-clockwise and right to rotate clockwise",
10, 0
DrawText "Press Esc To Exit.", 10, 20

'If the player presses Left, rotate four degrees Left, If he presses Right, rotate
four degrees Right
If KeyDown (KEY_LEFT)
        rotation = rotation - 4
ElseIf KeyDown (KEY_RIGHT)
        rotation = rotation + 4
EndIf

SetRotation rotation

'Draw the ship
DrawImage shipimage, 400,300
SetRotation 0
Flip
Wend
'End OF MAIN LOOP
```

As you can see from the `Flip` and the `Cls` commands, this program uses page flipping. The rest of the program is pretty self-explanatory. If the user presses left, the ship is rotated counter-clockwise four degrees. If the user presses right, the ship is rotated four degrees clockwise. Figure 6.32 shows the program running.

Notice that I set `SetRotation` to 0 after drawing the ship. Why did I do that? Well, try out demo06-12.bmx if you are unsure. You can see what happens in Figure 6.33.

Because I didn't reset the rotation, the text is rotated too! Kind of a cool effect, huh?

We are now going to talk about parallaxing. Think about it, with a word as cool as parallaxing, how can it not be fun?

## Parallaxing

Parallaxing is a very interesting topic, and we are going to jump right into it. Using parallaxing, you can create the effect of movement through 3D space from a fixed viewpoint. You could think of parallaxing as scrolling, if you want; in

**Figure 6.32**
The demo06-11.bmx program.

essence, you are scrolling two or more backgrounds at the same time to simulate movement.

### What Is Parallaxing?

Remember the last time you were in a car on the freeway? When you looked outside (assuming you weren't playing a videogame), did you notice that the objects that were closer to you moved faster than the objects that were farther away? The road markers that lined the road shot by you while the trees on the mountains far away moved much slower. Parallaxing creates this effect in games: one part of the background moves faster than the other part, based on distance from the player's viewpoint.

Before we can actually begin parallaxing, we need to go over tiling.

## TileImage

Because parallaxing effects begin in the background, we must first learn how to create backgrounds. Easier said than done, huh? Fortunately, BlitzMax provides a function for tiling backgrounds: TileImage.

**Figure 6.33**
The demo06-12.bmx program.

**Note**

What's tiling? Tiling takes a single image and plasters it all over your program's background in a tiled pattern. Just like kitchen tiles: each tile is exactly the same as the next one.

Here is the definition for `TileImage`.

```
TileImage image, [x,y,frames]
```

Table 6.7 lists each parameter. As you can see, the only required parameter is `image` (the image you want to be tiled). x and y move the starting point of the tiles to a location other than the default 0,0. Frames is used with animation, which will be discussed in the next chapter.

Using `TileImage` is really easy. Call the function you want to use with the image you want to tile. For our next demo program, we will be using the image in Figure 6.34.

The following program is called demo06-13.bmx. It only has four calls—one that initializes the graphics, one that loads the background image, and one that tiles the image using `TileImage`. The program's last call is to `WaitKey` so that the user can see the program before it closes. Figure 6.35 shows a sample screenshot of the program.

**Table 6.7**  TileImage's Parameters

| Parameter | Description |
| --- | --- |
| image | The handle of the image you want tiled |
| [x] | Optional; the beginning x coordinate of the tiling procedure |
| [y] | Optional; the beginning y coordinate of the tiling procedure |
| [frames] | Optional; allows you to use frames in animation |

**Figure 6.34**
The tiled image.

The call to TileImage is very simple.

```
'Tile the image
TileImage backgroundimage
```

As you can probably guess, backgroundimage was previously loaded.

Now that you have tiled the image, we need to figure out how to scroll it up and down. Scrolling causes the game to appear in motion; therefore, it will seem like you are actually flying in space. The following program is located on the CD as demo06-14.bmx.

The program begins as it usually does, with graphics initialization and whatnot (I don't think I have ever said *whatnot* before, ever). The initialization also creates the variable scrolly, which is used in the TileImage command. We then load the background, which is the same as the image in Figure 6.34. Now we enter the main loop.

```
'MAIN LOOP
While Not KeyDown(KEY_ESCAPE)
Cls
'Tile the background at the y position of scrolly
TileImage backgroundimage,0,scrolly
```

**Figure 6.35**
The demo06-13.bmx program.

```
'Scroll the background a bit by incrementing scrolly
scrolly=scrolly+1

'If scrolly gets too big, reset it to zero
If scrolly >= ImageHeight(backgroundimage)
      scrolly = 0
EndIf


Flip
Wend
'END OF MAIN LOOP
```

The loop begins as you probably expect. The first line inside the loop is a
TileImage command. This line tiles the background image, but it includes the
optional parameter scrolly for y. Because scrolly is incremented each frame in
the next line of code, the image is tiled a little bit higher each frame. This tiling

**Figure 6.36**
The closer (left) and distant (right) stars.

effect creates a scrolling effect. The last important line in the main loop, the If statement, resets scrolly when the program has scrolled the image one full time. In other words, if backgroundimage is 64 pixels high, every 64th frame will be identical.

Just in case you want to know, ImageHeight returns the height of the given image in pixels.

The last thing we have to do is scroll two images at once. Two images will create the effect of distance, because some stars will appear closer (by scrolling them faster) and others will appear farther away (by scrolling them slower). In addition, the closer stars are brighter. Figure 6.36 shows both star images.

Following is the full program demo06-15.bmx. As you can see, we loaded two images and scrolled them.

```
'demo06-15.bmx - A Parallaxing Program
Graphics 800,600

'Set AutoMidHandle to true
AutoMidHandle True

'IMAGES
'The close and quickly scrolled background
backgroundimageclose = LoadImage("stars.bmp")

'The further and slowly scrolled background
backgroundimagefar = LoadImage("starsfarther.bmp")

'Create scrolling tracker variable
scrolly = 0
```

```
'MAIN LOOP
While Not KeyDown(KEY_ESCAPE)

'Clear the screen
Cls

'Tile both backgrounds at proper speed
TileImage backgroundimagefar,0,scrolly
TileImage backgroundimageclose,0,scrolly*2

'Increment scrolly
scrolly=scrolly+1

'Reset tracker variable if it gets too large
If scrolly >= ImageHeight(backgroundimageclose)
      scrolly = 0
EndIf



Flip
Wend
'END OF MAIN LOOP
```

The major difference when comparing this program to the previous one is the loading and tiling. Instead of loading one image, this program loads two: backgroundimageclose and backgroundimagefar. The TileImage command tiles both images, but the second image is set to scroll twice as fast. Therefore, it gives the impression of being farther away. Figure 6.37 shows a screenshot of this program.

**Note**

Notice that I drew the closer stars after drawing the distant stars. This is kind of important—if I drew the closer ones first, they would appear to be under the distant ones. This would ruin the effect of parallaxing.

Well, that's it for image parallaxing. If you want to have some fun, try adding another image to the mix. Can you do it?

For the final program of the chapter, demo06-16.bmx, I simply took the KONG program from Chapter 1 and added a parallaxing star field on the background. It's the same as regular KONG, but now it's in space. Figure 6.38 shows the new KONG running.

**Figure 6.37**
The demo06-15.bmx program.

**Figure 6.38**
The demo06-16.bmx program.

## Summary

Whew, that was one long chapter. Hopefully, you've grasped all the topics we have covered so far. In this chapter, we learned:

- The different types of buffers

- How buffers are used in page flipping

- Translating

- Scaling

- Proportions

- Scaling images

- Scaling shapes

- Rotation

- Parallaxing

This chapter is a stepping-stone to the next chapter: Animation. Get ready, because you are going to learn how to load and display multiple images to animate an object, making it move, walk, run, jump, explode—anything you want!

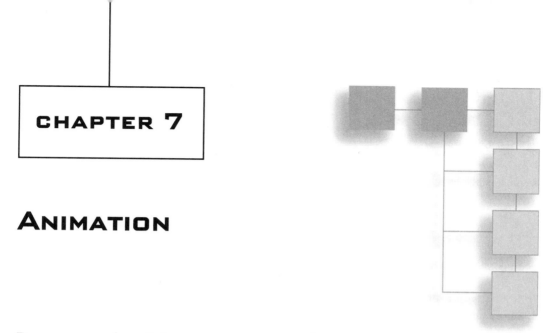

# CHAPTER 7

# ANIMATION

Do you remember all those parameters named [frame] that we left set to 0? Well, those parameters are very useful once you understand what they are there for, and that is what you will learn from this chapter. You are going to learn the sweet skill of animation.

As you know, each iteration of the main loop produces one image frame of the actual game. When the image frames are drawn in rapid succession, it seems as if the images on screen are moving fluidly. With the type of animation introduced in this chapter, you will learn how to simulate movement onscreen; for example, you will be able to animate a character and make it appear as if it is walking.

Let's get straight into the meat of the chapter. First things first, we need to review bitmaps again. "Again?" you might (whiningly) say, but this time we are using bitmaps in a different way.

## Using Bitmaps in Animation

We have used single bitmaps extensively throughout the book so far. A single bitmap contains only one frame of one static image. However, an image that supports frames contains numerous images—images that are usually related to one another.

Take, for example, Figure 7.1. As you can see, this is a single image.

Now, let's put this boy into a program.

**Figure 7.1**
A single, static image.

```
'demo07-01.bmx - A moving static image

Graphics 800,600

'Make back buffer default and set AutoMidHandle to true
AutoMidHandle True

'IMAGES
'Load the image that will be drawn on screen
playerimage = LoadImage("staticboy.bmp")

'TYPES
'This type defines the coordinate position of the player
Type TPlayer
 Field x,y
End Type

'Create the player
player:TPlayer = New TPlayer

'Set up beginning values for player
player.x = 400
player.y = 300


'MAIN LOOP
While Not KeyDown(KEY_ESCAPE) 'While user does not press Esc

'Clear the screen
Cls

'Print text
DrawText "X Coordinate: " + player.x, 0,0
DrawText "Y Coordinate: " + player.y, 0,12
```

```
'If player presses left, move bitmap left
If KeyDown (KEY_LEFT)
 player.x = player.x - 5
EndIf

'If player presses right, move bitmap right
If KeyDown(KEY_RIGHT)
 player.x = player.x + 5
EndIf

'If player presses up, move bitmap up
If KeyDown (KEY_UP)
 player.y = player.y -5
EndIf

'If player presses down, move bitmap down
If KeyDown (KEY_DOWN)
 player.y = player.y + 5
EndIf

'Draw the player on screen
DrawImage playerimage, player.x,player.y

Flip

'Slow it down a little
Delay 50

Wend
'END OF MAIN LOOP
```

This program loads an image and displays it on the screen. The coordinates are changed based on the key presses of the players: if they press up, down, left, or right, the boy moves accordingly. Figure 7.2 is a screenshot taken from the program.

Even though this program runs smoothly, it's very boring. All that you see is a moving image—the boy doesn't even move his legs. The image almost looks as if it is floating.

To fix this problem, we are going to make the image appear to walk. To do this, we will use an image with eight frames. Figure 7.3 shows the image.

**Figure 7.2**
The demo7-01.bmx program.

**Figure 7.3**
The frames of the walking image.

As you can see, each frame is slightly different from the previous frame. When we put these frames together, as we did with the main loop, we will create the effect of animation.

Some important parts of the program must change. First off, we have to load the image. Loading an animated image is not quite the same as loading a static image. The most obvious change is that we use the function `LoadAnimImage()` instead of `LoadImage()`.

`LoadAnimImage()` is defined like this:

```
LoadAnimImage (filename:String, width, height, first, count)
```

There are a few more parameters than `LoadImage()`. The first parameter, `file-name$`, acts just as the parameter with the same name in `LoadImage()`. `filename$` is just the file name of the image you want to load. The next two parameters, `width` and `height`, are the measurements of the width and height of each of the frames. For example, in Figure 7.3, the measurement of each frame is 71 × 95 pixels.

**Note**

> Notice that the width and height values of each frame are exactly the same in the previous example. Make sure you remember that all of the frames of an image must be the same; otherwise, your program will not run.

The parameter `first` tells which frame you want to begin loading. You almost always want to begin with the first frame, so you will set this value to 0, because, in computer languages, counting begins with 0. Rarely, you might want to load the images starting with a later frame than the first one. If this is the case, you will use a different value for `first`. The final parameter, `count`, informs `LoadAnim-Image()` how many total frames you are loading.

Table 7.1 summarizes each of `LoadAnimImage()`'s parameters. Now, we can load our animated image using the function

```
playerimage = LoadAnimImage("animatedboy.bmp", 95,71,0,8)
```

All right, loading now looks good. In the following program, demo07-02.bmx, we will be creating a type with the player's x and y coordinates. We are also going to need to add another variable to the type, `frame`. `frame` tells the program which frame should be drawn at that specific time. Following is the entire initialization section of the new program, demo07-02.bmx.

**Table 7.1**  LoadAnimImage()'s Parameters

| Parameter | Description |
| --- | --- |
| `filename:string` | The filename of the image you want to load |
| `width` | The width in pixels of each frame |
| `height` | The height in pixels of each frame |
| `first` | The number of the frame that you want to begin with (usually 0) |
| `count` | The total number of frames you want to load |

```
'demo07-02.bmx - A moving animated image

Graphics 800,600

AutoMidHandle True

'IMAGES
'Load the animated image of the boy
playerimage = LoadAnimImage("animatedboy.bmp",95,71,0,8)

'TYPES
'Load the player type
Type TPlayer
  Field x,y      'The x and y coordinate position
  Field frame    'The frame that should be drawn
End Type

'Create the player
player:TPlayer = New TPlayer

'Give the player its starting values
player.x = 400
player.y = 300
  player.frame = 0
```

We have changed the loading call to make it load the animated image. Also, the player type now includes a field frame, which is initialized to 0.

Now we enter the main loop. In order to make the image move, we must increment the frame whenever a key is pressed. Therefore, we add the line

```
player.frame = player.frame + 1
```

under the key tests that move the player up and right, and we add

```
player.frame = player.frame - 1
```

to the tests that move the player down and left. In other words, whenever the player presses a button, the image moves to the next frame, and in doing so, the boy seems to walk.

Of course, because there are only eight frames, we need to make sure that player.frame never goes above 7 (remember that frame begins at 0). We also must make sure that if the user goes below frame 0, the frame is reset to 7, so that the animated image resets itself and continues to animate. This is accomplished with this block of code:

```
If player.frame > 7
        player.frame = 0
ElseIf player.frame < 0
        player.frame = 7
 EndIf
```

Following is the full source for the main loop.

```
'MAIN LOOP
While Not KeyDown(KEY_ESCAPE)

'Clear the screen
Cls


'Position text at the top left corner of the screen
DrawText "X Coordinate: " + player.x, 0,0
DrawText "Y Coordinate: " + player.y, 0,12


'If player presses left, move him left and decrement the frame number
If KeyDown (KEY_LEFT)
 player.x = player.x - 5
 player.frame = player.frame - 1

EndIf

'If player presses right, move him right and increment the frame number
If KeyDown(KEY_RIGHT)
 player.x = player.x + 5
 player.frame = player.frame + 1
EndIf

'If player presses up, move him up and increment the frame number
If KeyDown (KEY_UP)
 player.y = player.y - 5
 player.frame = player.frame + 1
EndIf

'If player presses down, move him down and decrement the frame number
```

```
If KeyDown (KEY_DOWN)
 player.y = player.y + 5
 player.frame = player.frame - 1
EndIf

'If the frame gets too high, reset it back to zero.
If player.frame > 7
 player.frame = 0

'If the frame gets too low, reset it to 3
ElseIf player.frame < 0
 player.frame = 7
EndIf

'Draw the player at the correct position and the correct frame
DrawImage playerimage, player.x,player.y, player.frame

'Wait a while
Delay 100
Flip
Wend
 'END OF MAIN LOOP
```

And there we have it. Figure 7.4 is a screenshot from this program. There is one thing I want you to notice in the loop. See the DrawImage command? There is an extra parameter that we haven't seen before.

If you remember from long ago, the declaration of DrawImage is as follows:

```
DrawImage handle, x, y, [frame]
```

We have not used the final optional parameter until now. The [frame] parameter allows you to change which frame of an animated image is drawn, as we did in the previous program. Cool, huh?

## Making Bitmaps

Now that we know how to load bitmaps, you probably want to know how to create them. First off, decide what the animated image will look like. Usually, each frame will look almost the same, with only one or two small changes.

Take a look at Figure 7.5. This image, as you can see, is a rectangle. Say we wanted to animate this rectangle.

**Figure 7.4**
The demo07-02.bmx program.

**Figure 7.5**
A soon-to-be animated rectangle.

Now, we want to animate this image. Let's rotate it 45 degrees ($\frac{1}{8}$th of a complete turn). It looks like Figure 7.6.

As you can see, this rectangle has been turned a little sideways. Now, to put these together in a bitmap, we need to use our favorite paint program (I use Paint Shop Pro, which is included on the CD). I created both images, and then I put them

**Figure 7.6**
The second frame of the animated rectangle.

**Figure 7.7**
The double-framed image.

together in one single image. The final image is shown in Figure 7.7. If you are interested in learning more about designing images, check out *Game Art for Teens*, also published by Course PTR.

**N o t e**

Make sure that you put the frames back to back, with absolutely no space in between. If you happen to add space, the frames will become distorted and you will end up with a `Not enough frames in image` error. If your frames overlap, the program will display some of frame two in frame one, some of frame three in frame two, and so on. You can double-check this by adding up the sum of the widths/heights of all the frames you should have and making sure that the sum equals the actual width and height of your final image.

Now here is the trick: the width and height of *each frame* must be the width and height of the largest frame. In Figure 7.7, each frame is 250 pixels by 250 pixels, but only because the larger frame (frame 2) requires that size. Take a look—see the first frame? There is a lot of black space around it. The first frame is closer to 200 × 200, but it ends up larger because of the next rotated frame.

Now that we have this image ready to go, we need to write a program around it. The following listing is from demo07-03.bmx. Begin with the initialization.

```
'demo07-03.bmx - Demonstrates rotating a rectangle
Graphics 800,600

'Handle images from the center
AutoMidHandle True

'Load the animated rectangles
rectanglesimage = LoadAnimImage("rectangles.bmp",250,250,0,2)

'Create variable that counts how many rotations occurred
rotationcount = 0
```

Obviously, this section just sets up the graphics and loads the image. Make sure you notice that the LoadAnimImage() command states that rectanglesimage has two frames, each being 250 × 250 pixels. Also, the variable rotationcount is created to count how many times the rotation occurs.

Now move to the important part of this program.

```
'MAIN LOOP
While Not KeyDown(KEY_ESCAPE)
'Clear the screen
Cls

'Print the number of rotations
DrawText "Number of Rotations: " + rotationcount, 0, 0

'Draw the rectangle image with the proper frame
DrawImage rectanglesimage,400,300,rotationcount Mod 2

'Increment the rotation count variable
rotationcount = rotationcount + 1

'Wait a while
Delay 100

Flip
Wend
  'END OF MAIN LOOP
```

Figure 7.8 shows a screenshot from the program.

**Figure 7.8**
The demo07-03.bmx program.

Okay, let's start from the top. As usual, the Cls clears the screen, so the rotation does not leave streaks. Figure 7.9 shows what the program will look like if you remove the Cls command.

The DrawText command displays how many rotations have occurred in the program using the rotationcount function.

The program then draws the actual image. The parameters here are pretty clear, except for the final one. As you know, the last frame is the [frame] parameter. We want the program to alternate between 1 and 2 for [frame], and to do this, we use the Mod operator.

If you remember from long ago, the Mod operator returns the remainder of the first operand divided by the second. In other words, 1 Mod 2 returns 1, because 1 divided by 2 leaves a remainder of 1, and 2 Mod 2 returns 0, because 2 divided by 2 leaves a remainder of 0.

Table 7.2 shows the return value of Mod for 1-10 Moded by 2.

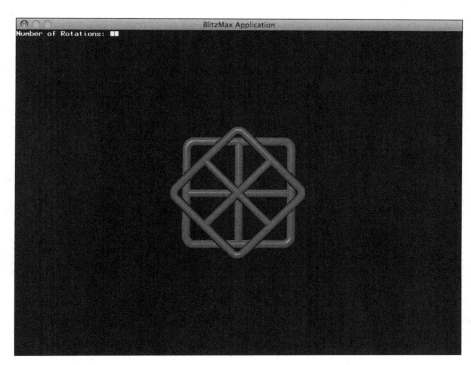

**Figure 7.9**
Removing `Cls` from demo07-03.bmx.

**Table 7.2**  Results of Mod

| First Operand | Second Operand | Result |
|:---:|:---:|:---:|
| 1 | 2 | 1 |
| 2 | 2 | 0 |
| 3 | 2 | 1 |
| 4 | 2 | 0 |
| 5 | 2 | 1 |
| 6 | 2 | 0 |
| 7 | 2 | 1 |
| 8 | 2 | 0 |
| 9 | 2 | 1 |
| 10 | 2 | 0 |

In other words, depending on the value of `rotationcounter` (if it is even or odd), it will display the first or second frame. If you wanted to expand the image to three frames, you would make the `[frame]` parameter equal to `rotationcount Mod 3`.

The next two lines of the code update the value of rotation count and delay the program by 100 milliseconds, respectively. If you remove the Delay command, the program runs so fast you can't see the frame changes!

All right, that's how you make a bitmap. Let's go on to something else now—movement.

## Displaying Movement

If you remember the previous chapter, you learned how to have BlitzMax deal with rotations for us. However, this does not always work. Sometimes, you will decide to put brightness or lighting on one area of the image, but you won't want that lighting rotated. Other times, you might want to have an image walk in numerous directions.

The first thing we need to do is to create the bitmap. This example starts with the image in Figure 7.10.

Okay, now that we have the base, we also need to have the animations. Because this is not going to be rotated, but rather turned around, BlitzMax cannot do the work for us. Figure 7.11 shows some of the frames of the image.

Excellent, huh? Now we are going to put the images together into one bitmap that will be used in the program, Figure 7.12. Notice that the bitmap is split into four sections: one section contains the animation for moving left, another for moving up, one more for moving right, and the last for moving down.

**Figure 7.10**
The about-to-be moved image.

**Figure 7.11**
The frames of movement.

**Figure 7.12**
The loaded player image.

Okay, now that we have the image ready, we need to get into the program. We first begin with the actual coding for demo07-04.bmx. As usual, create the back buffer and set the graphics first.

```
'demo07-04.bmx - Demonstrates sprite movement

Graphics 800,600
'Set up backbuffer and AutoMidHandle
AutoMidHandle True
```

After this, we write in the constants that will be used in the program.

```
'CONSTANTS
'These constants define the direction that is begin faced
Const DIRECTIONLEFT = 1      'When direction is left
Const DIRECTIONUP = 2      'When direction is up
Const DIRECTIONRIGHT = 3      'When direction is right
Const DIRECTIONDOWN = 4      'When direction is down

'These constants define how many pixels are moved per frame
Const MOVEX = 5      'How many pixels moved left/right per frame?
Const MOVEY = 5      'How many pixels moved up/down per frame?
```

These constants are used throughout the program, and are very useful. Basically, the DIRECTION* constants allow the players to have a different direction value based on which direction they are going. For example, if the users are heading up, their direction will be 2, if they are heading right, their direction will be 3.

The MOVE* parameters define the number of pixels the player will be moved per frame. Feel free to change them if you want.

**Table 7.3** demo07-04.bmx's Constants

| Constant | Value | Description |
| --- | --- | --- |
| DIRECTIONLEFT | 1 | The direction value for the player heading left. |
| DIRECTIONUP | 2 | The direction value for the player heading up. |
| DIRECTIONRIGHT | 3 | The direction value for the player heading right. |
| DIRECTIONDOWN | 4 | The direction value for the player heading down. |
| MOVEX | 5 | The number of pixels the player can move left or right per frame. |
| MOVEY | 6 | The number of pixels the player can move up or down per frame. |

Table 7.3 summarizes each of these parameters.

Alright, next we move on to the player type.

```
'TYPES
'The player type is used for the character on the screen
Type TPlayer
  Field x,y        'The coordinate position
  Field direction     'The direction that is being faced (one of the DIRECTIONXXX
constants)
  Field frame       'The frame that should be drawn
  Field image       'The image that should be drawn
  End Type
```

x and y indicate the coordinate position of the player, direction identifies which direction the player is facing, and frame chooses which frame of the player image is drawn. image tells the program which image is loaded and animated.

Table 7.4 explains each parameter.

Now we need to set up the player type.

```
'Create the player
player:TPlayer = New TPlayer

'Give the player starting variables
player.x = 400
player.y = 300
player.direction = DIRECTIONLEFT
player.frame = 0
'Load the player's image
player.image = LoadAnimImage("monkeyanim.bmp",48,40,0,8)
```

**Table 7.4**  demo07-04.bmx's Type Fields

| Field | Description |
| --- | --- |
| x | The x coordinate of the player. |
| y | The y coordinate of the player. |
| direction | The direction the player is facing, based upon the DIRECTION* constants. |
| frame | The frame of the player image that is to be drawn. |
| image | The image that will be loaded and animated. |

As usual, when creating a type, you must create an instance of the type by calling the New command. Here, we create player, based upon the player type. We then get into the actual fields.

The player begins existence directly in the center of the screen (400,300). I then decided to begin the player heading left, so player.direction is set to DIREC-TIONLEFT. The frame is then set to 0, so that the player will begin facing the correct direction with the correct starting point.

Note that we set AutoMidHandle to true earlier in the program. This allows the object to be centered and displayed correctly. Notice that I did this right before the following LoadAnimImage() command. LoadAnimImage() loads the player picture with the proper parameters: each frame is 48 × 40, and there are eight frames (beginning with 0 and ending with 7).

Okay, now that that is over with, we move on to the actual loop. At this point, the player is facing left, and is displaying frame 0. In the game loop, we want the player to be able to move the image around.

First off, begin the loop with some setup.

```
'MAIN LOOP
While Not KeyDown(KEY_ESCAPE)

'Clear the screen
Cls

'Print player info
DrawText "Player X: " + player.x,0,0
DrawText "Player Y: " + player.y,0,12
DrawText "Player Direction: " + player.direction,0,24
DrawText "Frame: " + player.frame,0,36
```

These lines display the values of all the fields of the player type (besides `image`, of course).

Now, I want to stop you for a moment. The next part of the code is going to be hard to comprehend, so I'm going to only show you one part of it and explain it to you before showing you the rest.

We now have to allow the player to change the direction of the character on the screen. To do this, we first test to see what has been pressed.

```
If KeyDown(KEY_LEFT)
```

Therefore, the following lines of code will occur only when the user presses left. Now you actually need to move the user left, by changing his x coordinate.

```
player.x = player.x - MOVEX
```

As you might expect, this pushes the user a bit left. Next, we change the direction the user is facing.

```
player.direction = DIRECTIONLEFT
```

This just tells the computer that the player is facing left.

The next line is probably the most difficult to understand. It computes the frame that's displayed based on the direction that the player is facing.

```
player.frame = (player.frame + 1 )Mod (2) + (2 * (player.direction)-2)
```

Whew! That's a big math problem. Let me show you what happens.

1. `player.frame` is incremented by 1. In this example, `player.frame`, which began the program as 0, is now equal to 1.

2. `player.frame` is divided by 2, and the remainder is returned using the `Mod` function. In this example, `player.frame`, which is equal to 1, is divided by 2. Because 1 / 2 leaves a remainder of 1, `(player.frame + 1 )Mod (2)` returns 1.

3. 2 multiplied by the direction of the player, and −2 is added to the frame value. This expression gives the appropriate value of the frame depending on the direction of the player. In this example, `2 * player.direction` (which is equal to 1) − 2 = 0, which is added to `player.frame` (which, according to step 2, is equal to 1). Thus, `player.frame` is equal to 1.

**Table 7.5** Each Frame's Values

| Frame Number | Direction | 2 * player.direction − 2 |
|:---:|:---:|:---:|
| 0 | 1 | 0 |
| 1 | 1 | 1 |
| 2 | 2 | 2 |
| 3 | 2 | 3 |
| 4 | 3 | 4 |
| 5 | 3 | 5 |
| 6 | 4 | 6 |
| 7 | 4 | 7 |

Hopefully, most of this isn't *that* hard to comprehend, except for the expression 2 * player.direction − 2. Basically, think of this equation as analogous to global and local coordinates. If you remember, with global and local coordinates, you find the position of something at its own local space and add it to the position of the screen. The same thing is occurring here; you are determining the difference in the frame (either 0 or 1, the local coordinates), and adding it to the 2 * player.direction − 2 (between 0 and 7, the global coordinates). Table 7.5 lists all the possible values for player.frame, complete with the value of 2 * player.direction − 2 for that frame.

### Note

Make sure you understand that the expression 2 * player.direction − 2 only works because there are two frames for each direction. If there were three frames for each animation (for a total of 12 frames, if there are still only four directions), the equation would be 3 * player.direction − 3. If there were five frames per direction, the expression would be 5 * player.direction − 5, and so on.

Now that you (hopefully) understand how we find the frame of the player, at least for when he moves left, let me show you the entire game loop.

```
'MAIN LOOP
While Not KeyDown(KEY_ESCAPE)

'Clear the screen
Cls

'Print player info
DrawText "Player X: " + player.x,0,0
```

```
DrawText "Player Y: " + player.y,0,12
DrawText "Player Direction: " + player.direction,0,24
DrawText "Frame: " + player.frame,0,36

'If player hits left, move him left, and find the correct direction and frame
If KeyDown(KEY_LEFT)
 player.x = player.x - MOVEX      'Move him left
 player.direction = DIRECTIONLEFT      'face him left
 player.frame = (player.frame + 1 )Mod (2) + (2 * (player.direction)-2)      'find
frame

'If player hits up, move him up, and find the correct direction and frame
ElseIf KeyDown(KEY_UP)
 player.y = player.y - MOVEY      'Move him up
 player.direction = DIRECTIONUP      'face him up
 player.frame = (player.frame + 1 )Mod (2) + (2 * (player.direction)-2)      'find
frame

'If player hits right, move him right, and find the correct direction and frame
ElseIf KeyDown(KEY_RIGHT)
 player.x = player.x + MOVEX      'move him right
 player.direction = DIRECTIONRIGHT      'face him right
 player.frame = (player.frame + 1 )Mod (2) + (2 * (player.direction)-2)      'find
frame

'If player hits down, move him down, and find the correct direction and frame
ElseIf KeyDown(KEY_DOWN)
 player.y = player.y + MOVEY      'Move him down
 player.direction = DIRECTIONDOWN      'face him down
 player.frame = (player.frame + 1 )Mod (2) + (2 * (player.direction)-2)      'find
frame
EndIf

'Draw the player at correct position and frame
DrawImage player.image,player.x,player.y, player.frame

'wait a (fraction of a) sec
Delay 50

Flip
Wend
'END OF MAIN LOOP
```

**Figure 7.13**
The demo07-04.bmx program.

Cool, huh? Figure 7.13 shows a screenshot of this program.

The final parts of the program react just as you would expect them to. When you press Right, the player moves five pixels to the right, as shown by the following line of code.

```
player.x = player.x + MOVEX
```

The same thing, only with y values, occurs when the user presses Up or Down.

At the end of the program, the image is drawn onscreen with the DrawImage command.

```
DrawImage player.image,player.x,player.y, player.frame
```

This draws the selected frame (player.frame) of the player's image (player.-image) and the player's x and y coordinates (player.x,player.y).

The program ends by delaying for 50 milliseconds. Without the delay, the animation occurs very quickly—sometimes so quickly, it is almost hard to see the actual movement!

**Figure 7.14**
The tiled grass.

**Figure 7.15**
The demo07-05.bmx program.

Well, that's it for demo07-04.bmx. Just for fun, I wrote demo07-05.bmx. The program is exactly the same as demo07-04.bmx, but this time the player is walking on grass instead of nothing. Figure 7.14 shows the grass that is tiled.

Figure 7.15 shows a screenshot from demo07-05.bmx.

This chapter is nearly complete, so let's review some of the most important things to remember when creating bitmaps.

- Make sure each frame of your bitmap is the same size.

- Make sure that all the bitmaps are lined up directly next to one another.

Also, remember that it is easier to understand animations when you make the bitmaps line up. For example, on demo07-04.bmx (and also demo07-05.bmx), I created four sets of two animations. The same would be done for other rotations. For example, say you were rotating a ship 12 times. Put the first four rotations (from facing up to facing right) in one row, the next four rotations (facing right to facing down) in another row, and so on.

## Summary

Alright, we did it! That's the end of this chapter. In this chapter, you learned the following concepts.

- Using bitmaps in animation

- Making bitmaps

- Displaying movement

Are you ready for the next chapter? We are moving up to collision detection. Whoopee!

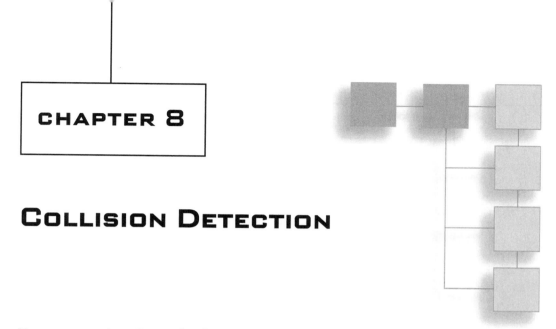

# CHAPTER 8

# COLLISION DETECTION

You are nearing the end of Part II. This chapter explains the art of collision detection. Collision detection allows your program to determine whether an object on your screen has been hit by another object, and performs actions based on the check. For example, if you made a space shooter, and you wanted to determine whether a missile hit an enemy ship, you would use collision detection. If the ship had been hit, you might decrease its hit points or destroy it altogether.

There are a few ways to check for collision detection, and we are going to go through them now. We can use bounding boxes, both rectangular and circular, and pixel-perfect collisions. Let's start off checking collision with a single pixel.

## Basic Collisions

Before we learn how to check for collisions of objects (images, shapes, and so on), let's go over basic pixel collisions. To determine whether a pixel collision has occurred, you just check the pixel you are tracking and make sure that its x and y values are not the same as the object you are testing it against. See Figure 8.1 for an example.

For the following program, demo08-01.bmx, we will allow the player to control a single pixel that can be moved up, down, left, or right. If the pixel hits a wall (the wall being the edge of the screen), the pixel position will be reset and the collision counter will be updated.

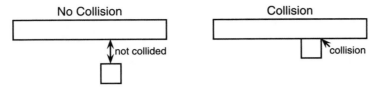

**Figure 8.1**
Difference between a collision and no collision.

## Following is the source for demo08-01.bmx:

```
'demo08-01.bmx - Demonstrates Pixel Collisions
Graphics 400,300

'create variables that define coordinate position of pixel
Global x = 200
Global y = 150

Cls

'This variable contains the amount of times a collision has occurred
collisions = 0


'MAIN LOOP
While Not KeyDown (KEY_ESCAPE)

'Print intro
DrawText "Press the arrow keys to move the pixel around.",0,0

'Print the number of collisions
DrawText "Collisions: " + collisions,0,12

'Move player around depending on the key he pressed
If KeyDown(KEY_UP)
  y = y - 5
ElseIf KeyDown(KEY_DOWN)
  y = y + 5
ElseIf KeyDown(KEY_LEFT)
  x = x - 5
ElseIf KeyDown(KEY_RIGHT)
  x = x + 5
EndIf
```

```
'Call the CheckForCollisions function and determine if a collision occurred
collisions = CheckForCollisions(collisions)

'Draw the pixel on the screen
Plot x,y

'wait a (fraction of a) sec
Delay 100

Flip


Wend
'END OF MAIN LOOP


'FUNCTIONS

'Function CheckForCollisions(collisions) - Returns number of total collisions,
tests for new ones
'collisions: the number of collisions at the time of calling the function
Function CheckForCollisions(collisions)

'If the pixel is offscreen, report a collision
If x <= 0 Or x >= 400 Or y <= 0 Or y >= 300
 collisions = collisions + 1      'increment collisions
 Cls       'clear the screen
 DrawText "A Collision Has Occurred", 100, 150
 Flip
 Delay 1000      'wait a sec
 Cls       'clear screen again
 Flip
 Cls


 x = 200      'reset x
 y = 150      'reset y
EndIf

'return the amount of collisions
Return collisions
Cls
 End Function
```

This program works pretty much as you would expect it to. It begins by setting the graphics and creating the variables x,y, and collisions. It then enters the main loop.

**Note**

Notice that while x and y are global variables, collisions is not. This fact will be important later in the program.

Inside the main loop, the program determines whether any arrow keys have been pressed. If so, it increments the x and y variables accordingly. The program also displays the number of collisions at the top of the screen.

Near the end of the loop, the program calls the function CheckForCollisions(). It includes collisions as a parameter. It also sets collisions equal to the return value of the function. Table 8.1 details the parameter.

Consider the CheckForCollisions() function further. The first and hardest part of the function to understand is the test. The test looks like this:

```
If x <= 0 Or x >= 400 Or y <= 0 Or y >= 300
```

This test determines whether the point has gone offscreen. Referring to Figure 8.2, you see that the x tests pertain to the right and left walls of the screen and the y tests pertain to the upper and lower walls.

Now, if the program finds that the point has hit one of the walls, it begins its reset procedure. First, it adds 1 to collisions, which increases the collision counter by 1. It then displays "A Collision Has Occurred" on the screen. The x and y coordinates are then reset.

Whether or not a collision occurs, the function returns the value of collisions to the main loop. If there was no collision, collisions will remain the same; if there was a collision, collisions increases by one.

**Table 8.1** CheckForCollisions()'s Parameter

| Parameter | Description |
| --- | --- |
| collisions | The number of collisions that have occurred thus far in the program. The number of collisions is also returned by the function. |

**Figure 8.2**
The wall tests.

**Figure 8.3**
The demo08-01.bmx program.

The rest of the main loop draws the pixel on the screen and delays the program for 1/10 of a second.

That's it for demo08-01.bmx. Figure 8.3 is a screenshot from the program.

## Bounding Circles

Now that we know how to check single pixels for collision, we need to learn how to check for collision of objects. Objects are shapes, images, and the like. There are a few ways to check shapes for collisions.

Bounding circles is the first method. Basically, it involves placing invisible circles around the objects we are testing. If the circles overlap, a collision has occurred. See Figure 8.4 for an example.

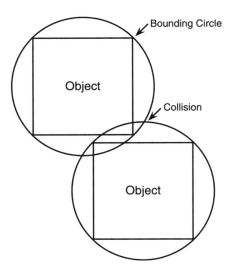

**Figure 8.4**
Overlapping circles.

If you look carefully at Figure 8.4, you will notice that the objects didn't actually collide—only their bounding circles did. This usually isn't a big deal; because the objects are so close to one another that it appears as if there was a collision.

Before I can show you how this works, you need to understand two concepts: one about distance between points, and one about the radius of a circle.

## Distance between Points

When we use bounding circles, we will have to compare the distances of points. To find the distance of two points, we can use a mathematical equation. Following is the equation.

```
distance = sqrt((x2-x1)^2 + (y2-y1)^2)
```

### Note

Have you ever seen the ^ symbol? It means "to the power of." In this case, ^2 means you raise the number by a power of two, or you square it. To square a value means to multiply a value by itself. In other words, 10^2 is read as "10 squared," and is equal to 10 × 10, or 100.

How do you read this? To find the distance between two points, you take the second x coordinate minus the first x coordinate and the second y coordinate

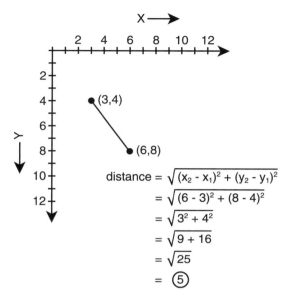

**Figure 8.5**
Testing distance.

minus the first y coordinate. You then square (multiply each of the values by itself) each number and add their results together. Finally, you take the square root of the final number. Figure 8.5 shows how you might compare the distance between two different points.

Difficult to understand, huh? Well, don't worry about it. I wrote the following function, `Distance()`, just for you.

```
Function Distance(x1,y1,x2,y2)
        dx = x2 - x1
        dy = y2 - y1
        Return sqr((dx*dx) + (dy*dy))
End Function
```

There's a new concept or two introduced here. Let's go over them.

First, notice that I computed what `x2-x1` and `y2-y1` were equal to before actually finding the distance. This makes reading the code much easier. If I had neglected to pre-compute those numbers, the function's return statement would look something like this.

```
Return sqr(((x2-x1)*(x2-x1)) + ((y2-y1)*(y2-y1)))
```

Much uglier, huh? Finding out the values made my code much easier to read and comprehend.

Also, notice the function sqr(). This function returns the square root of the number that it is provided. The square root is a number that when multiplied by itself gives the given number. Huh? Basically, if you multiply the square root of a number by itself, you achieve the number. For example, the square root of 4 is 2. You can prove this by multiplying 2 by itself. Because 2 × 2 = 4, 2 is the square root of 4 (so is -2, but that is a different matter altogether).

To find the square root by hand is an incredibly complex procedure. That is why BlitzMax provides the sqr() function for you. Following is the declaration for sqr().

Sqr (value:Float)

Table 8.2 lists the parameter for sqr().

Well that's just about it for finding the distance between two points. Just for reference, following is the declaration for the Distance() function.

Distance(x1,y1,x2,y2)

Table 8.3 lists each of Distance()'s parameters.

Okay, now we move on to finding the radius of a circle.

**Table 8.2**  Sqr()'s Parameter

| Parameter | Description |
| --- | --- |
| value:Float | The value you want to square root. |

**Table 8.3**  Distance()'s Parameters

| Parameter | Description |
| --- | --- |
| x1 | The x coordinate for the first point you want to compare. |
| y1 | The y coordinate for the first point you want to compare. |
| x2 | The x coordinate for the second point you want to compare. |
| y2 | The y coordinate for the second point you want to compare. |

## Radii

Is your brain hurting from the distance section? Well don't worry, this part is much easier. First off, the radius (plural radii, a very cool word) of a circle is equal to 1/2 of the diameter of the circle.

In a circle, there is one point directly in the center. From here on, I will call this point the "center of the circle." Well, anyway, the diameter of a circle is the distance from any point on a circle to another point on a circle, provided it crosses through the "center of the circle." What do I mean? Check out Figure 8.6.

Notice that the diameter shown in Figure 8.6 is just one of many. In fact, can you guess how many diameters there are in a circle? If you guessed 1, you are wrong. 360? Nope, wrong again. There are actually infinite diameters in a circle. That's right; there are an *infinite* number of diameters in a circle. However, all of them must extend from side to side and through the center of the circle, thus their lengths are all the same.

Anyway, getting back to radii, the radius of a circle is 1/2 the diameter. You might be thinking, isn't that the same as the distance from the "center of the circle" to the actual circle? You are absolutely correct! Figure 8.7 shows the radius of a circle.

Make sure you understand that any point on the circle is exactly the same distance from the "center of the circle" as any other point on the circle. Ready for another cool word? Each point on the circle is *equidistant* from the "center of the circle."

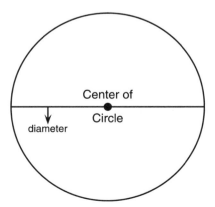

**Figure 8.6**
The diameter of a circle.

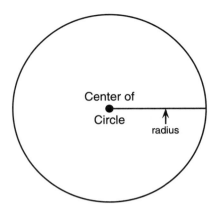

**Figure 8.7**
The radius of a circle.

Okay, we are now good to go. How can we find the radius of an object? It's a big problem, so let's figure out how to do it.

We are going to use code to figure this out. First, we load an object—say, an image.

```
imagehandle = LoadImage("image.bmp")
```

Not too terribly difficult, eh? Now we have to find the radius. Before we can do that, we need to go over two very basic functions. These functions are `ImageWidth()` and `ImageHeight()`.

These two functions return the width and height in pixels of the image whose handle you provide. Following are their declarations.

```
ImageWidth(imagehandle)
ImageHeight(imagehandle)
```

Tables 8.4 and 8.5 list their parameters.

Anyway, getting back to the actual coding, we now need to find the radius of our image. Let's define the radius of the image as the distance from the center of the image to the outer parts of the image. Make sure you understand that every bitmap is rectangular and not circular in nature. Therefore, the radius collision test will not be perfectly accurate.

You might be thinking that we can just take the result of either `ImageHeight()` or `ImageWidth()` and divide it by two to get a radius. However, this isn't a good idea. Because the images are not square, but rather rectangular, taking only the width

**Table 8.4**   ImageWidth()'s Parameters

| Parameter | Description |
| --- | --- |
| imagehandle | The handle to the image whose width in pixels is returned by the function. |

**Table 8.5**   ImageHeight()'s Parameters

| Parameter | Description |
| --- | --- |
| imagehandle | The handle to the image whose height in pixels is returned by the function. |

**Table 8.6**   FindRadius()'s Parameter

| Parameter | Description |
| --- | --- |
| imagehandle | The handle to the image whose approximate radius is returned by the function. |

or only the height into account can give you an inaccurate radius. What we are going to do is take the average of one-half of the height and width of the image. Let's write such a function, FindRadius().

```
Function FindRadius(imagehandle)
    Return ((ImageWidth(imagehandle)/2) + (ImageHeight(imagehandle)/2) / 2)
End Function
```

This function returns the approximate radius of the image it is given. Table 8.6 lists the parameters.

Okay, now we need to know how to test the image from FindRadius() with another object for collision. All that we do is test the point to determine whether its distance from the image is less than the distance of the radius. The following program, demo08-02.bmx, demonstrates how to do this. It's a long one, so I don't want to list it all out in the book. Let me show you some cool parts, though.

We haven't read about using the EachIn keyword in for loops lately. Let's review how they work.

First of all, we have to create a type. In this program, we used a type for every point. The type is defined like this.

```
'the point type defines each object that can be hit by the ship
Type TPoint
  Field x,y      'the x and y coordinate of the ship
End Type
```

Now, we want to create a lot of these points. This is accomplished through the EachIn loop.

```
'Create NUMBEROFOBJECTS new points with random x and y coords
For counter = 0 To NUMBEROFOBJECTS
  point:TPoint = New TPoint
  point.x = Rand (0,800)
  point.y = Rand (0,600)
  ListAddLast pointlist, point
Next
```

This loop creates NUMBEROFOBJECTS points and gives them all random x and y values.

If you are wondering what the constant NUMBEROFOBJECTS means, check out Table 8.7.

Sound good? Good. Now that we have created each of the objects, we also need to know how to delete all of the objects. We delete the objects when the level is reset.

```
'Delete every point on screen
For Local point:TPoint = EachIn pointlist
  'Delete point
  ListRemove(pointlist, point)
Next
```

This deletes all of the points that have been created previously.

By the way, if you don't remember how the EachIn loop works, check out Chapter 3, "Loops, Functions, Arrays, and Types," for a review.

**Table 8.7** demo08-02.bmx's Constants

| Constant | Value | Description |
| --- | --- | --- |
| NUMBEROFOBJECTS | 50 | The number of points that can be hit by the player's ship. |
| MOVEX | 5 | The number of pixels the player can move left or right per frame. |
| MOVEY | 5 | The number of pixels the player can move up or down per frame. |

Okay, the next thing I want to go over is `TestCollisions()`. This function tests all of the objects on the screen to determine whether the ship hit them.

```
'FUNCTION TestCollisions() - Tests the objects and the ship for collisions
'No input parameters
'Returns 1 if there was a collision, 0 if there was none
Function TestCollisions()

'Check every object to see if it is within player's radius. If it is, return that
there was a collision.
For point:TPoint = EachIn pointlist
  If Distance(player.x,player.y,point.x,point.y) < player.radius
        Return 1
  EndIf
Next

'If there was no collision, return 0
Return 0 'There was no collision

  End Function
```

Not too bad, huh? It checks each point to determine whether the point is within the radius of the ship. If so, 1 is returned. In the main loop, if there was a collision, the level is reset and the number of collisions is incremented by one.

Quite a few functions are defined in this program, so Table 8.8 lists them all.

All right, that's just about it for this section of the code. Next, we move on to bounding boxes. By the way, Figure 8.8 shows a screenshot from the program.

**Table 8.8** demo08-02.bmx's Functions

| Function | Description |
| --- | --- |
| ResetLevel() | Deletes and renews all the objects; resets the player's starting coordinates. |
| TestCollisions() | Tests all objects to see whether they have collided with the spaceship, and returns 1 if a collision took place. |
| TestKeys() | Tests the keyboard to see whether any keys have been pressed. |
| Distance() | Finds the distance between two points. |
| FindRadius() | Finds the radius of an image. |

**Figure 8.8**
The demo08-02.bmx program.

## Bounding Boxes

Okay, now that we have learned how to use bounding circles, let's learn how to use bounding boxes. Bounding boxes are just like bounding circles, except that instead of comparing overlapping circles, it compares overlapping rectangles. Check out Figure 8.9 for an example of a bounding rectangle.

If you check out Figure 8.10, you will notice that a collision does not always occur even though a collision is reported. This is usually not a big deal, though, because the collision is pretty close.

Unlike using bounding circles, BlitzMax provides a way to test for collisions using bounding boxes. You'll read about this in a minute, after I show you how to do it manually.

We have to use ImageHeight() and ImageWidth() again, but this time in a different way. The bounding box for the rectangle is going to be the outer edge of the image. See Figure 8.11 for an example.

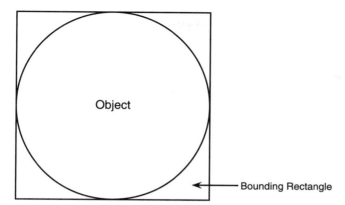

**Figure 8.9**
A bounding rectangle.

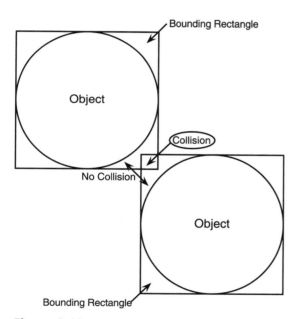

**Figure 8.10**
An imperfect collision.

**Figure 8.11**
A bounding box.

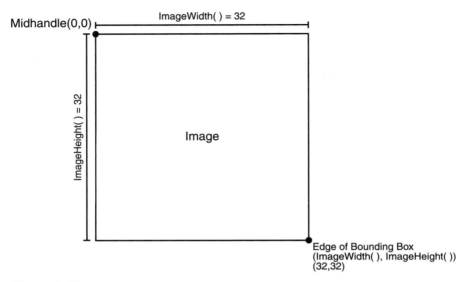

**Figure 8.12**
A bounding box with the mid handle at the upper-left corner.

Now, how are we going to go about finding this bounding box? First of all, remember that when we use images, the handling point is directly in the center of the image. This is defined by AutoMidHandle. Because it is in the center, we need to determine the upper-left and lower-right corners to find the bounding box.

If the mid handle had been set to the top-left corner of the image, this would be an easy problem to fix. We would begin with the mid handle for the upper corner. The mid handle's x coordinate plus ImageWidth() would be the lower-right corner's x coordinate, and the lower-right corner's y coordinate would be the mid handle's y coordinate plus ImageHeight(). Check out Figure 8.12 for an example of how this works with an image that is 32 pixels wide by 32 pixels high.

Well, now, here's the thing. Because the mid handle isn't at the top-left corner, we need to use another formula. Basically, the bounding box will have an upper-left corner of:

$-1/2$ * ImageWidth(), $-1/2$ * ImageHeight()

And a lower-right corner of:

$1/2$ * ImageWidth(), $1/2$ * ImageHeight().

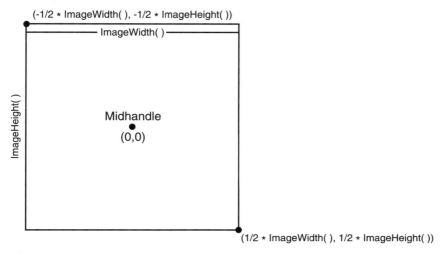

**Figure 8.13**
A bounding box with mid handle at the center.

Figure 8.13 illustrates this.

How does this work? Well, `AutoMidHandle` sets up the handling point directly in the center of the image rectangle. We need to move the handling point to the top-left corner of the image so that we can draw a rectangle around the bitmap. Because the handling point is directly in the center, we need to move the handling point 1/2 of the height of the rectangle up, and 1/2 of the width of the rectangle left. This allows you to grab the rectangle by the top-left corner.

Okay, now, before we write our collision detection program, let's write a program that demonstrates the bounding box technique. The following program, demo08-03.bmx, draws a rectangle around the bounding box of a spaceship.

```
'demo08-03.bmx - Draws a bounding box

Graphics 800,600

AutoMidHandle True

'IMAGES
'Load the ship image
Global shipimage = LoadImage("ship.bmp")
```

```
'Give the ship default parameters
Global x = 400
Global y = 300



'CONSTANTS
'These constants define how many pixels are moved per frame
Const MOVEX = 5
Const MOVEY = 5

'MAIN LOOP
While Not KeyDown(KEY_ESCAPE)
'Clear the screen
Cls

'Find out if any important keys on the keyboard have been pressed
TestKeys()

'Draw the bounding box around the player
DrawPlayerRect()

'Draw the image of the ship
DrawImage shipimage,x,y

Flip

'Slow it down
Delay 20

Wend
'END OF MAIN LOOP


'FUNCTION DrawPlayerRect() - Draws a bounding rectangle
Function DrawPlayerRect()

'find the width of the image
iw = ImageWidth(shipimage)

'Find the upper left hand coordinates
x1 = ((-ImageWidth(shipimage)/2) +x)
y1 = ((-ImageHeight(shipimage)/2) + y)
```

```
'Draw the entire bounding box
DrawOutlineRectangle(x1, y1, ImageWidth(shipimage), ImageHeight(shipImage))

End Function

'FUNCTION DrawOutlineRectangle(x1,y1,width,height) - draws a bounding box
Function DrawOutlineRectangle(x1, y1, width, height)

 DrawLine x1, y1, x1 + width, y1
 DrawLine x1, y1, x1, y1 + width
 DrawLine x1 + width, y1, x1 + width, y1 + width
 DrawLine x1, y1 + width, x1 + width, y1 + width

End Function
'FUNCTION TestKeys() - Tests all of the keys to see if they were hit
Function TestKeys()

'If up is hit, move player up
If KeyDown(KEY_UP)
 y = y - MOVEY
EndIf

'If down is hit, move player down
If KeyDown(KEY_DOWN) 'If down was hit
 y = y + MOVEY
EndIf

'If left is hit, move player left
If KeyDown(KEY_LEFT)
 x = x - MOVEX
EndIf

'If right is hit, move player right
If KeyDown(KEY_RIGHT)
 x = x + MOVEX
EndIf

End Function
```

To me, the most difficult thing to understand is the function DrawPlayerRect().

DrawPlayerRect() draws the bounding box around the player's image. If you remember correctly, I said that the bounding box extends from $-1/2 *$ ImageWidth(),

$-1/2$ * `ImageHeight()` to $1/2$ * `ImageWidth()`, $1/2$ * `ImageHeight()`. However, the `DrawPlayerRect()` function seems to make the bounding box look a lot different.

```
'FUNCTION DrawPlayerRect() - Draws a bounding rectangle
Function DrawPlayerRect()

'find the width of the image
iw = ImageWidth(shipimage)

'Find the upper left hand coordinates
x1 = ((-ImageWidth(shipimage)/2) + x)
y1 = ((-ImageHeight(shipimage)/2) + y)

'Draw the entire bounding box
DrawOutlineRectangle(x1, y1, ImageWidth(shipimage), ImageHeight(shipImage))

End Function

'FUNCTION DrawOutlineRectangle(x1,y1,width,height) - draws a bounding box
Function DrawOutlineRectangle(x1, y1, width, height)

  DrawLine x1, y1, x1 + width, y1
  DrawLine x1, y1, x1, y1 + width
  DrawLine x1 + width, y1, x1 + width, y1 + width
  DrawLine x1, y1 + width, x1 + width, y1 + width

End Function
```

First of all, take the variable $x1\#$. As you can see, instead of being set to $1/2$ * `ImageWidth()`, it is set to `ImageWidth()/2`. However, $1/2$ * `ImageWidth()` and `ImageWidth()/2` are equivalent. Multiplying something by $1/2$ is the same as dividing something by 2. Therefore, $1/2$ * `ImageWidth()` is the same as `ImageWidth()/2`.

Also, notice that I added the x coordinate to the rectangle when finding $x1\#$. This places the bounding box into the actual player space—if I forgot to add it, the rectangle would begin at the top-left corner of the screen. This is the same as global and local coordinates. Finding the bounding box is finding the local coordinates, but by adding the proper x value, you move it to the correct global coordinates. We do the same thing with the $y1\#$ variable.

Last, the `DrawOutlineRectangle()` call might be a little confusing. This function simply draws four lines, given a starting point and a `width` and `height`.

**Figure 8.14**
The demo08-03.bmx program.

Remember that? Anyway, as you know, the rectangle begins at x,y. We already figured out what x and y are in the previous two variables, x1 and y1. We then need to determine the width and height of the rectangle. The rectangle's width and height are the width and height of the image. This is achieved by using ImageWidth() and ImageHeight(). Figure 8.14 shows a screenshot from the program.

By the way, there is a much easier way to grab the image by the top-left corner than using ImageHeight() and ImageWidth(). BlitzMax provides a function named SetHandle that lets you choose where on the image you want your handle (grabbing point) to be located. SetHandle is declared like this.

```
SetHandle x, y
```

To set the grabbing point to the top-left corner, you would just call SetHandle as follows.

```
HandleImage 0, 0
shipimage = LoadImage("shipimage.bmp")
AutoMidHandle True
```

By setting `AutoMidHandle` to `true` after loading your ship, the newly loaded images will be grabbed at the center.

All right, we are now ready to determine whether an object has collided with the spaceship using bounding boxes. This program, demo08-04.bmx, is the same as the one in demo08-02.bmx, except it does not use bounding circles.

Let's go over the changes in the program. First of all, the player type has changed from this:

```
'The player type is the spaceship on the screen
Type TPlayer
      Field x,y        'the x and y coordinate of the player
      Field collisions      'the number of collisions that have occurred
      Field radius       'the radius of the player image
      Field image       'the actual image of the player
End Type
```

to this:

```
'The player type is the spaceship on the screen
Type TPlayer
   Field x,y        'the x and y coordinate of the player
   Field collisions      'the number of collisions that have occurred
   Field image       'the actual image of the player
End Type
```

Yeah, that's right. We got rid of the `radius` field! Anyway, getting back to the program, we changed the `TestCollisions()` function quite a bit.

```
'FUNCTION TestCollisions() - Tests the objects and the ship for collisions
'No input parameters
'Returns 1 if there was a collision, 0 if there was none
Function TestCollisions()

'Check every object to see if it is within player's radius. If it is, return that
there was a collision.
For point:TPoint = EachIn pointlist

   'Find players bounding box
   x1 = -ImageWidth(player.image)/2 + player.x
   x2 = ImageWidth(player.image)/2 + player.x
   y1 = -ImageHeight(player.image)/2 + player.y
   y2 = ImageHeight(player.image)/2 + player.y
```

```
        'If the point is within collision boundary, return 1
        If (point.x > x1) And (point.x < x2) And (point.y > y1) And (point.y < y2)
                Return 1
        EndIf
Next 'Move on to next point

'If there was no collision, return 0
Return 0 'There was no collision

    End Function
```

As you can see, the function begins by finding the size of the rectangle. Recall that the bounding rectangle extends from $-$ImageWidth()/2 + x, $-$ImageHeight()/2 + y to ImageWidth()/2 + x, ImageHeight()/2 + y. The If statement determines whether any of the points are within the bounding box, and if so, a collision is reported.

Also, one last major change. The FindRadius() and the Distance() functions have been changed to this:

Yep! Those functions are no longer necessary, so they have been deleted.

## Image Collisions

One thing you might have noticed is that these programs test the ship only against single pixels. What if we want to test an image against another image? Say, a bullet against a ship, or a missile crash? BlitzMax provides an excellent way to do this.

There is a function provided by BlitzMax called ImagesCollide(). It is defined like this:

```
ImagesCollide (image1,x1,y1,frame1,image2,x2,y2,frame2)
```

Table 8.9 explains all the parameters.

Now, let's write a program that uses this function. The following, demo08-06.bmx, allows you to control a ship. If you hit the randomly moving ship that is also onscreen, a collision occurs.

The program is pretty easy to follow, so I am just going to list some important parts. Following are the types from the program, and the initial values for these types.

**Table 8.9** ImagesCollide()'s Parameters

| Parameter | Description |
|---|---|
| image1 | The handle to the first image you want to test for collision. |
| x1 | The x coordinate of the first image. |
| y1 | The y coordinate of the first image. |
| frame1 | The frame of the first image you want to check—unless you are using animation, set this to 0. |
| image2 | The handle to the second image you want to test for collision. |
| x2 | The x coordinate of the second image. |
| y2 | The y coordinate of the second image. |
| frame2 | The frame of the second image you want to check—unless you are using animation, set this to 0. |

```
'MAIN LOOP
While Not KeyDown(KEY_ESCAPE)
Cls

'Make sure all text appears in top left corner

DrawText "Collisions: " + player.collisions, 0, 0

'Find out if enemy hit a wall
TestEnemyCollisions()

'Test keyboard
TestKeys()

'If player and enemy overlap, increment collisions and reset player and enemy
If (ImagesCollide(player.image,player.x,player.y,0,enemy.image,enemy.x,
enemy.y,0))
          player.collisions = player.collisions + 1
          player.x = 400
          player.y = 400
          enemy.x = 400
          enemy.y = 200
          enemy.xv = Rand(-5,5)
          enemy.yv = Rand(-5,5)
EndIf

'Move the enemy
enemy.x = enemy.x + enemy.xv
enemy.y = enemy.y + enemy.yv
```

```
'Draw the player and the enemy
DrawImage enemy.image,enemy.x,enemy.y
DrawImage player.image,player.x,player.y

Flip

'Slow it down
Delay 20

Wend
```

The main loop does this: it prints out how many collisions have occurred, it calls TestEnemyCollisions() and TestKeys(), it determines whether any collisions have occurred, it moves the enemy, and it draws the two ships. The only major line of interest is the test.

```
(ImagesCollide(player.image,player.x,player.y,0,enemy.image,enemy.x,enemy.y,0))
```

This determines whether the player's image and the enemy's image have overlapped. Figure 8.15 shows a screenshot from the program.

**Figure 8.15**
The demo08-05.bmx program.

That's just about it for pixel-imperfect collisions. Next, you'll learn how to find out whether collisions have actually occurred using pixel-perfect collisions.

## Summary

Whoo-hoo! We have now reached the end of Chapter 8, and also, the end of Part II. In this chapter, you learned how to use several types of collision-detection methods. Don't forget them, because they will be useful in your programs!

In this chapter, we covered these concepts:

- Basic collisions
- Bounding circles
- Distance between points
- Radii
- Bounding boxes
- Image collisions

Starting with the next chapter, we are going to learn more topics of BlitzMax, and we will progress toward our own final game. Cool, huh?

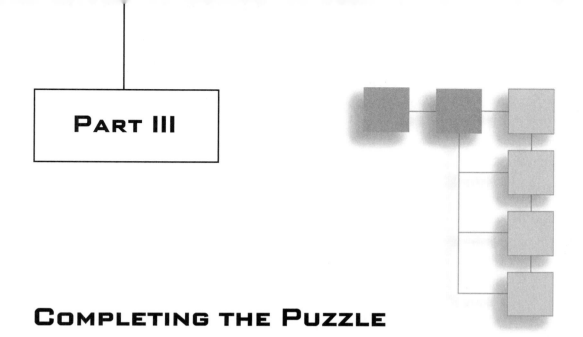

# PART III

# COMPLETING THE PUZZLE

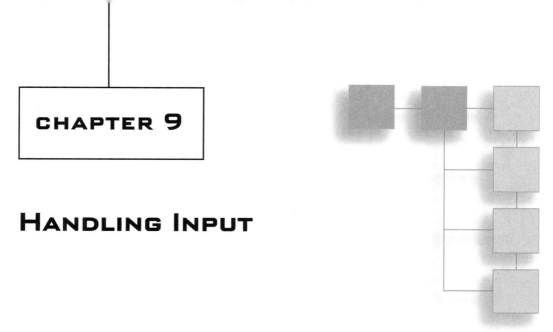

# CHAPTER 9

# HANDLING INPUT

We are finally on the last part of the book! When you're finished with this part, you will know everything you need in order to make games. So, let's get started with making decisions based on user input. Of course, every game requires handling of input. Otherwise, it isn't a game; instead, it's a movie. Sometimes you might want to include movies and other sections of games that don't accept user input in your game—*cinematics,* for instance, are bits of a game that explain the storyline without any actual game play. The main part of your game, however, will rely on input from the user.

Although there are a number of ways that the player can interact with the game (using game pads, racing wheels, and so on), BlitzMax simplifies all of the choices to three input sources: the mouse, the keyboard, and the joystick. This chapter covers the first two and introduces the third. First up: the keyboard!

## Handling the Keyboard

You use the keyboard every time you use your computer; heck, I am using it to type these words right now. So, of course, the keyboard is probably going to be a common source of input for most games you make. We better get crackin' if we want to figure out what the player wants to do.

We have read about the keyboard's role in a very limited way thus far: basically, you know how to determine whether the users have pressed the Esc key and a few select other keys. The following sections review what we know and then teach you a bit more. So, let's begin by reviewing the functions `KeyDown()` and `KeyHit()`.

## KeyDown()

We have been using this function throughout the book, so you most likely already know what it does. First off, let's go over the declaration of `KeyDown()`.

`KeyDown (keycode)`

Memories, huh? Anyway, `KeyDown()` tests the keyboard to determine whether the key code has been pressed. If you don't remember, let me redefine *key code* for you. A scan code is a code that represents a certain key. Each key on your keyboard is represented by a certain scan code.

If the key has been pressed, `KeyDown()` returns 1. If a key was not pressed, `KeyDown()` returns 0.

Table 9.1 explains the parameters of `KeyDown()`.

There are numerous scan codes that are built into BlitzMax, and all of them are listed in Appendix A. However, I decided to list a few of them right here, in Table 9.2.

**Table 9.1**  KeyDown()'s Parameter

| Parameter | Description |
| --- | --- |
| keycode | Tests if the key represented by key code has been pressed. |

**Table 9.2**  Relevant Scan Codes

| Key | Scan Code |
| --- | --- |
| Esc | KEY_ESCAPE |
| #'s 0-9 | KEY_0 – KEY_9 |
| Return | KEY_RETURN |
| Spacebar | KEY_SPACE |
| F10 | KEY_F19 |
| Up | KEY_UP |
| Left | KEY_LEFT |
| Right | KEY_RIGHT |
| Down | KEY_DOWN |
| A-Z | KEY_A – KEY_Z |

Flip to Appendix A to see a list of all the key codes you could ever use.

So how do we use this information? Well, usually we test KeyDown() with an If statement. For example, if we wanted to determine whether the user pressed the spacebar, we would write something like this.

```
If KeyDown(KEY_SPACE)
     'Do Something
 Endif
```

Let's go through this code in depth. As you know, the If statement performs the following actions if what it tests amounts to true. If you remember, in computer speak, 1 is equal to true, and 0 is equal to false. KeyDown() returns 1 if the key specified by its scan code is pressed on the keyboard. Therefore, the statements inside the If...Endif block are executed if and only if the user pressed the spacebar.

Let's write a program around this. The following program, demo09-01.bmx, moves an outerspace background when the user presses the up, down, left, and right keys.

```
'demo09-01.bmx - Demonstrates usage of KeyDown()

'Initialize Graphics
Graphics 800,600

'Load the background image
backgroundimage = LoadImage("stars.bmp")

'scrollx and scrolly define how much the image should be moved
scrollx = 0
scrolly = 0


'MAIN LOOP
While Not KeyDown(KEY_ESCAPE)

Cls

'If the player hits up, we will scroll the background up
If KeyDown(KEY_UP)
 scrolly = scrolly - 5 'scroll background 5 pixels up
EndIf
```

```
'If the player hits left, we will scroll the background left
If KeyDown(KEY_LEFT)
  scrollx = scrollx - 5 'scroll background 5 pixels left
EndIf

'If player hits right, we will scroll the background right
If KeyDown(KEY_RIGHT)
  scrollx = scrollx + 5 'scroll background 5 pixels right
EndIf

'If player hits down, we will scroll the background down
If KeyDown(KEY_DOWN)
  scrolly = scrolly + 5 'Scroll background 5 pixels down
EndIf

'Tile the background image on the screen so it looks like actual outerspace
TileImage backgroundimage,scrollx,scrolly

'Wait a fraction of a second.
Delay 35
Flip

  Wend 'END OF MAIN LOOP
```

This program demonstrates the concepts of KeyDown() quite well. Let's begin at the top. I created a section of constants that define the keys that will be used throughout the program. Constants, as you probably remember, are variables whose values cannot be changed; thus, they are perfectly suited to hold the scan code numbers.

Anyway, back to the code. We move on to the main loop. As you can see, the main loop only functions as long as the Esc key is *not* pressed, as seen by this line of code.

```
While Not KeyDown(KEY_ESCAPE)
```

Like the If statement, While only functions as long as the following statements are true, or equal to 1. Because KeyDown() returns 0 unless the key is pressed, and Not flips 0 into 1 and 1 into 0, Not KeyDown(KEY_ESCAPE) is 1 (true) as long as the key is not being pressed. Therefore, the main loop executes only as long as the Esc key is not pressed.

The program then moves into the actual key tests. Following is the test for the up key.

```
'If the player hits up, we will scroll the background up
If KeyDown(KEY_UP)
        scrolly = scrolly - 5 'scroll background 5 pixels up
 EndIf
```

Here, the statements execute as long as KEY_UP is pressed. The statements change the value of the scrolly variable, and the background scrolls up a little.

The previous test is repeated three more times to test all four arrow keys: up, down, left, and right. Figure 9.1 is a screenshot taken from the program.

Notice that when the map scrolls left, it seems like you are moving right, and vice versa. The same happens when you scroll up. It's a cool effect, don't you think?

Okay, I think you get the gist of that. However, I want to go over one problem with using KeyDown(). Sometimes when you type something on your keyboard, KeyDown() believes that you held the key down for longer than one frame. This happens because the game loop iterates extremely fast, and you might be holding the key down for more than one frame at a time. Of course, this is what you want to happen on some games, especially with movement. When you are performing

**Figure 9.1**
The demo09-01.bmx program.

an action like moving a spaceship around the screen, you want the player to be able to simply hold down the key to move the character around. However, every once in a while, you will have a case where you don't want the users to be able to hold down the keys for more than one frame.

Take this, for example: when you are creating a game, you usually want the player to be able to quit the game by pressing Esc. Now, maybe you want to show something on the screen before the game actually closes, so you print "Press any key to exit" on the screen. The program then waits for a keypress by using the function WaitKey, which pauses the program until a key is pressed. WaitKey has no parameters; it just stops a program's execution. Here is the problem, though: when the player presses Esc, the key is carried over to the WaitKey statement and the program exits immediately.

You have to find a way to halt the program from retrieving the key immediately. There is one easy way to do this.

What we need to do is clear the computer's memory of what keys have been pressed. This will cause the computer to forget about any previously held down keys. To perform this action, we use the function FlushKeys. FlushKeys's declaration is extremely simple:

```
FlushKeys
```

There are no parameters—just call the function by itself. Anyway, by calling FlushKeys, you clear the key input memory. Thus, any key that was held down previously is deleted.

Let's move on to the next keyboard input function: KeyHit().

## KeyHit()

This is the last function that we will be going over for keyboard input. KeyHit() acts an awful lot like KeyDown(), except for a small but important difference. Whereas KeyDown() allows the player to hold down a key, KeyHit() only lets the player press the keyboard once. Thus, you can only read which key the player pressed one time. Take, for example, demo09-02.bmx. This program draws a spaceship on a tiled space background. It allows the player to move the spaceship using KeyHit(). Figure 9.2 is a screenshot taken from this program.

In demo09-02.bmx, you will find the KeyHit() command nested in If statements. Following is the source from the program that uses KeyHit().

**Figure 9.2**
The demo09-02.bmx program.

```
'If the player hits up, move player up
If KeyHit(KEY_UP)
 y = y - 5 'move player 5 pixels up
EndIf


'If the player hits left, move player left
If KeyHit(KEY_LEFT)
 x = x - 5 'move player 5 pixels left
EndIf


'If player hits right, move player right
If KeyHit(KEY_RIGHT)
 x = x + 5 'move player 5 pixels right
EndIf


'If player hits down, move player down
If KeyHit(KEY_DOWN)
 y = y + 5 'move player 5 pixels down
EndIf
```

**Table 9.3**  KeyHit()'s Parameter

| Parameter | Description |
|-----------|-------------|
| keycode | The scan code of the key you want to test for input. |

By the way, KeyHit()'s declaration is exactly the same as KeyDown()'s declaration.

```
KeyHit (keycode)
```

Table 9.3 examines the parameter.

If you run the program, you will notice that you can only move the player by pressing the arrow keys multiple times. Usually, you would rather allow the player to move around by holding down the arrow keys, but sometimes you might prefer to only let the player do something by pressing the key over and over again.

Let's take a space-simulation game, for example. We want to allow the player to be able to move around the screen and fire bullets. To do this, we will allow the players to hold down the arrow keys for movement, but they have to press the spacebar to produce a bullet.

Following is the initialization section from demo09-03.bmx.

```
'demo09-03.bmx - A Space Simulation with KeyHit()

Graphics 800,600

'Set AutoMidHandle to true
AutoMidHandle True

'TYPES

'Bullet type = hold the information for each bullet
Type TBullet
  Field x,y    'the coordinates of the bullet
End Type



'Player type - holds the actual player
Type TPlayer
  Field x,y    'the coordinates of the player
End Type
```

```
'Create player and initialize field
Global player:TPlayer = New TPlayer
player.x = 400
player.y = 500

Global bulletlist:TList = CreateList()


'IMAGES
playerimage = LoadImage("ship.bmp")
Global bulletimage = LoadImage("bullet.bmp")
backgroundimage = LoadImage("stars.bmp")

'Create a scrolling indicator variable
scrolly = 0
```

The initialization section acts pretty much how you would expect it to. It begins by setting the graphics mode and setting AutoMidHandle to true. After that, it sets the starting buffer to be the back buffer. Next, it creates the types that are used in the program.

The first type is the bullet type. Every bullet that is to be created uses this type. The next type is the player type. Both TBullet and TPlayer have the same fields: x and y. As you probably have guessed, x and y define the coordinates for the bullet's and player's positions.

After creating the types, the program initializes the player type. Of course, there is only one player, so a single player is created. The player's beginning x and y coordinates are defined at 400,500, which starts the player roughly in the middle of the screen near the bottom. We create a bulletlist to keep track of all our bullets.

The next two sections define the constants and the images. The constants are the scan codes for each of the keys that are used in the game. The program loads three images: playerimage, bulletimage, and backgroundimage. Notice that bulletimage is global, implying that it is used in other functions, not just the main function.

The final section of the initialization creates scrolly. This indicator variable defines how far the background should scroll at any instant.

Next up, consider the main loop.

```
'MAIN LOOP
While Not KeyDown(KEY_ESCAPE)

Cls

'Increment scrolling variable
scrolly = scrolly + 1

'Tile the background
TileImage backgroundimage,0,scrolly

'Reset the scrolling variable when it grows too large
If scrolly > ImageHeight(backgroundimage)
 scrolly = 0
EndIf

'Test input keys
TestKeys()

'Update (move) each bullet
UpdateBullets()

'Draw the player
DrawImage playerimage, player.x, player.y

'Wait a bit
Delay 50

'Flip the front and back buffers
Flip

Wend    'END OF MAIN LOOP
```

The main loop begins by tiling the background. It increments the indicator variable, scrolly, and then tiles the background. When scrolly grows too large, its value is reset to 0. Following that, the program calls two user-defined functions: TestKeys() and UpdateBullets(). The first function tests the keyboard to determine if any input has occurred, and the second function moves and updates each bullet on the screen.

The main loop ends by drawing the player's ship and his or her current position. It then flips the front and back buffers using the command Flip.

The rest of the program lists the two user-defined functions: TestKeys() and UpdateBullets(). Following is the source for TestKeys().

```
'FUNCTIONS
'Function TestKeys() - Tests what buttons have been pressed by player
Function TestKeys()

'If the player hits up, we move him 5 pixels up
If KeyDown(KEY_UP)
 player.y = player.y - 5 'move player 5 pixels up
EndIf

'If the player hits left, we move him 5 pixels left
If KeyDown(KEY_LEFT)
 player.x = player.x - 5 'move player 5 pixels left
EndIf

'If player hits right, we move him 5 pixels right
If KeyDown(KEY_RIGHT)
 player.x = player.x + 5 'move player 5 pixels right
EndIf

'If player hits down, we move him 5 pixels down
If KeyDown(KEY_DOWN)
 player.y = player.y + 5 'move player 5 pixels down
EndIf




'If player hits spacebar, we will create a new bullet at the player's current
position
If KeyHit(KEY_SPACE)
 bullet:TBullet = New TBullet
 bullet.x = player.x
 bullet.y = player.y
 ListAddLast bulletlist, bullet
EndIf

End Function
```

The TestKeys() function, although not short, is pretty easy to comprehend. The function tests each key to determine whether it has been pressed, and if so, it

**Table 9.4**  demo09-03.bmx's Keys

| Key | Function |
| --- | --- |
| Up arrow | Moves the player five pixels up. |
| Left arrow | Moves the player five pixels left. |
| Right arrow | Moves the player five pixels right. |
| Down arrow | Moves the player five pixels down. |
| Spacebar | Creates a new bullet to be drawn onscreen. |

changes something in the program. Table 9.4 explains what each key does when pressed.

As you can see, the arrow keys do pretty much what you expect them to do. The only new key is the spacebar.

When the player presses the spacebar, a new bullet is created. The code that performs this action follows.

```
If KeyHit(KEY_SPACE)
        Bullet:TBullet = New TBullet
```

Notice that the function uses KeyHit() instead of KeyDown() for the creation of new bullets. This prevents the player from holding down the spacebar and creating hundreds of bullets quickly. Figure 9.3 shows what happens if you exchange KeyDown() with KeyHit().

By creating a new bullet, the program adds a new bullet to the bullet type. If you remember, when creating multiple members of the same type, the most recent one becomes active. Thus, the following lines

```
bullet.x = player.x
bullet.y = player.y
```

only relate to the most recent bullet (the one that was just created a few milli-seconds earlier). The new bullet is created at the player's current position.

Okay, the next and final function updates each bullet. Following is the source for UpdateBullets().

```
'Function UpdateBullets() - Moves each bullet on screen
Function UpdateBullets()

'For every bullet, move it up 5 pixels. If it goes offscreen, delete it, otherwise,
draw it
```

**Figure 9.3**
Exchanging `KeyDown()` with `KeyHit()`.

```
For Local bullet:TBullet = EachIn bulletlist
 bullet.y = bullet.y - 5     'Move bullet up

 'If bullet moves offscreen, delete it, otherwise, draw it onscreen
 If bullet.y < 0
      ListRemove bulletlist, bullet
 Else
      DrawImage bulletimage, bullet.x, bullet.y     'Draw the bullet
 EndIf

Next    'move to next bullet

End Function
```

The function begins with an `EachIn` loop that tests every created bullet. The function moves each existing bullet five pixels up. The program then determines whether the bullet is offscreen. If so, the bullet is deleted. If not, the bullet is drawn onscreen.

The function ends by moving on to the next bullet, and returning to the main function after every bullet has been processed.

**Figure 9.4**
The demo09-03.bmx program.

Well, that is it for demo09-03.bmx. The screenshot in Figure 9.4 was taken from that program.

By the way, try changing KeyHit() into KeyDown() on the TestKeys() function. Seriously, it can provide hours of fun—especially for those who like shiny and fast moving objects (like me!).

Before you move on to mouse input, I want to explain one thing about KeyHit(). KeyHit() does provide a return value. The function returns the number of times the user pressed a key since the previous KeyHit() call (or since the beginning of the program if there are no earlier KeyHit() calls). The following demo, demo09-04.bmx, demonstrates what it can do.

```
'demo09-04.bmx - Demonstrates the return value of KeyHit()

'Set up graphics so that you can read all of the text, make it windowed
Graphics 800,600
```

```
'Begin introductory text
DrawText "You know what's cool? Game Programming.",0,0
DrawText "Although Maneesh ain't that uncool, either.",0,12

Flip

'Continue text
DrawText "Anyway, press Esc as many times as you can in the Next 5 seconds.",
0,36
DrawText "At the end of the program, the number of times will be printed.",0,48

Flip

numberofhits=0

'Allow the player 5 seconds to hit esc as many times as possible
timerbegin=MilliSecs()

While timerbegin>MilliSecs()-5000
  If KeyHit(KEY_ESCAPE)
        numberofhits = numberofhits + 1
  EndIf
Wend




'Print the number of times Esc was hit
DrawText "Esc was hit " + numberofhits + " times.",0,60
DrawText "You gotta love KeyHit(), huh?",0,72


Flip

'Hold on a sec so the player can see the final text
Delay 5000
```

The main part of the program sets numberofhits to KeyHit(KEY_ESCAPE) and adds the value of the function to numberofhits—it adds one to numberofhits every time the user pressed Esc since the beginning of the program. Figure 9.5 is a screenshot taken from demo09-04.bmx.

Well, that is all for keyboard input. Now we move on to mouse input.

**Figure 9.5**
The demo09-04.bmx program.

## Mapping the Mouse to the Screen

Handling the mouse is a lot easier than handling the keyboard. Just look at them: compared to the 105 keys on your keyboard, there are only two or three buttons on your mouse (well, maybe more, depending on the make). Thus, you only have to test the input of three keys maximum. However, when using the mouse, you also have to test the coordinate position on the screen.

Unlike a keyboard, which is ever-present, the mouse only exists onscreen at a certain location. By moving the mouse, you move the mouse cursor on your screen (usually designated by an arrow), and you change where your mouse points. This pointer technology allows you to select or choose anything onscreen by moving your mouse to the location and clicking.

In old versions of Blitz, the mouse was hidden on the screen. Fortunately, in BlitzMax, the mouse cursor is visible. This saves us a lot of difficulty in displaying a mouse cursor on the screen. In the old editions of this book, I spent a number of pages explaining how to draw a mouse cursor on the screen. Fortunately, you don't have to be bored with all that information. Here is what you should know about the mouse before we move on.

1. A mouse cursor (that looks like Figure 9.6) is displayed by default.

2. If you want to get rid of the cursor, use the command `HideMouse` with no parameters.

3. To detect the position of the mouse cursor at any given time, use `MouseX()` and `MouseY()`.

Easy eh?

## What Was That? Handling Mouse Key Presses

Like a keyboard, a mouse also has keys that you can click on the screen. You might use the mouse for many actions throughout your games. For example, say you have a side-scroller game, like *Super Mario Brothers*. You might allow the user to move onscreen by clicking with the left mouse button, and allow the player to jump by using the right mouse button.

Figure 9.7 shows an average mouse. Notice that it has a mouse wheel. Many mice have mouse wheels, and we will learn how to use the mouse wheel as well as the other two mouse buttons.

Anyway, on to the functions.

**Figure 9.6**
The mouse cursor.

**Figure 9.7**
A common mouse.

### MouseDown()

BlitzMax offers mouse-input functions that are similar to the keyboard-input functions. The function that we will learn about in this section, MouseDown(), acts just like its keyboard counterpart KeyDown().

MouseDown() has the declaration as follows.

```
MouseDown (button)
```

button is the button that you are checking for: the left mouse button, the right mouse button, or the middle mouse button. Table 9.5 lists all the possibilities for button.

Easy, huh? How can we use MouseDown()? Well, for example, to determine whether the user clicked the left mouse button, you would do something like this.

```
If MouseDown(1)
     'perform actions
 Endif
```

Whatever you want to happen when the left mouse button is clicked is placed between the If and the Endif statements.

MouseDown() returns true (1) if the mouse key was clicked, and false (0) if it was not clicked.

I'm neglecting to write a sample program for MouseDown() right now; instead, I will use it in a sample program with the next function: MouseHit().

### MouseHit()

I bet you can guess the difference between this function and MouseDown(), huh? Whereas you can hold down MouseDown(), you must click the mouse button over and over when using MouseHit() to initiate the action.

**Table 9.5**  MouseDown()'s Button Possibilities

| Button | Key Code |
| --- | --- |
| Left mouse button | 1 |
| Right mouse button | 2 |
| Middle mouse button | 3 |

This difference is the same as KeyDown() versus KeyHit(), the keyboard-input functions. Just like KeyHit(), MouseHit() also records the number of times you click the button.

MouseHit() is declared like this:

MouseHit (button)

button can be any of those listed in Table 9.5.

Anyway, let's rewrite demo09-03.bmx to use mouse input. Instead of using keys to move the player's ship, the ship is located at the coordinates of the mouse. For this program, we do not need a mouse cursor, because the ship serves as a sign of the mouse's position.

Also, the mouse buttons have been changed. Although pressing the left mouse button still creates a bullet, holding down the right mouse button creates a laser. Let's try it.

Most of the program has changed, so I am going to copy the source section by section. It begins with the initialization section of demo09-06.bmx.

```
'demo09-06.bmx - A Space Simulation with MouseDown() and KeyDown()

Graphics 800,600

'Set AutoMidHandle to true
AutoMidHandle True

'TYPES

'Bullet type = hold the information for each bullet
Type TBullet
 Field x,y 'the coordinates of the bullet
 Field bullettype 'LASER or NORMALBULLET (see constants)
End Type



'Player type - holds the actual player
Type TPlayer
 Field x,y 'the coordinates of the player
End Type

'Create player and initialize field
```

```
Global player:TPlayer = New TPlayer
player.x = 400
player.y = 500


'CONSTANTS
'The following constants are used for testing key presses (mouse and keyboard)
Const LEFTMOUSEBUTTON = 1, RIGHTMOUSEBUTTON = 2
'The following constants are used for the bullets, BULLET is a regular bullet,
LASER is a laser
Const NORMALBULLET = 1, LASER = 2



'IMAGES
playerimage = LoadImage("ship.bmp")
Global bulletimage = LoadImage("bullet.bmp")
backgroundimage = LoadImage("stars.bmp")
Global laserimage = LoadImage("laser.bmp")

'change handle for the laser image
SetImageHandle laserimage, ImageWidth(laserimage)/2, ImageHeight(laserimage)


'VARIABLES
'Create a scrolling indicator variable
scrolly = 0

'Number of times left and mouse buttons were hit
Global leftmouseclicks = 0
Global rightmouseclicks = 0

Global bulletlist:TList = CreateList()
```

Okay, let's go through this section. The program begins just like normal, with the setting of the graphics mode, the creation of the back buffer, and setting Auto-MidHandle to true. In the next part, the types have changed a bit.

The TBullet type looked like this in demo09-03.bmx:

```
Type bullet
    Field x,y 'the coordinates of the bullet
  End Type
```

Notice the new field: bullettype. This type defines whether the bullet is a normal bullet or laser. We assign this field at the time of the bullet's creation, depending on whether the player clicks the left mouse button or the right mouse button.

The next major change in the program takes place in the constants section. As you can see, we have deleted all of the key code constants besides Esc. Esc remains because we use it to determine whether the program should exit in the main loop.

In the key codes place, we created a set of new constants. The first two new constants are LEFTMOUSEBUTTON and RIGHTMOUSEBUTTON. These two constants are used in the MouseHit() and MouseDown() tests later in the program—they tell the program which mouse buttons were clicked. The other two constants, NORMALBULLET and LASER, are used in the bullettype field of the bullet type. If bullettype is equal to NORMALBULLET, the bullets are regular run-of-the-mill bullets. If bullettype is LASER, the bullet is a laser.

We loaded a new image, laserimage, which is the image of each laser bullet shot by clicking the right mouse button. Figure 9.8 shows what the laser looks like. It is the straight line down the middle.

The laser is very long because it extends from one end of the screen to the other. Thus, the height of the laser is the height of the screen.

**Figure 9.8**
The laser image.

We then set the handle to the bottom-center of the image with the line

```
SetImageHandle laserimage, ImageWidth(laserimage)/2, ImageHeight(laserimage)
```

This line might be a little difficult to understand, so let's go over it. First off, we need to know what `SetImageHandle` does.

`SetImageHandle` allows you to choose where the handling point of an image is. `AutoMidHandle` automatically assigns the handling point of any image to the direct center. What does the handling point do? Well, when you move the image around, it moves by its handling point. Imagine picking up a playing card. If you pick it up in the exact center, you will notice that the card extends in all directions from your finger. This is what `AutoMidHandle` does. See Figure 9.9 for an example.

As you can see in Figure 9.9, the handling point, which is where your finger is, is directly in the center of the card. The card's points extend in all directions from the center point. When you move your hand around, the card is still grasped from the center, and thus, the edges of the card always extend from 0,0.

When using the laser image, however, we want the image to be grasped from the bottom. We will be making the laser extend from the front of the player's spaceship to the upper wall of the screen, and because it must begin right on the player, we have to set the handle to the bottom edge of the laser. Figure 9.10 shows what it would look like to set the handle to the bottom of the playing card.

`SetImageHandle` allows you to set the handle of the laser image to the coordinates you want. In the line

```
SetImageHandle laserimage, ImageWidth(laserimage)/2, ImageHeight(laserimage)
```

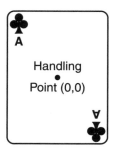

**Figure 9.9**
`AutoMidHandle` on a playing card.

Handling Point (0,0)

**Figure 9.10**
The lower handle on a playing card.

ImageWidth( )/2, ImageHeight( )

**Figure 9.11**
The handle on the laser image.

the handle is set to ImageWidth(laserimage)/2, ImageHeight(laserimage). What does this mean? The x coordinate of the handle is located at ImageWidth (laserimage)/2. This is half of the width of the image, which is in the center of the image. The y coordinate, ImageHeight(laserimage), puts the handle at the bottom of the image. See Figure 9.11 for help.

Okay, hopefully we understand the laser image's handle now. Moving on in the initialization section of the program, we get to two new variables, leftmouse-clicks and rightmouseclicks. These two variables record how many times each of their respective buttons were clicked.

Next up is the main loop. Check it out.

```
'MAIN LOOP
While Not KeyDown(KEY_ESCAPE)

Cls
'Increment scrolling variable
scrolly = scrolly + 1

'Tile the background
TileImage backgroundimage,0,scrolly

'set up text
DrawText "Player X: " + MouseX(),0,0
DrawText "Player Y: " + MouseY(),0,12
DrawText "Number of times left mouse button was hit: " + leftmouseclicks,0,24
DrawText "Number of times right mouse button was hit: " + rightmouseclicks,0,36

'Reset the scrolling variable when it grows too large
If scrolly > ImageHeight(backgroundimage)
     scrolly = 0
EndIf

'Test mouse buttons
TestMouse()

'Update (move) each bullet
UpdateBullets()

'Draw the player
DrawImage playerimage, player.x, player.y


'Slow it down
Delay 20

'Flip the front and back buffers
Flip

Wend 'END OF MAIN LOOP
```

This loop is almost exactly the same as the one in demo09-03.bmx, except for two changes. We added some text to the screen that tells the users their position and how many times they have clicked the left and right mouse buttons. The second change is a change in name: TestKeys() has been changed to TestMouse(), which is the function we examine next.

```
'FUNCTIONS
'Function TestMouse() - Tests what mouse buttons have been pressed and where
player is located
Function TestMouse()

'set the player at the position of the mouse
player.x = MouseX()
player.y = MouseY()

'If the player hits left mouse button, create a bullet
If MouseHit(LEFTMOUSEBUTTON)
 bullet:TBullet = New TBullet      'create bullet
 bullet.x = player.x     'place bullet at player's x coordinate
 bullet.y = player.y     'place bullet at player's y coordinate
 bullet.bullettype = NORMALBULLET      'make it a normal bullet

 ListAddLast bulletlist, bullet
 'increment left mouse clicks
 leftmouseclicks = leftmouseclicks + 1
EndIf

'If the player hits left, we will scroll the background left
If MouseDown(RIGHTMOUSEBUTTON)
 bullet:TBullet = New TBullet      'create bullet
 bullet.x = player.x      'place bullet at player's x coordinate
 bullet.y = player.y      'place bullet at player's y coordinate
 bullet.bullettype = LASER      'make it a laser

 ListAddLast bulletlist, bullet
 'add amount of right mouse clicks since last frame
 rightmouseclicks = rightmouseclicks + MouseHit(RIGHTMOUSEBUTTON)
EndIf
 End Function
```

Whew, big difference, huh? This function had a massive overhaul, because you are no longer using the keyboard. The function begins by assigning the coordinates of the ship to the coordinates of the mouse using the functions MouseX() and MouseY(). If you remember, MouseX() and MouseY() return the coordinates of the mouse at the given time.

After this, we determine whether the player has clicked any mouse buttons. If so, the program creates a bullet. The tests for the left and the right mouse button begin in the same way: a new bullet is created with the coordinates of the player. This creates the bullet directly under the player, giving the illusion that the player's ship actually fired the bullet. The next line marks a difference between the left mouse test and the right mouse test. If the player clicked the left mouse button, the bullet type of the bullet is set to NORMALBULLET, whereas if the player clicked the right mouse button, the bullet type is set to LASER.

The last section of each of the tests increments either the left mouse-click counter or the right mouse-click counter, depending on which button was clicked. You can see that the actions taken to increment the counter are different in each test, and if you need help understanding why, see the accompanying note.

**Note**

Look at the end of each of the mouse input tests for both the left mouse button and the right mouse button: do you notice how each line is different? Both lines increment their respective counters that detail how many times a laser or bullet has been fired, but they do so in a different way. The first test, MouseHit(LEFTMOUSEBUTTON), adds 1 directly to the left mouse-click counter, whereas the second test, MouseDown(RIGHTMOUSEBUTTON) adds the return value of a MouseHit(RIGHTMOUSEBUTTON) to its counter. Why can't we just add 1 to the right mouse-button counter? Well, in the first test, we used MouseHit() to determine whether the left mouse button was clicked. If you remember, MouseHit() always returns 1 when the key (here, the left mouse key) is clicked once. Because we are calling MouseHit(), we know for a fact that the key was clicked once, so we add one to the counter. On the other hand, we use Mouse-Down() for the right mouse button test. MouseDown() returns 1 as long as the button is being held down, not only if the button is being pressed (like MouseHit() does). In other words, a new bullet can be created even though the key was not released and then pressed again—the new bullet is created just because the key is being held down. Because of this fact, we add KeyHit(RIGHTMOUSEBUTTON) to the counter, which will add one if the right key is released and then pressed again, and zero if it is simply held down.

Anyway, we can now move on to the final function: UpdateBullets().

```
'Function UpdateBullets() - Moves each bullet on screen
Function UpdateBullets()
```

```
'For every bullet, move it up 5 pixels. If it goes offscreen, delete it; otherwise,
draw it
```

```
For bullet:TBullet = EachIn bulletlist


    'If bullet moves offscreen, delete it; otherwise, draw it onscreen. Draw
    laserimage if it is a laser, bulletimage if it is a bullet
    If bullet.y < 0
        ListRemove bulletlist, bullet
    ElseIf bullet.bullettype = NORMALBULLET
        bullet.y = bullet.y - 5       'Move bullet up
        DrawImage bulletimage, bullet.x, bullet.y       'Draw the bullet
    ElseIf bullet.bullettype = LASER
        If player.x <> bullet.x
            ListRemove bulletlist, bullet
        Else
            DrawImage laserimage, bullet.x, bullet.y       'Draw the laser
        EndIf
    EndIf

Next      'move to next bullet

  End Function
```

This function begins by moving each bullet upward five pixels. The function then determines whether the bullet is on the screen or if it has moved offscreen. If the bullet's y coordinate is less than 0, the bullet is offscreen. When this happens, the bullet is deleted using the `ListRemove` function. If the bullet wasn't deleted, the function tests to see what type the bullet is, using `bullet.bullettype`. If the bullet is a normal bullet, the program draws the bullet at the proper coordinates. If the bullet is a laser, the program must do a few more tests.

Because the laser follows the player around, and it stretches to the end of the screen, we do not want the player's x coordinate to be any different from the laser's x coordinate. Therefore, we test the player's x against the bullet's x using the Not Equal To operator `<>`. If `player.x` and `bullet.x` are not equal to one another, the laser is deleted. If the player's x and the bullet's x are equal to one another, the laser is drawn on the screen.

That is it for demo09-06.bmx. Figure 9.12 is a screenshot taken from the program.

All right, I hope you understand basic mouse input now. Before we move on to joystick input, I want to go over the middle mouse wheel.

**Figure 9.12**
The demo09-06.bmx program.

## The Middle Mouse Wheel

As you know, many mice have a middle mouse button in addition to the normal right and left mouse buttons. Often, the middle mouse button is a scrolling wheel, which can be used in programs such as Internet Explorer to scroll up and down. BlitzMax provides support for the middle mouse wheel, both in clicking and in scrolling.

You already know how to determine whether the middle mouse button was clicked. To do this, just call MouseDown() or MouseHit() with 3 as its parameter. The difference between the two is the same between KeyDown() and KeyHit(): MouseDown() is true if the button is being held down, whereas MouseHit() only is true if the key was pressed, but not held down. You would write something like this in your program:

```
If MouseHit(3)
     'perform actions
 EndIf
```

Not that difficult, eh? Determining whether the mouse was scrolled is almost as easy.

upwards, MouseZ( ) increases

downwards, MouseZ( ) decreases

**Figure 9.13**
Scrolling a mouse wheel.

Remember at the beginning of the mouse input section, where we used the two functions MouseX( ) and MouseY( )? If you remember, MouseX( ) and MouseY( ) gave the coordinate position of the mouse. BlitzMax provides the function MouseZ( ) that tests the mouse wheel to determine whether it has scrolled.

MouseZ( ) begins at 0 when your program begins. As you scroll the mouse wheel away from you (upward), MouseZ( ) increases. As you scroll the mouse wheel toward you (downward), MouseZ( ) decreases. See Figure 9.13; it might help illustrate what scrolling the mouse "upward" and "downward" means.

Anyway, to test for what MouseZ( ) is, you simply call the function. There are no parameters or anything to look for. So, let's try a sample program, demo09-07.bmx. This program scrolls the background 20 pixels as you scroll the mouse wheel.

```
'demo09-07.bmx - Demonstrates use of MouseZ( )

'Set up graphics and backbuffer
Graphics 800,600

'Load images
backgroundimage = LoadImage("stars.bmp")
shipimage = LoadImage("ship.bmp")

'MAIN LOOP
While Not KeyDown(KEY_ESCAPE)

Cls

'Scroll the background 20 pixels with each mouse wheel scroll
scrolly = MouseZ() * 20
```

```
'Tile the background
TileImage backgroundimage,0,scrolly


'Draw the player
DrawImage shipimage, MouseX(), MouseY()

Flip
Wend
'END OF MAIN LOOP
```

As you can see, the program sets `scrolly` to `MouseZ() * 20`. Multiplying `MouseZ()` by 20 forces the scrolling variable to change by 20 pixels with each change in the mouse wheel. This means that the background will scroll faster and easier. Try changing 20 to a different number and see what happens. If you set 20 to a smaller number, you will notice that the background scrolls much slower, whereas making it larger makes the background scroll faster.

The following figure, Figure 9.14, is a screenshot directly from demo09-07.bmx.

**Figure 9.14**
The demo09-07.bmx program.

Okay, before we move on to the next section, there are a few miscellaneous mouse functions that you should know. Like FlushKeys(), BlitzMax provides the function FlushMouse(). This function clears the computer's memory of keys that have been pressed on the mouse.

WaitMouse() is another function that has a keyboard counterpart, WaitKeys(). This function waits for the player to press a button on the mouse before resuming the program's execution.

Last, BlitzMax provides the function MoveMouse(). This function has the declaration

```
MoveMouse x,y
```

This function moves the mouse to the coordinates you feed it. Therefore, if you type MoveMouse(0,0), the mouse moves to the top-left corner of the screen.

All right, that is it for mouse input!

## Summary

Whew, that was a long chapter. Hopefully, you now understand the basis of input. Mouse, keyboard, and joystick input are used in all games, and it is of the utmost importance that you have a firm grasp of these concepts. This chapter covered the following concepts:

- Receiving keyboard input with KeyDown() and KeyHit()

- Displaying a mouse cursor

- Handling mouse key presses with MouseDown() and MouseHit()

- Using the middle mouse wheel

Even though BlitzMax provides you with a large number of functions (I didn't even go over them all), only a few are absolutely necessary. You will almost definitely be using either KeyDown() or MouseDown() in your programs. Other functions, such as FlushKeys(), only occasionally.

Anyway, get ready for the next lesson. We are moving on to something really fun: sound. You will learn how to use sound in your games to give the effect of action!

# CHAPTER 10

# Sounds and Music

If you've played any games lately, you know the difference that sound can make. Sound not only makes you feel like you are part of the game, but it can also provide clues about what's around the corner. Many newer games even support *multi-channel sound*, which allows you to hear sound in more than one direction. In multi-channel sound, you have more than two speakers (many systems have as many as five, and sometimes even more located around the player). All of these speakers, or channels, can play different sounds at the same time. You can hear someone approaching from behind you (from the speakers that are located to your back), yet when you turn around to face him, the footsteps are emitted from your front speakers!

BlitzMax provides a lot of support for both sound and music, and this chapter teaches you how to use both. First up, sound!

## Sound

In the introduction, I said that we will learn about both sound and music in this chapter, and you might be thinking that they are the same. Nope! BlitzMax refers to sounds and music as two different entities. Unlike music, sound is played dynamically. What does this mean? The game does not play sound files over and over. Instead, the sound is only played at specific times. Take, for example, a gun. You don't want a gunshot to ring over and over; you want it to make a sound only when the gun actually shoots.

For this book, we will be using the .WAV file format for the sound files. What is the .WAV file format, you might ask? It is a file format that represents a sound on the computer. This sound format does not have any quality loss like some other file formats (which we will discuss later), so the sound from a .WAV file is "cleaner." I have included a number of royalty-free sound files on the CD, most in .WAV format, that you can use in your programs.

Anyway, let's get started. First off, we need to know how to load sounds.

## Loading Sounds

Remember images? It was extremely easy to load them, right? We just used the LoadImage() function. Well, BlitzMax makes loading sounds just as easy: we use the LoadSound() function. LoadSound() is declared as follows:

LoadSound (filename:String)

Table 10.1 describes the parameter for LoadSound().

You load sounds just like you load images.

*soundfile* = LoadSound ("*soundfile.wav*")

Change *soundfile* and *soundfile.wav* to the name of the variable and file of the sound you want to load into your program.

**Note**

From this point on, I use a certain style for my sound files. Whenever I load them, I call the variable that holds the file, xxxxxsound.wav, where xxxxx describes the sound. For example, to load the sound of a laser, I would call the sound lasersound, and I would load it as follows: lasersound = LoadSound (laser.wav).

By the way, there is something else you might want to know. The name of the variable that contains the sound (in the previous example, soundfile) is called a *handle*. Why is it called a handle? Well, basically, you use the handle variable as an address or reference to the object. So a "handle" helps you refer to something—in this case a sound file. When you want to manipulate a sound file, you need a handle to access it; it's like a key to a lock.

**Table 10.1** LoadSound()'s Parameters

| Parameter | Description |
|---|---|
| filename:String | The filename of the sound file you want to load. |

All right, I hope you understand this. Let's move on to the next section, which teaches you how to actually play the sounds.

## Listen Closely—Playing Sounds

You've gotten this far into the chapter, and you probably want to learn how to actually listen to those beautiful sounds that you just learned to load. BlitzMax provides us with an easy way to play sounds.

This command is called `PlaySound`. (Predictable, huh?) It is declared as follows.

```
PlaySound sound_variable, [channel]
```

Take a wild guess what `sound_variable` is. Yep, you got it: `sound_variable` is the handle of the sound file you loaded using `LoadSound()`. In other words, you can load a sound clip like this:

```
explosionsound = LoadSound("explosion.wav")
```

Then you play it like this:

```
PlaySound explosionsound
```

Crazy difficult, huh? Anyway, Table 10.2 summarizes `PlaySound`'s parameters.

Okay, let's use this function in a sample program. Let's begin with a scrolling background. (Why? Because it is easy and always fun to do.) Then we can add the nice-looking spaceship we use way too often. Then, and listen closely because this is the fun part, we allow the player to fire a bullet using the spacebar. The firing of a bullet creates a bullet-firing sound.

Let's also add an enemy spaceship to the mix. This enemy is like me: he moves in a random fashion, is never predictable, and has no self-defense capabilities whatsoever. Anyway, when the bullet hits this crazy mini-me, an explosion sound is played, and the enemy is destroyed. His ship is then reset.

**Table 10.2**  PlaySound()'s Parameters

| Parameter | Description |
| --- | --- |
| sound_variable | The handle to the sound file (loaded with LoadSound()) you want to play. |
| [channel] | The channel you want to play the sound through, a new one is created by default. |

**Table 10.3**  demo10-01.bmx's Keys

| Key | Action |
| --- | --- |
| Esc | Exits the game |
| Up arrow | Moves ship up |
| Down arrow | Moves ship down |
| Right arrow | Moves ship right |
| Left arrow | Moves ship left |
| Spacebar | Fires bullet |

Hey, I wanted to make this program a little weird, so I used a picture of myself for the enemy ship. Well, just watch.

Anyway, Table 10.3 explains the keys for the program.

I was going to show the entire source for the program, but I realized it takes up about five pages. I am in the mood to save some trees, so I will just display the important parts. The first code block I will show you is taken from the initialization section of demo10-01.bmx.

```
'SOUNDS
'Load the sound that is played when the player fires a bullet
Global bulletsound = LoadSound("zing.wav")

'Load the sound that is played when the player destroys the enemy
Global explosionsound = LoadSound ("explode.wav")
```

I bet you can guess what this does! This code loads both of the sounds that are used in the program.

Let's move on to using those loaded sounds. The following source is the UpdateBullets() function.

```
'Function UpdateBullets() - Moves and tests each bullet for collision
Function UpdateBullets()

'Loop through every bullet
For bullets:TBullet = EachIn bulletlist

        'Update the bullet's position by moving 5 pixels up
        bullets.y = bullets.y - 5


'Draw the bullet at its proper coordinates
        DrawImage bullets.image, bullets.x, bullets.y
```

```
'If the bullet hit the enemy, play the explosion and reset the level

        If ImagesCollide(enemy.image,enemy.x,enemy.y,0,bullets.image,
bullets.x,bullets.y,0)
                PlaySound explosionsound 'Play the explosion
                Cls
                DrawText "You destroyed the enemy! How could you?",260,300
                Flip
                Delay 4000
                ResetLevel() 'Reset all variables of the level
                Return 'Go back to main loop
        EndIf

'If the bullet goes off screen, delete it
        If bullets.y < 0
                ListRemove bulletlist, bullets
        EndIf


Next 'Move on to next bullet
End Function
```

As you probably guessed, this function updates all of the bullets onscreen. It begins by moving each bullet up five pixels, and it then draws the bullet. The bullet then tests for a collision.

The collision test uses the function ImagesCollide(). As you might remember, ImagesCollide() tests two images, here enemy.x and bullets.x, to see whether they have overlapped one another. If they have, the explosion sound is played using the command PlaySound.

```
PlaySound explosionsound 'Play the explosion
```

The rest of the function clears the screen and displays some text. It then resets the level, and, using the Return command, returns back to the main loop.

### Caution

You might be wondering why I used the Return command to go back to the main loop instead of just letting the function finish going through its instructions. Here is the reason why: Within the function ResetLevel() (which is called directly before the Return command), all of the bullets are deleted. This includes the bullet that was just being processed. Because the bullet no longer exists, how could we perform the actions of the next line, which tests to see whether the bullet has gone offscreen? There is no way, so in order to fix this situation, we just return back to the main loop and start from scratch.

The last part of the function just tests to see whether the bullet is offscreen. If it is, the bullet is deleted.

The PlaySound function is used once more in the program. The following block is ripped from the TestKeys() function.

```
'Create a new bullet if spacebar is hit
If KeyHit(KEY_SPACE)
        bullets:TBullet = New TBullet      'Create the bullet
        bullets.x = player.x    'Assign bullet to player's x
        bullets.y = player.y    'Assign bullet to player's y
        bullets.image = LoadImage("bullet.bmp")    'Load the bullet image

        'Play the bullet sound
        PlaySound bulletsound
EndIf
```

What does this do? Well, it begins by testing to see whether the player has pressed the spacebar. If he has, the program then creates a new bullet. The program then assigns the bullet's starting coordinates to the player's starting coordinates. The bullet's image is then loaded.

The block ends by playing bulletsound. This sound is created every time a new bullet is created.

That's it for this crazy program. Figure 10.1 shows the program in its full glory. That's me with a crazy face.

Okay, so we now know how to play a sound. We're not done yet, folks! BlitzMax provides some really cool tools that make sounds a lot more fun to use.

### What's the Difference Between a Sound and a Channel?

You might get confused by how I refer to sounds and channels in this section. Actually, sounds and channels are very related, so it's good to understand both. Essentially, a sound is just a sound, a gunshot or a laser zing, or whatever. A channel is what the sound is played through on your computer. Think of the sound as a CD, and the channel as the CD player—you need the channel to read and project the sound.

When you use PlaySound(), BlitzMax automatically creates a channel to play the sound. However, if you want to edit the sound channel, by adjusting volume or pan, you need to create a channel and adjust the channel's volume, not the sound's volume. You can create a channel by using AllocChannel().

**Figure 10.1**
The demo10-01.bmx program. Could you ever shoot someone with so cute a face?

### SetChannelVolume

I bet you can guess what SetChannelVolume does. Simply put, changing the volume of a sound adjusts how loud or quiet the sound is.

Here is the declaration:

```
SetChannelVolume channel, volume:Float
```

channel is the handle to the channel that you want to change the volume of. How do you get a channel? Use AllocChannel().

```
Channel:TChannel = AllocChannel()
```

Volume is a floating-point variable between 0 and 1.000. The closer to 1 volume# is, the louder the sound is. Table 10.4 summarizes the parameters.

Cool? Let's make a program. demo10-02.bmx draws a randomly moving spaceship, and plays a laser sound every time you press the spacebar. The farther away the enemy ship is from your ship, the quieter the sound. If the ship is really close, the sound is played loudly.

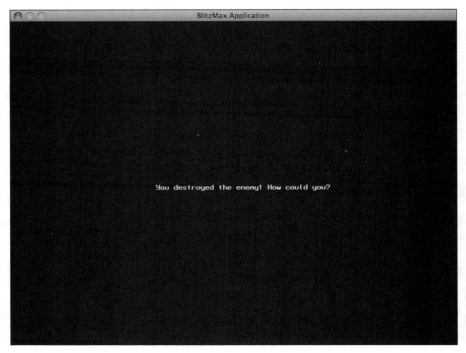

**Figure 10.2**
How could you do that!

| Table 10.4   SetChannelVolume()'s Parameters | |
| --- | --- |
| **Parameter** | **Description** |
| channel | The handle to the sound file you want to work with. |
| Volume:Float | The volume you want to set channel to. Can be between 0 and 1.000. |

This program is a long one, so I am just going to show two parts of it. The first is ripped from the user-defined function FindCorrectVolume().

```
'Function FindCorrectVolume - Sets volume# to the correct value depending on
distance from player to enemy
Function FindCorrectVolume()

'Find distance between player and enemy
dist = Distance(player_var.x,player_var.y,enemy_var.x,enemy_var.y)

'Assign the volume number to volume# depending on how far the distance is. The
farther the distance, the quieter the sound
```

```
If dist < 100
  volume# = 1.000
ElseIf dist < 200
  volume# = .700
ElseIf dist < 300
  volume# = .400
ElseIf dist < 400
  volume# = .1000
Else
  volume# = 0.000
EndIf

  End Function
```

The first thing this function does is find the distance between the enemy and the player using the `Distance()` function we wrote in Chapter 8, "Collision Detection." (I copied the source from the `Distance()` function into this program.) It then assigns `volume` to a number depending on how high `dist` is. If `dist` is higher, the spaceship is farther away; therefore, the sound should be quieter. The block of `If...ElseIf...Else` statements determines how loud the volume should be.

This next part loads the sound and channel.

```
'SOUNDS
'The following sound is produced each time the player hits spacebar
Global bulletsound = LoadSound("zing.wav")
Global bulletchannel:TChannel = AllocChannel()
'Create a volume tracker variable and set it to half volume (.5)
Global volume:Float = .5

'Synchronize the sound with the volume
SetChannelVolume bulletchannel, volume
```

Notice how we create a channel and a sound. We then assign the volume to the channel, not the sound.

The next and last part of demo10-02.bmx actually uses the `SetChannelVolume` function.

```
'Create a new bullet if spacebar is hit
If KeyHit(KEY_SPACE)
```

```
'Find what volume# should be
FindCorrectVolume()

'Assign bulletsound to volume#
SetChannelVolume bulletchannel, volume

'Play the bullet
PlaySound bulletsound,bulletchannel
EndIf
```

This code is executed when you press the spacebar. It calls `FindCorrectVolume()`, which assigns `volume#` to its correct value. The code then adjusts the volume of `bulletsound` depending on the `volume#` variable. The block finally plays the sound clip of the bullet.

Figure 10.3 is a screenshot taken from demo10-02.bmx.

All right, that's it for `SetChannelVolume`. We only have one more function to learn about before we move on to playing music!

**Figure 10.3**
The demo10-02.bmx program.

**Table 10.5**  SetChannelPan()'s Parameters

| Parameter | Description |
|---|---|
| `channel_variable` | The handle to the sound you want to pan. |
| `pan:Float` | The amount between −1.000 and 1.000 you want to pan the sound. |

### SetChannelPan

`SetChannelPan` offers a very cool effect: it allows you to create the illusion of moving sound by letting you pick which speaker the sound plays out of. You can have the program play sound out of the left speaker, the right speaker, or both. This allows you to make the players feel like the sounds are actually moving around them.

`SetChannelPan` is declared like this:

```
SetChannelPan channel_variable, pan:Float
```

Now this is the cool part: because `pan` is a floating-point variable, you can have the sound panned a little to the left but still playing slightly on the right. What do I mean? Well, if you set `pan` to −0.75, the sound would play 75% out of the left speaker and 25% out of the right speaker.

`channel_variable`, as you probably know, is the handle to the channel you want to edit. `Pan` contains the amount you want to pan the sound. `Pan` can be between −1.000 and 1.000—if the number is negative, it will play predominantly out of the left speaker, and if it is positive, it will play mostly out of the right speaker.

Table 10.5 summarizes the `SetChannelPan` parameters.

Cool? Let's write a program. This thing is going to be easy: an enemy ship moves left and right. When the player presses the spacebar, the sound is played. If the enemy is to the left of the player, the sound is played completely out of the left speaker. If the enemy is to the right of the player, the sound is played out of the right speaker. If the enemy is directly in front of the player, the sound is played out of both speakers. The following is the main loop that is taken from demo10-03.bmx.

```
'MAIN LOOP
While Not KeyDown(KEY_ESCAPE)
```

```
'Tile the background
Cls
TileImage backgroundimage, 0, scrolly
'increment the scrolling variable
scrolly = scrolly + 1

If scrolly > ImageHeight(backgroundimage)
 scrolly = 0
EndIf

'Print all text at top-left corner
DrawText "Panning variable: " + pan,0,0

'set up player coordinates
player.x = MouseX()
player.y = MouseY()




'if enemy is to the left of player, make sound come out of left speaker
If enemy.x < player.x
 pan = -1.000
 'If enemy is to right of player, make sound come out of right speaker
ElseIf enemy.x > player.x
 pan = 1.000
 'If enemy is in front of player
Else
 pan = 0
EndIf

'Pan the sound
SetChannelPan bulletchannel, pan


'If player presses spacebar, play the sound
If KeyHit (KEY_SPACE)


 PlaySound bulletsound, bulletchannel
EndIf

'Move the enemy according to his velocity
```

```
enemy.x = enemy.x + enemy.xv

'If the enemy goes offscreen, reflect his velocity
If enemy.x < 0 Or enemy.x > 800
 enemy.xv = - enemy.xv
EndIf

'Draw the player and the enemy
DrawImage player.image,player.x,player.y
DrawImage enemy.image,enemy.x,enemy.y

'Slow it down a little
Delay 20

Flip


Wend
```

Not that bad, eh? The main part is finding what the pan variable should be. pan is used as a parameter for SetChannelPan, and it determines how far to the left or right the sound should pan. To find what pan should be, we use the following code block.

```
'if enemy is to the left of player, make sound come out of left speaker
If enemy.x < player.x
 pan = -1.000
 'If enemy is to right of player, make sound come out of right speaker
ElseIf enemy.x > player.x
 pan = 1.000
 'If enemy is in front of player
Else
 pan = 0
 EndIf
```

This code sets pan to −1 (left speaker) if the enemy is to the left of the player, 1 if the player is to the right, and 0 if he is directly in front of the player. The last part of the main loop I want to show you actually uses the SetChannelPan function.

```
'Pan the sound
SetChannelPan bulletsound, pan'
```

Pretty cool, huh? This function synchronizes the bullet sound with the pan' variable.

**Figure 10.4**
The demo10-03.bmx program.

Figure 10.4 is a screenshot taken from the program.

Whew! That's it for sounds! Now we get to move on to using music in our games.

## Music

You've gotten this far, but you might not quite understand the difference between music and sound, at least on a computer. Here's the thing; you have used sound so far to produce gunfire and explosion sounds. You can see that these sounds are played only at the time of the actual explosion or at the time when the bullet is actually fired. Music, however, is played in the background while your game is running. Therefore, it is much easier to use, because you can rig it up to play at the beginning of the game, and not worry about the music from then on.

For the music examples in this book, I use the .OGG format. BlitzMax doesn't allow MP3s, I think for legal reasons, so .OGG is a good alternative. There's a lot of information out there if you want to learn about the other formats. Special thanks to Thomas Stenbäck and everyone else at Interim Nation for letting me use their music on the CD. You can visit Interim Nation, the composers for the music on the CD, at http://www.interimnation.com.

To begin understanding music in BlitzMax, we first need to discuss *channels*.

## Channels and Music

What is a channel? We talked about it a little, let's do it again. Well, imagine you have a sibling who is talking to you. At that point, the only thing you can hear is your sibling. Now, imagine that a phone located near you begins to ring. Suddenly, you can hear two things at once, right? Well, at this moment, there are two channels playing: the sibling channel and the telephone-ringing channel.

Now, the cool thing about channels is that you can edit each channel independently. What does this mean? Well, for instance, say your sibling, who is currently on the sibling channel, begins to whisper to you. The volume of this voice has decreased. Using channels, you can change the volume of one channel while leaving another the same. If you take a look at Figure 10.5, you can see an example of how channels might work. There are two boxes, both emitting sounds. One is on the right and one is on the left; thus, using the magic of channels, the one on the left is panned far to the left and the one on the right is panned to the right.

All we need now is to learn how to get control of a channel. Unlike handles, which you retrieve by loading sounds, you must *play* a sound in order get access to a channel.

The most common way to get a channel is to use the function `PlaySound()`, as you know.

Say you wanted to load a techno song named technosong.mp3. This is what you would do:

**Figure 10.5**
Channels and panning.

```
technosong = LoadSound("technosong.mp3")
musicchannel = PlaySound("technosong.mp3")
```

As you can see, the function uses the `PlaySound()` function and assigns the song to a channel variable. This variable can be used later for sound editing. `PlaySound`, by default, returns a channel variable.

Notice that this line of code actually plays the music. That means that at the time of using this line of code, technosong.mp3 will begin to play. If you want to load the sound before using the sound file in the program, use the `LoadSound()` function, and then play the sound on a specific channel. Okay, now that we know how to load a music file, let's find out what we can do with those channels.

## Messing with 'Da Channels

The last section taught you how to play music files and load channels, and this section teaches you how to use them. Following is a list of all the functions and their declarations that can be used with channels.

- `StopChannel channel_handle`

- `PauseChannel channel_handle`

- `ResumeChannel channel_handle`

You know some other ones already: `SetChannelVolume` and `SetChannelPan`. Most of these don't even require parameters beyond the obligatory channel variable, and those that do aren't tough. Anyway, let me help you understand what these functions do.

These functions (`Stop`, `Pause`, and `ResumeChannel`) work much like the Stop, Pause, and Resume buttons on a CD player. The `StopChannel` function stops a song immediately. The song is shut down and can only be restarted from the beginning. `PauseChannel` and `ResumeChannel`, however, allow you to pause and begin playing a music file anywhere within the song. `PauseChannel` pauses the song and `ResumeChannel` picks up the song from the same point that was left off.

You can use these functions in numerous situations. Say you have a game with a monster alien at the end. The music plays in the background, and when you get to the monster, you want the music to stop playing while the monster says or does something. What you do is call `PauseChannel` right when the monster appears onscreen, and after he finishes his speech or video or whatever, you call `ResumeChannel` to begin the music right from the starting point.

**Table 10.6**  Stop/Pause/Resume Channel's Parameters

| Parameter | Description |
| --- | --- |
| `channel_handle` | The channel you want to stop/pause/resume. |

**Table 10.7**  demo10-04.bmx's Keys

| Key | Action |
| --- | --- |
| Left Arrow | Pans music to left by −.1 |
| Right Arrow | Pans music to right by .1 |
| 'A' key | Increases volume by .1 |
| 'Z' key | Decreases volume by .1 |
| 'P' key | Pauses sound |
| 'R' key | Resumes sound |
| 'S' key | Stops sound |

Anyway, Table 10.6 explains the parameters in the `StopChannel`, `PauseChannel`, and `ResumeChannel` functions.

All right, cool. Next up is the second group, which consists of the functions `ChannelVolume`, `ChannelPan`, and `ChannelPitch`.

Okay, I included a program, demo10-04.bmx, that allows you to play with a music file. You can change its volume, pan it, and change its pitch. You can also pause, stop, and resume the song. Table 10.7 details all of the keys for demo10-04.bmx.

The source for demo10-04.bmx is very long, so it's not included in the book. Feel free to check it out on the CD. By the way, listen to the song included in the demo—it's very cool.

Figure 10.6 is a screenshot from demo10-04.bmx.

There is another channel that you might want to know a bit more about. The function, `ChannelPlaying()`, tests to see whether a channel is currently playing. If the music file is playing, `ChannelPlaying()` will return 1; if it is not playing, `ChannelPlaying()` returns 0.

**Figure 10.6**
The demo10-04.bmx program.

## Summary

BlitzMax really makes it easy to use sound and music within games, and sound and music really make a difference in a game. They provide a nice tone and setting for the game. Using background music, you can give the player the feeling of a frenetic action mission or a slow searching mission.

To review, the main topics that we covered are:

- Loading sounds

- Playing sounds

- Editing channels

By the way, there are a lot of sounds and music files on the CD. Thomas Stenbäck provided all the music files, and they sound great.

In the next chapter, we are going to cover artificial intelligence. You will learn how to make computers think and act—well sorta!

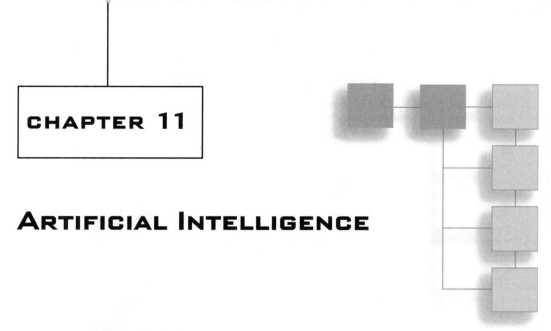

# CHAPTER 11

# ARTIFICIAL INTELLIGENCE

As we near the end of this book, we get more to the heart of computer game programming. Unlike any other program that you will find on computers, games need to be able to actually make the computer think! Well, maybe not think, but at least appear as if it were thinking :). In games that have enemies that are not human-controlled, the computer has to take over and play against the player. This chapter provides you with the tools to make any enemy appear to act as a human would.

The art of artificial intelligence can be extremely complicated and tough to follow; therefore, this chapter is a very quick primer to some easier parts of artificial intelligence. There are many more interesting topics above and beyond what I'll teach you, and if you want to learn about some of them, I suggest you seek out other books on the topic.

I'm sure you're itchin' to get started, so I'm going to conclude the introduction right now. I mean, now. Seriously, the intro is over. I'm not joking.

## Random Numbers

The first part of artificial intelligence we're going to learn is how to use random variables in programs. Using random variables in programs isn't really intelligent, but it's a first step, right?

**Random Variables: Really Random?**

Here is an interesting bit of information about random numbers in computers: finding a true random number is almost impossible. Computers only take input, process it, and produce output—they are not built to produce random numbers, for the most part. Therefore, computers can only produce pseudo-random numbers. What is a pseudo-random number? It is a number that, even though it might appear to be random, isn't truly random. For example, if you print out ten million random numbers, you shouldn't be able to detect any patterns, and there should be an equal distribution between the numbers. However, if you try this on a computer, you will see patterns and you will see slight unevenness in the numbers. For the purposes here, though, the pseudo-random numbers are close enough to random!

In order to generate random numbers, we need to call two functions. The first one we call is named `SeedRnd`.

`SeedRnd` is declared like this:

```
SeedRnd seed
```

What is a seed? Well, `SeedRnd` works like this: it feeds the computer a number that will be used later to create pseudo-random numbers. We need to make `seed` equal to a number that changes every time the game is played; otherwise, the "random" numbers will always be the same every time the game is played.

The function `MilliSecs()` is a function that changes every time the program runs. This function returns the number of milliseconds in the system timer (since the computer last started up). Because the time on the system timer changes continuously, `MilliSecs()` is a good choice for a value to feed `SeedRnd`.

At the beginning of a program that uses random variables, we call `SeedRnd` as follows:

```
SeedRnd MilliSecs()
```

Pretty cool, huh? After doing that, we can continue to use random numbers. Note that `SeedRnd` doesn't actually perform any noticeable functions in a program; it simply sets up the program to use random variables later in the program.

Now that we have set up the random generator (by calling `SeedRnd`), we are able to actually find those random numbers. There are two functions that are provided by BlitzMax. These functions are `Rnd` and `Rand`.

Both of these functions have similar declarations.

```
Rand ([start], end)
Rnd (start:Float, end:Float)
```

As you can see, they are almost the same. First of all, let me help you understand what those parameters are.

The parameter names for both `Rand()` and `Rnd()` are the same. The `start` parameter is the smallest possible value for the random number, and `end` is the largest possible value for the random number. That was probably a little hard to comprehend, so let me explain it better. When using one of the random functions, you will usually feed it two parameters. For example, you might do something like this:

```
randomvalue = Rand (100,200)
```

Because you handed `Rand()` the parameters 100 and 200, `randomvalue` will now contain a number between 100 and 200. You can change the parameters slightly to see what I mean. If you changed the 100 to 50 in the previous call, `randomvalue` would contain a number between 50 and 200.

Also, one other thing. You might have noticed that the [start] parameter in `Rand()` is optional (as signified by the brackets). Because it is optional, you are only required to provide `Rand` with one parameter. If you neglect to include [start], BlitzMax will assume that you want the [start] parameter to equal to 1. Therefore, calling `Rand()` as follows

```
Rand (205)
```

returns a random number between 1 and 205.

Both `Rand()` and `Rnd()` have the same parameters, except `Rand()`'s are integers and `Rnd()`'s are floating points. Remember, an integer is a number without a decimal point (for example, 314), whereas a floating-point variable has a decimal attached (for example, 314.13, where ".13" is the decimal).

The fact that `Rnd()` allows you to provide it with floating-point parameters means that you can make your random variables contain numbers with decimal points. If you call `Rnd()` like this:

```
Rnd (1.000,14.000)
```

the function will return a number between 1.000 and 14.000. It could end up being a number such as 3.133 or something like that.

If you decided to call `Rand()` in the same way, the number would end up being only an integer, such as 4 or 9. Take a look at Figure 11.1 to see what happens when you call the `Rand()` function with floating parameters. As you can see, even

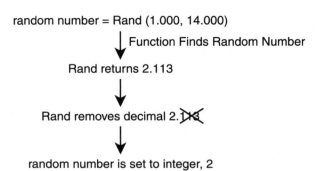

**Figure 11.1**
Using `Rand()` with floating-point parameters.

if you provide `Rand()` with floating-point numbers as parameters, it will still return an integer. It does this by finding the random number and deleting the decimal point.

All right, excellent. Hopefully you understand how to determine random numbers. Now, let's put this into a program.

Following is the source to demo11-01.bmx.

```
'demo11-01.bmx - Demonstrates random variables
Graphics 800,600

'Set up AutoMidHandle
AutoMidHandle True

'Make sure we seed the random generator
SeedRnd MilliSecs()

'Now we load the image that we will use.
flyimage = LoadAnimImage ("fly.bmp",64,64,0,4)
'create a starting frame value
frame = 0

'create the x and y values for the fly
flyx = 400
flyy = 300

'MAIN LOOP
While Not KeyDown (KEY_ESCAPE)
```

```
'Clear the screen
Cls

DrawText "Fly X: " + flyx,0,0
DrawText "Fly Y: " + flyy,0,12

'move the fly a random amount
flyx = flyx + Rand(-15,15)
flyy = flyy + Rand(-15,15)

'Draw the fly on screen
DrawImage flyimage,flyx,flyy,frame

'increment the frame
frame = frame + 1

'If frame gets too large or small, reset it
If frame > 3
 frame = 0
ElseIf frame < 0
 frame = 3
EndIf

'Flip the buffers
Flip

'Wait a little bit
Delay 25

Wend
 'END OF MAIN LOOP
```

Figure 11.2 is a screenshot taken from demo11-01.bmx.

All right, the program is nice and all, but it's not smooth, is it? The fly is extremely jerky and looks terrible when drawn on the screen. The reason for this is that the fly's x and y variables are updated every single frame, which means his position changes drastically more than 30 times a second (because usually about 30 frames per second occur during games such as these).

Let's redo this program, but instead of changing the fly's coordinates 30 times every second, we will do it only once every few seconds. How are we going to do this? Well, first of all, we need to learn the art of making a timer using the MilliSecs() function.

**Figure 11.2**
The demo11-01.bmx program.

## Creating a MilliSecs() Timer

You have probably noticed the frequent use of MilliSecs()—we use it to seed our random generator with the SeedRnd command. If you remember, the reason we use milliseconds to seed the random generator is because MilliSecs() is never the same twice. So, if it is never the same twice, how can we use this to create a timer?

MilliSecs()'s value increases every millisecond that the computer is running. For example, if MilliSecs() is equal to 100123 right now, in exactly one millisecond, it will be equal to 100124. A millisecond is equal to one one-thousandth of a second (in other words, there are 1000 milliseconds in a second), so 101123 occurs exactly one second later than 100123. Now, we need to use MilliSecs() to create a timer. Even though MilliSecs() will never be called at the exact same time, this isn't a big problem. What we are going to do is create a variable that holds MilliSecs() at the starting time. We then check MilliSecs() every frame until its value is equal to or greater than the starting variable we created at the beginning plus the amount of time we want the timer to last.

So, let's put a timer into code. The following snippet shows how a three-second timer would work.

```
'Create timerbegin which holds the value of the starting timer
timerbegin = MilliSecs()

'We would begin the main loop here

'test if the current number of MilliSecs() is equal to the timerbegin + 3 secs
If MilliSecs() >= timerbegin + 3000
        'Do Something
 EndIf
```

### Caution

If you happened to cut and paste this code into a program, it would not work correctly. The timer would never run out! The reason is that the timer would reset every frame because of the `timerbegin = MilliSecs()` line, and the `If MilliSecs() >= timerbegin + 3000` would never stray more than a few milliseconds from `timerbegin`. In order for the program to work, we need to separate the initialization of the timer and the timer test. If you need to use the timer only once, you can just place the initialization at the beginning of the program and insert the test in the main loop.

Let's go through this line by line. First of all, we created the timer.

```
'Create timerbegin which holds the value of the starting timer
timerbegin = MilliSecs()
```

This creates a timer with a value equal to the amount of `MilliSecs()` at the time of the creation of the timer.

Next, we need to test the timer to determine whether it has been in existence long enough.

```
'test if the current number of MilliSecs() is equal to the timerbegin + 3 secs
If MilliSecs() >= timerbegin + 3000
```

How does this work? Well, the function tests the current value of `MilliSecs()` against `timerbegin` plus three seconds (3000 milliseconds). If you remember, `timerbegin` is equal to the value of `MilliSecs()` at the time of creation of the timer. Because `MilliSecs()` increases every millisecond that the computer is running, the test will return true three seconds after the timer was created.

Pretty sweet, if I do say so myself. The following is the full source to demo 11-02.bmx.

```
'demo11-02.bmx - Demonstrates random variables
Graphics 800,600

'Set up AutoMidHandle
AutoMidHandle True

'Make sure we seed the random generator
SeedRnd MilliSecs()


'CONSTANT
'this constant regulates how long it takes before the fly changes directions
Const CHANGEDIRECTIONS = 1500       'the fly changes every 1.5 seconds

'The fly type
Type TFly
  Field x,y     'the coordinate position
  Field xv,yv    'the fly's velocity
  Field image    'The fly's image
End Type

'let's create the fly
fly:TFly = New TFly

'Start the fly in the center of the screen
fly.x = 400
fly.y = 300

'Give the fly a random velocity
fly.xv = Rand(-15,15)
fly.yv = Rand(-15,15)

'Now we load the fly image
fly.image = LoadAnimImage ("fly.bmp",64,64,0,4)

'create a starting frame value
frame = 0

'Create starting timer
timerbegin = MilliSecs()

'Create a variable that says the timer does not need to be reset
timeractive = 1
```

```
'MAIN LOOP
While Not KeyDown (KEY_ESCAPE)

'Clear the screen
Cls

DrawText "Fly X: " + flyx,0,0
DrawText "Fly Y: " + flyy,0,20
DrawText "Current time remaining on timer: " + ( CHANGEDIRECTIONS - MilliSecs() +
timerbegin ),0,40


'If the counter has run through, update the fly's velocities
If MilliSecs() >= timerbegin + CHANGEDIRECTIONS

  'move the fly a random amount
  fly.xv = fly.xv + Rand(-10,10)
  fly.yv = fly.yv + Rand(-10,10)

  'make sure timer is reset
  timeractive = 0
EndIf

'If the timer is inactive, reset the timer
If timeractive = 0
  timerbegin = MilliSecs()
  timeractive = 1
EndIf



'Move the fly
fly.x = fly.x + fly.xv
fly.y = fly.y + fly.yv

'Test if fly hit any walls
If fly.x <= 0 Or fly.x > 800
  fly.xv = -fly.xv
EndIf

If fly.y <= 0 Or fly.y >= 600
  fly.yv = - fly.yv
EndIf
```

```
'Draw the fly on screen
DrawImage fly.image,fly.x,fly.y,frame

'increment the frame
frame = frame + 1

'If frame gets too large or small, reset it
If frame > 3
  frame = 0
ElseIf frame < 0
  frame = 3
EndIf

'Flip the buffers
Flip

'Wait a little bit
Delay 75

Wend      'END OF MAIN LOOP
```

I only made a few small changes from the demo11-01.bmx program, which I will address now.

First of all, I created a constant that determines how long the pause is between the changes in speed and direction for the ship. This constant is named CHANGEDIRECTIONS.

The next part of the program that I changed was the fly itself. I created a type around the fly and set up its starting variables. Following is the code from the source that creates and initializes the fly.

```
'The fly type
Type TFly
  Field x,y     'the coordinate position
  Field xv,yv    'the fly's velocity
  Field image    'The fly's image
End Type


'let's create the fly
fly:TFly = New TFly

'Start the fly in the center of the screen
fly.x = 400
fly.y = 300
```

```
'Give the fly a random velocity
fly.xv = Rand(-15,15)
fly.yv = Rand(-15,15)

'Now we load the fly image
 fly.image = LoadAnimImage ("fly.bmp",64,64,0,4)
```

As you can see, the TFly type makes it a lot easier to identify all the variables that pertain to the fly. We start the fly in the center of the map, give him random coordinates, and load his image in the previous section.

The next thing I changed was directly before the main loop. I added a section that creates the timer.

```
;Create starting timer
timerbegin = MilliSecs()

;Create a variable that says the timer does not need to be reset
 timeractive = 1
```

You already know what timerbegin does, but you might be wondering what timeractive is there for. timeractive is equal to 1 when the timer is working correctly, but when the timer completes, timeractive is set to 0. The timer then resets, and timeractive is set to 1 again.

Next we move on to the main loop. We go through the usual process of clearing the background and drawing out the pertinent info on the screen. In this program, the x and y coordinates, as well as the time remaining on the timer, are written on the screen.

The following If...EndIf statement does the grunt work for the timer.

```
'If the counter has run through, update the fly's velocities
If MilliSecs() >= timerbegin + CHANGEDIRECTIONS

        ;move the fly a random amount
        fly.xv = fly.xv + Rand(-5,5)
        fly.yv = fly.yv + Rand(-5,5)

        ;make sure timer is reset
        timeractive = 0
EndIf
```

This block begins with a test to determine whether the timer has finished. It does this by testing the current value of MilliSecs() against the value of

MilliSecs() when the timer began (timerbegin), plus the length of the counter (CHANGEDIRECTIONS). If the test returns true, the timer has run through. That means that the commands within the block are executed.

When the timer runs out, the fly gets new random x and y velocities, which move the fly in a different direction at a different speed. The timeractive variable is then set to 0, which means that the timer is unusable and needs to be reset. The code that resets the timer occurs directly after the previous code. It looks something like this:

```
;If the timer is inactive, reset the timer
If timeractive = 0
       timerbegin = MilliSecs()
       timeractive = 1
EndIf
```

This section of the code resets the starting point of the timer to the current value of MilliSecs(). Because the timer no longer needs to be reset (at least until the new timer has completed), timeractive is set to 1.

Two other changes were made from the first program to the second program of this chapter. The first is the addition of code that determines whether the fly has hit any walls. The code looks like this.

```
'Test if fly hit any walls
If fly.x <= 0 Or fly.x > 800
       fly.xv = -fly.xv
EndIf

If fly.y <= 0 Or fly.y >= 600
       fly.yv = - fly.yv
  EndIf
```

This code tests whether the fly has moved offscreen, and if it has, it reverses the direction the fly is traveling.

The other change was the addition of velocity values in the program. In the first program, we only changed the x and y coordinates of the fly, and in this program we used x and y coordinates along with x and y velocities. Figure 11.3 shows what the new demo looks like.

All right, that's the end of the first part of this chapter. The next section introduces you to chasing and evading.

**Figure 11.3**
The demo11-02.bmx program.

# Chasing and Evading

Well, now that we know how to use random variables and timers, we need to learn how to create artificial intelligence that actually works for a reason. Chasing and evading are very good ways to demonstrate this. Both are easy and interesting: chasing makes one object follow another and evading makes one object run away from another.

Without further ado, chasing!

## Chasing

Chasing entails finding the coordinates of one object and moving another based on where the first one is located. That might be a complex explanation, so let's break it down.

Let's say you have a spaceship following another spaceship; in fact, we will be writing a program that does this in a few minutes. Well, the program starts with the two ships onscreen in such a manner that ship A is following ship B. When

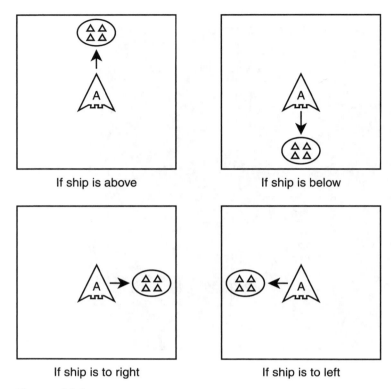

**Figure 11.4**
Following, chasing, tracking, or stalking? You be the judge.

ship B is to the left of ship A, ship A begins to move left. When ship B is to the right of ship A, ship A moves right. The same thing happens when ship B is above or below ship A: when above, ship A moves up; when below, ship A moves down. Figure 11.4 demonstrates chasing.

So, because everything we do in this book uses spaceships, let's make a chasing game in BlitzMax.

```
'demo11-03.bmx - Demonstrates chasing algorithms
Graphics 800,600

'Set up AutoMidHandle
AutoMidHandle True

'IMAGES
'player and enemy ships
```

```
playership = LoadImage ("spaceship.bmp")
enemyship = LoadImage ("enemyship.bmp")

'Load background
backgroundimage = LoadImage ("stars.bmp")


'CONSTANTS
'the following constants define how fast the player and the enemy move
Const PLAYERSPEED = 10
Const ENEMYSPEED = 5

'position player on bottom center of screen
playerx = 400
playery = 400

'position enemy on Upper center of screen
enemyx = 400
enemyy = 200

'set up scrolling variable
scrolly = 0

'MAIN LOOP
While Not KeyDown(KEY_ESCAPE)

Cls
'tile the background image
TileImage backgroundimage, 0, scrolly

'move the background up a little
scrolly = scrolly + 1

'If scrolly gets too big, reset it
If scrolly > ImageHeight(backgroundimage)
 scrolly = 0
EndIf



'Test the keypresses of the player
'If the player hits up, we move him up
```

```
If KeyDown(KEY_UP)
 playery = playery - PLAYERSPEED
EndIf

'If the player hits left, we move him left
If KeyDown(KEY_LEFT)
 playerx = playerx - PLAYERSPEED
EndIf

'If player hits right, we move him right
If KeyDown(KEY_RIGHT)
 playerx = playerx + PLAYERSPEED
EndIf

'If player hits down, we move him down
If KeyDown(KEY_DOWN)
 playery = playery + PLAYERSPEED
EndIf



'Now, we move the enemy depending on where the player is
'If the player is above the enemy, move the enemy up
If playery > enemyy
 enemyy = enemyy + ENEMYSPEED
EndIf

'If the player is to the left of the enemy, move the enemy left
If playerx < enemyx
 enemyx = enemyx - ENEMYSPEED
EndIf

'If the player is to the right of the enemy, move the enemy right
If playerx > enemyx
 enemyx = enemyx + ENEMYSPEED
EndIf

'If the player is below the enemy, move the enemy down
If playery < enemyy
 enemyy = enemyy - ENEMYSPEED
EndIf
```

```
'draw the player and enemy on the screen
DrawImage playership, playerx, playery
DrawImage enemyship, enemyx, enemyy


'Delay for a bit
Delay 25

'Flip the front and back buffer
Flip

Wend
'End OF MAIN LOOP
```

As you can see, this program is a lot of fun to watch when it runs on the screen. No matter where you go, that tenacious spaceship won't go away! Check out Figure 11.5 for a screenshot from the program.

**Figure 11.5**
The demo11-03.bmx program.

There is only one section of the program I want to discuss: the tracking section. The tracking code looks like this:

```
'Now, we move the enemy depending on where the player is
'If the player is above the enemy, move the enemy up
If playery > enemyy
  enemyy = enemyy + ENEMYSPEED
EndIf

'If the player is to the left of the enemy, move the enemy left
If playerx < enemyx
  enemyx = enemyx - ENEMYSPEED
EndIf

'If the player is to the right of the enemy, move the enemy right
If playerx > enemyx
  enemyx = enemyx + ENEMYSPEED
EndIf

'If the player is below the enemy, move the enemy down
If playery < enemyy
  enemyy = enemyy - ENEMYSPEED
  EndIf
```

Let's start off with the first line, If playery > enemyy. What does this do? Well, this just checks the y coordinate of the player against the y coordinate of the enemy. Because the higher on the screen the object is, the lower the y coordinate is (remember that the top of the screen is y = 0), when playery is greater than enemyy (this is tested in the first If...EndIf statement), the player is below the enemy. Therefore, the enemy moves down a little bit.

The same thing happens in the following If...EndIf statements. When playerx is less than enemyx, the player is to the left of the enemy, and the enemy moves left. When playerx is more than enemyx, the player is to the right of the enemy, and the enemy moves right. Finally, when playery < enemyy, the enemy moves down.

Well, that's it for tracking. All that's left in this chapter is the extremely difficult concept of evasion.

## Evading

A lot of times, when I tell a joke, my friends comment that they can't determine whether the statement I said was true or if I was simply kidding them. The final

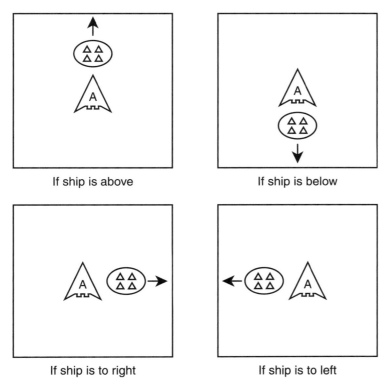

If ship is above          If ship is below

If ship is to right       If ship is to left

**Figure 11.6**
Evasion.

sentence of the last section would be an example of that. Just to let you know, evading isn't the "extremely" difficult concept I made it out to be. But you probably already knew that, right?

Either way, I'm sure you want to know all the ins and outs of evasion. Actually, you already do. Evasion is the opposite of chasing, because the enemy is running *away* from you. Check out Figure 11.6 to see how evasion works, with the player being the ship marked "A." As you can see, the ship always moves away from the player.

Anyway, take a guess as to how you would use evasion. If you guessed that all you do is take the tracking algorithm and change the pluses to minuses and the minuses to pluses, you are right!

demo11-04.bmx shows evasion, and it is almost exactly the same as its predecessor, demo11-03.bmx. In fact, I only made two changes. Here is the first one.

```
'Now, we move the enemy depending on where the player is
'If the player is above the enemy, move the enemy down
If playery > enemyy
        enemyy = enemyy - ENEMYSPEED
EndIf


'If the player is to the left of the enemy, move the enemy right
If playerx < enemyx
        enemyx = enemyx + ENEMYSPEED
EndIf


'If the player is to the right of the enemy, move the enemy left
If playerx > enemyx
        enemyx = enemyx - ENEMYSPEED
EndIf


'if the player is below the enemy, move the enemy up
If playery < enemyy
        enemyy = enemyy + ENEMYSPEED
 EndIf
```

Does this look familiar? As I said, it is exactly the same as demo11-03.bmx, but the pluses and minuses have been flipped. Now, when the enemy is to the right of the player, it continues to move right. When the enemy is to the left, the player moves even farther left. When the player is above the enemy, the player moves up, and when the player is below the enemy, the player moves down.

I also added one new section to the program. This section makes sure that the enemy ship doesn't run offscreen, as you would expect it to because it is fleeing the player.

```
'if enemy goes offscreen, move him back onscreen
If enemyx <= 0
        enemyx = 0
ElseIf enemyx >= 800
        enemyx = 800
EndIf
If enemyy <= 0
        enemyy = 0
ElseIf enemyy >= 600
        enemyy = 600
 EndIf
```

This code checks the enemy's coordinates to see whether he is onscreen or offscreen. If he is offscreen, the code makes sure he cannot move any farther in that direction and keeps him onscreen.

## Summary

Beautiful, ain't it? One more chapter and we will have created a real game.

In this chapter we lightly touched on the concepts of Artificial Intelligence. There are a lot (I mean A LOT) of other things that can be done with artificial intelligence, some of which are really interesting and exciting. Some programmers are coming up with ways to model the human genome (genetic algorithms) and even the human brain (neural networks)!

Keep practicing artificial intelligence, and you will likely stumble upon some concepts of your own. Just keep in mind; it is impossible to actually make a computer think. Your job, as a programmer, is to make the computer appear to be thinking. If it seems to be doing the expected, that is all that is required.

In this chapter, we went over the following topics:

- Random variables
- Timers
- Chasing
- Evasion

Hopefully you will be able to put these topics to use in your upcoming games and programs! If you would like to learn more about artificial intelligence, check out *AI Techniques for Game Programming* by Mat Buckland (published by Premier Press, ISBN: 1-931841-08-X).

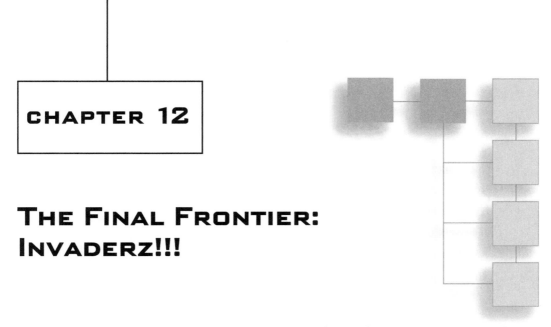

# CHAPTER 12

# THE FINAL FRONTIER: INVADERZ!!!

Are you ready to finish this? Well guess what! It's the final game—the last demo!

When I wrote Invaderz!!!, I planned on copying and pasting the entire source into the book, and then I was going to explain all the code to you step by step. Unfortunately, the code is 17 pages long. That's right, 17 pages! In other words, the full source is on the CD!

What we can do is go over the most important sections and algorithms of the code. I won't be explaining the easy sections, just the tough ones. The good thing, though, is the code is heavily commented, and you can probably figure out most of what you want to just by reading through the source.

**Note**

I'm going to make a recommendation right now. As you read this chapter, please, please, PLEASE keep a copy of the source code open! It's named invaderz.bmx, and it's on the CD. It will be a heck of a lot easier to view the entire source from the file, and you will understand the major points a lot better.

## Let's Bust It: Planning the Game

So, I knew I wanted to make a game for the final program in the book. What kind of game do you think I chose to make? You guessed it: a space shooter. I decided I wanted the game to be like *Space Invaders* (if you have ever played it before, you know what I am talking about). The point of the game is, as the player, to fire bullets at the enemy UFOs as they appear on the screen. The player is a human

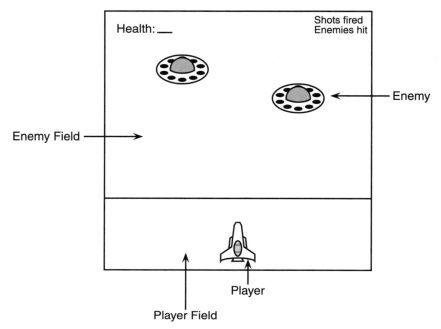

**Figure 12.1**
A sketch of the final game's playing field.

ship, and the enemy is alien ships. Now, I'll give you a little history on how I created it, and then we'll walk through the specifics together.

First of all, I planned out what the game would look like. I designed it so that the enemy UFOs appear from the top of the screen, and the player is on the bottom of the screen. As the enemies appear onscreen, the player shoots at the enemies, and they explode on contact.

My sketch for the game setup is shown in Figure 12.1. Well, actually my sketch was done in pencil, but I had it redrawn for this book.

I then had a basis for how the game would look and feel. Notice that in the sketch, I created a HUD that displays the health and the shots fired/enemies hit totals. This allowed me to spend my time on the actual game, instead of thinking about how the HUD should look later when writing the game. Now that I had the game plan ready, I created the images I would be using for the game. The most important ones, of course, were the player and the enemy images. The enemy bitmap looks like Figure 12.2.

And the player looks like Figure 12.3.

**Figure 12.2**
The enemy bitmap.

**Figure 12.3**
The player bitmap.

These images are used in the game. As you can see, they are animated; however, they are animated in different ways.

The enemy bitmap has a rather straightforward animation style—it just loops from the first frame to the last frame. What I mean is that when the enemy ship moves around, it plays each frame in the bitmap consecutively. The first frame of the game loop is the first frame of the spaceship, the second frame of the game loop is the second frame of the spaceship, and so on, until you reach the final frame of the enemy spaceship (the 10th frame). The 11th frame of the game loop is then the first frame of the bitmap again, and so on.

The player bitmap reacts a little bit differently. We want the game to make the player tilt left when the spaceship is moving left and tilt right when the spaceship is moving right. It will remain flat when not moving at all.

We have to use some interesting code to get this to work. First of all, load the bitmap in, as you might expect, with the command `LoadAnimImage()`.

```
Global playerimage = LoadAnimImage("player.bmp",35,32,0,13)
```

This assumes that each frame of the player bitmap is 35 × 32 pixels (and so it is), and that there are 13 frames (and so there are). Well, as you can see, the first frame is not a flat position, but instead a view of the spaceship tilting left. We want the player spaceship to rest on the seventh frame, and have the frames increase (move toward tilting right) when the player presses right, and, conversely, have the frames decrease (move toward tilting left) when the player presses left. Set the frame to rest on frame 7 when no key is pressed, like this:

```
player.frame = 7
```

Then, when the player presses right, the code will do this:

```
'tilt player right
player.frame = player.frame + 1
```

```
;don't let frame get too high
If player.frame >= 12
    Player.frame = 12
Endif
```

Can you see what is happening here? Note that this code occurs within the right key testing block, meaning this code is tested only when the right key is pressed. What is happening is that the frame is being incremented each frame, but only as long as the right key is pressed. (The right-key testing code occurs around the previous code, and is not visible in the book.) The code limits how high `player.frame` can get, however, because there are only 13 frames in the player spaceship image.

Why does it check to see if the `frame` variable is greater than or equal to 12, instead of 13? Remember that frame counts begin at 0, therefore, the final frame is $13 - 1$, or 12.

Okay, it's time to wrap up the planning section. There are a lot of other things you need to do, such as decide how to choose where the enemies come from, how many enemies are on each level, and the like. If you want to see how I did it, open up the invaderz.bmx program from the CD. It contains the source, and the comments will help you understand what I was thinking when I wrote the game.

By the way, I chose the name Invaderz!!! for the name of my game. Why? It's a cool name. And you can tell it's important because there are not one, not two, but three exclamation points after the word!

## Constants, Functions, and Types in Invaderz!!!

Let's take the time to go over each of the variables, constants, functions, and types used in Invaderz!!! First off, let's check out all of the constants.

There are only a few constants, but they are very important. Table 12.1 lists all the constants and their descriptions.

**Table 12.1** Constants in Invaderz!!!

| Constant | Value | Description |
| --- | --- | --- |
| CHANGEENEMYDIRECTION | 700 | The time (in milliseconds) between velocity changes for enemy UFOs. |
| TIMEBETWEENENEMYBULLETS | 1200 | The time (in milliseconds) between enemy bullet fire. |

So what do CHANGEENEMYDIRECTION and TIMEBETWEENENEMYBULLETS do? Well, let's go over both of them.

In this program, the enemies' movement is random. We need to move those UFOs in a random direction at the beginning. We don't want it to appear random, however, so we need to adjust their direction variables every once in a while to make it appear that they are moving. CHANGEENEMYDIRECTION determines the time between those direction changes. Each UFO changes direction every 700 milliseconds (or every 7/10 of a second).

TIMEBETWEENENEMYBULLETS does the same sort of thing. This constant determines how long a break there is between the bullet shots by the enemy. Instead of 700 milliseconds like the CHANGEENEMYDIRECTION constant, this constant has the enemies fire bullets every 1,200 milliseconds (1 and 1/5 of a second, or every 1.2 seconds).

Cool? Let's examine the functions. There are a lot of them!

Table 12.2 lists each function in Invaderz!!!

Not all these functions are called by the main loop, so I drew a function outline that explains how the functions interact with one another (see Figure 12.4).

That's all for functions. Last, we have the types used in Invaderz!!!

**Table 12.2** Functions in Invaderz!!!

| Function | Description |
| --- | --- |
| InitializeLevel() | Resets the level with the proper amount of enemies and resets all the starting variables. |
| DrawHUD() | Draws the health points remaining and the bullets fired/hit displays in the top of the window. |
| CreateNewEnemy() | Creates a new enemy ship onscreen. |
| DrawShips() | Draws the enemy and player spaceships. |
| EnemyAI() | Updates the directions and bullet fires of the enemy spaceships. |
| CreateBullet() | Creates a new bullet onscreen. |
| UpdateBullets() | Moves bullets and checks to see whether they collided against any opposing ships. |
| CreateExplosion() | Creates an explosion after a ship collision. |
| UpdateExplosions() | Rotates explosions through its frames and deletes the explosion when it is over. |
| GameOver() | Prepares the game for exit and quits to desktop. |

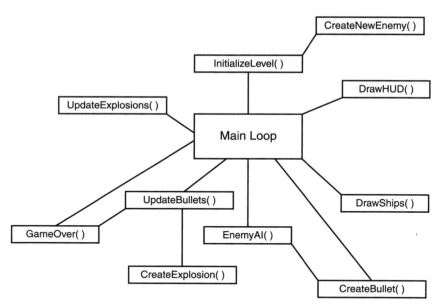

**Figure 12.4**
The function outline for Invaderz!!!

There are four types used in Invaderz!!! They are

- The TShip type

- The TUser type

- The TBullet type

- The TExplosion type

The TShip type refers to all the enemies that are created during the game, the TUser type is the player spaceship that is onscreen, the TBullet type describes each bullet that is fired during the game (both enemy and player bullets), and the TExplosion type refers to explosions that occur after a ship dies for either enemy or player.

I am going to list tables with all of the types' fields, in order to give you a feel for the Invaderz!!! program.

Table 12.3 lists the TShip type's fields.

Table 12.4 lists the TUser type's fields, which are used to make the player.

Notice, if you will, that the TShip and TUser types are very similar to one another. This is because they are both spaceships, and although they are opposing forces, both of them have to move in the same way. Their similarities remind me of

**Table 12.3**  The TShip Type's Fields

| Field | Description |
| --- | --- |
| x | The x coordinate of the ship. |
| y | The y coordinate of the ship. |
| hits | The hit points remaining on the ship. |
| xv | The x direction variable that governs how far left and right the ship moves per frame. |
| yv | The y direction variable that governs how far up and down the ship moves per frame. |
| frame | The frame of the animated image that will be drawn. (Refer to Figure 12.2.) |

**Table 12.4**  The TUser Type's Fields

| Field | Description |
| --- | --- |
| x | The x coordinate of the user. |
| y | The y coordinate of the user. |
| hits | The remaining hit points on the user. |
| frame | The frame of the animated image that will be drawn. (Refer to Figure 12.3.) |
| draw | Determines whether the user should be drawn on the screen or not. The user should be drawn if set to 1 and should not be drawn if set to 0. |

**Table 12.5**  The TBullet Type's Fields

| Field | Description |
| --- | --- |
| x | The x coordinate of the bullet. |
| y | The y coordinate of the bullet. |
| draw | Determines whether the bullet should be drawn on the screen or not. The bullet should be drawn if set to 1 and should not be drawn if set to 0. |
| from | Determines who fired the bullet. This is set to 1 if it was fired by the user and set to 2 if it was fired by an enemy. |
| frame | The frame of the animated image that will be drawn. |

comic book heroes and super villains: the super villains are almost exactly the same as the hero, and in fact, they are often friends growing up.

Table 12.5 lists the TBullet type's fields.

And last but not least, Table 12.6 lists the TExplosion type's fields.

Woo-hoo! Now, let's move on to actually playing the game.

**Table 12.6**  The TExplosion Type's Fields

| Field | Description |
| --- | --- |
| x | The x coordinate of the explosion. |
| y | The y coordinate of the explosion. |
| from | Determines who is exploding. This is set to 1 if the user exploded and set to 2 if the enemy exploded. |
| frame | The frame of the animated image that will be drawn. |

## Playing Invaderz!!!

We've gone through the motions of creating the game (or at least getting a feel for the game) and now we get to the fun part: playing the game!

Invaderz!!! is a very simple game to play. There are two ways to open it, but both require you to navigate to the Chapter 12 folder on the CD. Put the CD in your CD-ROM drive and find the Source folder, and then double-click Chapter 12. Once you have done this, you will see a bunch of files that relate to the Invaderz!!! game. To play the game directly, double-click the icon that looks like a rocket ship. This file is named invaderz.exe.

The other way to load Invaderz!!! is to run it from within the BlitzMax compiler and compile the code straight away. Do this by finding the file named invaderz.bmx and double-clicking it. It should load in the BlitzMax compiler within a few seconds. Look near the top of the screen and you will find a toolbar with a number of menus starting with File. Select the menu named Program and click Run Program. Another way to do this is to press the F5 key on your keyboard (after you load the program in BlitzMax).

### Note

If you want to run the game within the BlitzMax compiler, you will need to have BlitzMax installed on your machine. You probably already installed this program earlier in the book, but just in case you didn't, now is the time to do so. See Chapter 1 for instructions on installing the compiler.

You have just opened the game! You can now play it to your heart's content. There are only three functioning keys within the program, and Table 12.7 explains them.

Let me give you some tips for Invaderz!!! Note, by the way, that you can't "beat" the game. The game continually gets harder and harder until the player dies.

**Table 12.7** The Keys Used in Invaderz!!!

| Key | Description |
| --- | --- |
| Left Arrow | Moves the player ship left. |
| Right Arrow | Moves the player ship right. |
| Spacebar | Fires a bullet. |

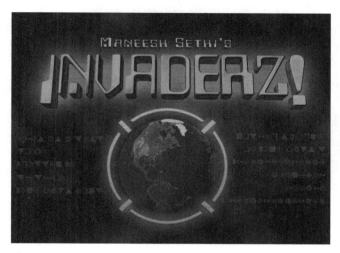

**Figure 12.5**
The Invaderz!!! title screen.

- Try to stay in one place and fire bullets as quickly as you can. When one of the enemies fires a bullet at you, however, get out of the way.

- Remember, the bullets not only hurt the enemy if it hits him head on, but also if the enemy runs into it.

- Try to judge how fast the enemy is moving when firing a bullet. Oftentimes, you can fire a bullet directly into the enemy's path simply by watching.

- On the contrary to the previous tip, remember that the velocities of each ship change every 7/10 of a second. If they are moving to the left quickly, their route might modify to move them up slightly. If they are moving right very slowly, they might reverse directions completely!

And that's it for the Invaderz!!! game. Take a look at the screenshots from the game, Figures 12.5 and 12.6.

**Figure 12.6**
The Invaderz!!! game.

## Epilogue

The game is over and the book is done. I've had a lot of fun traveling down this path with you, and I hope that what I have taught you will help you reach new limits in game programming and in life. I know this sounds clichèd, but really, I want you to use your new knowledge to make some new games!

Let's talk about the future of game programming—namely, yours. If you enjoyed what we have done with this book, you should know that there is a heck of a lot more out there to learn. Take a look at some of the sites listed in Appendix B to see what else you can learn. Play around with the compiler and the BlitzMax language and create your own games. Believe me, the best way to get better is to practice.

BlitzMax is an excellent language for learning programming. Now that you have the necessary skills of programming, you will understand a lot more if you choose to move on to other languages. Some concepts, such as loops and functions, have been hammered into your head in this book, and it won't be nearly as hard to understand them when doing the same in a different language.

Once you have reached the limits of BlitzMax, there are two paths you might consider. The first is to move on to three-dimensional game programming using Blitz3D. This language is made by the same people who brought you BlitzMax. It's a tough language, but the things you can do with Blitz3D are simply amazing. You can create entire game worlds with people and houses and the like. Amazing. My new book is coming out, *3D Game Programming for Teens, Second Edition*, which uses the Blitz3D language.

The other choice is to leave the Blitz language altogether. There is a language called C (and its successor, C++) that is the most common language for producing and actually publishing games. The reason C is used over Blitz is because C is a much more powerful language; it can reach into the hardware to perform functions, and it is faster as well. You might think about picking up a book on C or C++ and studying the language (C was the first language I ever taught myself).

As you well know, life is simply a maze of paths, and each choice you make leads you down a path you have to follow. Choose to continue programming, choose to continue making games, choose to enjoy what you are doing, or don't. It's that simple.

Anyway, my tirade is over. I want to hear from you, however! I will gladly help with any games or programs that you make and want me to see or help you with. Simply e-mail me the program at:

**maneesh@maneeshsethi.com**

I want you to go to my Web site and join the community! You can find forums that talk about this book also.

**http://www.maneeshsethi.com**

Lastly, if you liked this book, make sure you review it on amazon.com! It really helps sales! (Tell your friends, also.)

I will be organizing a contest on my Web site in the near future. Submit your best game, and you could win a free book or, if you are really lucky, a signed photo of me. ☺

Oh yeah, one more thing. Make sure you check out my other books. *Web Design for Teens* teaches you how to make Web sites, and *How to Succeed As A Lazy Student* will help you learn how to beat school without doing any work. Also, like I said, *3D Game Programming for Teens, Second Edition*, written by yours truly, is in the works. Keep your eye out for other things I will be putting out.

I would love to hear from you, so don't hesitate to e-mail me. Heck, just e-mail me and say hi, if you want.

"The greatest trick the devil ever pulled was convincing the world he didn't exist. And like that, *whoosh*, he's gone."

That's it from me. Maneesh Sethi, signing out.

# Part IV

# Appendixes

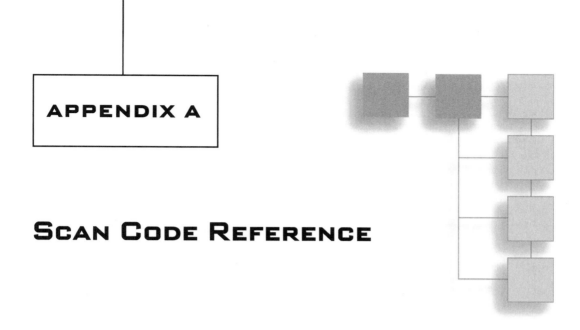

# APPENDIX A

# SCAN CODE REFERENCE

This appendix contains a list of all the scan codes you can use for input in your programs. Scan codes are used in functions such as KeyHit() or KeyDown() like this:

KeyDown(*scancode*)

Input the scan code for the key you want to test for, and this function will return 1 if the key was pressed.

Many of the following keys won't appear on your keyboard; some of them are international keys (like the symbol for the Yen), and some of them only exist on advanced keyboards that have extra keys (like the Calculator key). Anyway, you can find any key that you would ever think of using on this list, shown in Table A.1.

**Table A.1** The Scan Code Reference

| Mouse Button | Value | Modifier Key | Value |
|---|---|---|---|
| Left mouse button | MOUSE_LEFT | Shift modifier | MODIFIER_SHIFT |
| Right mouse button | MOUSE_RIGHT | Control modifier | MODIFIER_CONTROL |
| Middle mouse button | MOUSE_MIDDLE | Option modifier | MODIFIER_OPTION |
| | | System modifier | MODIFIER_SYSTEM |
| | | Command modifier | MODIFIER_COMMAND |

**Table A.1**  (*Continued*)

| Keyboard Key | Value | Keyboard Key | Value |
|---|---|---|---|
| Backspace | KEY_BACKSPACE | F | KEY_F |
| Tab | KEY_TAB | G | KEY_G |
| Clear | KEY_CLEAR | H | KEY_H |
| Return | KEY_RETURN | I | KEY_I |
| Enter | KEY_ENTER | J | KEY_J |
| Pause | KEY_PAUSE | K | KEY_K |
| Escape | KEY_ESCAPE | L | KEY_L |
| Space | KEY_SPACE | M | KEY_M |
| Page Up | KEY_PAGEUP | N | KEY_N |
| Page Down | KEY_PAGEDOWN | O | KEY_O |
| End | KEY_END | P | KEY_P |
| Home | KEY_HOME | Q | KEY_Q |
| Cursor (Left) | KEY_LEFT | R | KEY_R |
| Cursor (Up) | KEY_UP | S | KEY_S |
| Cursor (Right) | KEY_RIGHT | T | KEY_T |
| Cursor (Down) | KEY_DOWN | U | KEY_U |
| Select | KEY_SELECT | V | KEY_V |
| Print | KEY_PRINT | W | KEY_W |
| Execute | KEY_EXECUTE | X | KEY_X |
| Screen | KEY_SCREEN | Y | KEY_Y |
| Insert | KEY_INSERT | Z | KEY_Z |
| Delete | KEY_DELETE | Sys key (Left) | KEY_LSYS |
| Help | KEY_HELP | Sys key (Right) | KEY_RSYS |
| 0 | KEY_0 | Numpad 0 | KEY_NUM0 |
| 1 | KEY_1 | Numpad 1 | KEY_NUM1 |
| 2 | KEY_2 | Numpad 2 | KEY_NUM2 |
| 3 | KEY_3 | Numpad 3 | KEY_NUM3 |
| 4 | KEY_4 | Numpad 4 | KEY_NUM4 |
| 5 | KEY_5 | Numpad 5 | KEY_NUM5 |
| 6 | KEY_6 | Numpad 6 | KEY_NUM6 |
| 7 | KEY_7 | Numpad 7 | KEY_NUM7 |
| 8 | KEY_8 | Numpad 8 | KEY_NUM8 |
| 9 | KEY_9 | Numpad 9 | KEY_NUM9 |
| A | KEY_A | Numpad * | KEY_NUMMULTIPLY |
| B | KEY_B | Numpad + | KEY_NUMADD |
| C | KEY_C | Numpad - | KEY_NUMSUBTRACT |
| D | KEY_D | Numpad . | KEY_NUMDECIMAL |
| E | KEY_E | Numpad / | KEY_NUMDIVIDE |

**Table A.1** (*Continued*)

| Keyboard Key | Value | Keyboard Key | Value |
|---|---|---|---|
| F1 | KEY_F1 | Control (Left) | KEY_LCONTROL |
| F2 | KEY_F2 | Control (Right) | KEY_RCONTROL |
| F3 | KEY_F3 | Alt key (Left) | KEY_LALT |
| F4 | KEY_F4 | Alt key (Right) | KEY_RALT |
| F5 | KEY_F5 | Tilde | KEY_TILDE |
| F6 | KEY_F6 | Minus | KEY_MINUS |
| F7 | KEY_F7 | Equals | KEY_EQUALS |
| F8 | KEY_F8 | Bracket (Open) | KEY_OPENBRACKET |
| F9 | KEY_F9 | Bracket (Close) | KEY_CLOSEBRACKET |
| F10 | KEY_F10 | Backslash | KEY_BACKSLASH |
| F11 | KEY_F11 | Semicolon | KEY_SEMICOLON |
| F12 | KEY_F12 | Quote | KEY_QUOTES |
| Num Lock | KEY_NUMLOCK | Comma | KEY_COMMA |
| Scroll Lock | KEY_SCROLL | Period | KEY_PERIOD |
| Shift (Left) | KEY_LSHIFT | Slash | KEY_SLASH |
| Shift (Right) | KEY_RSHIFT | | |

# APPENDIX B

# USEFUL LINKS

This appendix lists some links where you might be able to learn more about Blitz Basic game programming.

## Blitz Links

There are some extremely good sites for learning Blitz programming. Check out the forums on each: they are active and helpful.

www.maneeshsethi.com is the official site for this book. You will find updates to this book and tutorials/programs on this site. You can also contact me directly from this site.

www.BlitzBasic.com is the official site of the BlitzMax program. You can find the actual BlitzMax program to download (this program is also included on the CD) along with some tutorials. The most updated version of the command reference is on this Web site. To get to the command reference, go to www.blitzbasic.com, click Community, and click Blitz3D Docs directly below. From there, you can choose to see the 2D command reference.

## General Game Programming Links

Although the number of Blitz Basic programming sites is limited, there are plenty more Web sites on general game programming. Following is one very useful one.

www.GameDev.net is one of the most widely known and most visited game programming sites on the Internet. The site boasts literally hundreds of articles and tutorials on game coding. This site can help introduce you to other languages, as well as provide theories and concepts that you can use in Blitz programming.

http://www-cs-students.stanford.edu/~amitp/gameprog.html is the site of Amit's Game Programming Information site. This site is an introduction to game programming. It has answers to some questions you might have about furthering your game programming knowledge.

# WHAT'S ON THE CD

The CD that is in the back of the book comes with a lot of useful programs and demos. Let me explain to you everything that you will find when you boot this baby up.

Check out the readme files in every directory! They will have instructions and updates to everything on the CD.

The directory structure for this CD should be pretty easy to follow. You will find everything arranged like this:

Source\

       Chapter01\

       Chapter02\

       . . .

       Chapter12\

Art\

     Book Art\

     Spritelib_Gpl\

Sounds\

      Sound\

      Music\

Programs\

Following is an explanation for all these categories.

## Source

On the CD, you will find all the source code from the examples in the book. I recommend that you copy all the code to your hard drive before playing around with it. You will be unable to compile the source if it is left on the CD, but moving it to the hard drive fixes the compilation errors. Also, executable files for each and every demo program are included.

## Art

I have included a section that contains all the art I have used in the book, along with a few other art libraries I have found. The main folder contains the art created by Edgar L. Ibarra for the book, and the subfolder named Spritelib_Gpl is a library of images made by Ari Feldman. The Spritelib_Gpl folder contains numerous subdirectories, each of which contains different images. Special thanks to Edgar and Ari for the art.

## Sounds

This section contains two subdirectories: Sound and Music. Inside the sound directory, you will find numerous sound effects that can be used in your programs, royalty free. The Music subdirectory has a few MP3 files and some MIDI music files that can be used in your programs, also. If you want to use the MP3 files for anything other than personal use (if you decide to sell your game, for example), please contact Thomas Stenbäck of Interim Nation for licensing info. You can contact Thomas at interimnation@hotmail.com.

## Programs

This section contains a few programs that you can use to help you in your conquest of the gaming world. Included are the demo files for the following programs.

- **BlitzMax**—This is the main software for this book. This is a 30-day trial version. There is a Mac version and a Windows version of the demo included on the CD. Only the Mac Intel version is included on the CD—if you have an old Mac, you might want to download the PPC version, available on the website.

- **BlitzPlus/Blitz3d**—Blitz Plus and Blitz 3d are Windows only, and can be used for making 2D and 3D games.

- **Corel Paint Shop Pro**—An art program, much like Microsoft Paint, but much more robust.

- **MilkShape 3D**—A 3D modeler for more advanced techniques.

- **CoolEdit Pro**—A sound-editing program.

Okay, that's about it for the CD. Have fun with everything that is included!

# INDEX

# You're a teen with a great imagination...

Written specifically for teens in a language you understand, on topics you're interested in! Each book in the *For Teens* series features step-by-step instructions to help you conquer the tools and techniques presented. Hands-on projects help you put your new skills into action. And the accompanying CD-ROM or web downloads provide tutorials, instructional videos, software programs, and more!

...unleash your creativity with the  series!!

**Computer Programming for Teens**
ISBN: 1-59863-446-1 • $29.99

**Web Comics for Teens**
ISBN: 1-59863-467-4 • $29.99

**3D Game Programming for Teens**
ISBN: 1-59200-900-X • $29.99

**Game Creation for Teens**
1-59863-500-X • $29.99

**Torque for Teens**
ISBN: 1-59863-409-7 • $29.99

**Web Design for Teens**
ISBN: 1-59200-607-8 • $19.99

**Microsoft Visual Basic
Game Programming for Teens**
Second Edition
ISBN: 1-59863-390-2 • $29.99

**Game Art for Teens**
Second Edition
ISBN: 1-59200-959-X • $34.99

# License Agreement/Notice of Limited Warranty